SPEECHES & DOCUMENTS

ON

INDIAN POLICY

SPEECHES & DOCUMENTS

ON

INDIAN POLICY

1750-1921

Editor by

A BERRIEDALE KEITH

IN TWO VOLUMES

VOL. II

Published by

Gyan Publishing House
5, Ansari Road
Daryaganj, New Delhi-110002
Phone: 011-47034999, 9811692060
E-mail: books@gyanbooks.com

Distribution Network
gyanbooks.com
India, USA, Canada, UK, Australia

ISBN: 978-93-7014-410-1 (Set)
978-93-7014-318-0 (PB)

First Published, 1922

2nd Impression 2025

Printed at: Gyan Press, Delhi.

SPEECHES & DOCUMENTS ON INDIAN POLICY (VOL. II)
Editor: A BERRIEDALE KEITH

The World's Classics

CCXXXII

SPEECHES AND DOCUMENTS

ON

INDIAN POLICY

SPEECHES & DOCUMENTS

ON

INDIAN POLICY

1750–1921

EDITED BY

PROFESSOR A. BERRIEDALE KEITH

D.C.L., D.LITT.

IN TWO VOLUMES

VOL. II

HUMPHREY MILFORD
OXFORD UNIVERSITY PRESS

LONDON   EDINBURGH   GLASGOW   COPENHAGEN
NEW YORK   TORONTO   MELBOURNE   CAPE TOWN
BOMBAY   CALCUTTA   MADRAS   SHANGHAI

*This volume of ' Speeches and Documents on Indian Policy '
was first published in ' The World's Classics ' in 1922.*

CONTENTS TO VOL. II

II

INDIA AS A BRITISH DEPENDENCY

1858–1914

B

1. *Sir Charles Wood, House of Commons,* 6 *June,* 1861.

I RISE to move for leave to bring in a Bill of the greatest possible importance to our Indian empire. It modifies to a great extent the Executive Government, and—what is of still greater importance—it alters the means and manner of legislation. I can assure the House that I never felt more responsibility than in venturing to submit to it a proposal of so important and grave a character. It is hardly necessary for me to mention that the power of legislating for 150,000,000 of people, and nearly 50,000,000 whose welfare it indirectly affects, is a matter of the gravest importance, and I am quite sure that to those who have ever studied India the inherent difficulties of the question will be no less apparent. We have to legislate for different races, with different languages, religions, manners, and customs, ranging from the bigoted Mahommedan, who considers that we have usurped his legitimate position as the ruler of India, to the timid Hindoo, who, though bowing to every conqueror, is bigotedly attached to his caste, his religion, his laws, and his customs, which have descended to him uninterruptedly for countless generations. But, added to that, we have English settlers in India differing in almost every respect from the native population,—active, energetic, enterprising, with all the pride of race and conquest, presuming on their superior powers, and looking down in many respects and I am afraid violating in others, the feelings and prejudices of the native population ; with whom, nevertheless, they must be subject to laws passed by the legislative body in India. I have always thought that the gravest question in modern times is the relation between civilized and less civilized nations, or between civilized portions of nations, when they came in contact. The difficulty is seen in America, in Africa, in New Zealand, but nowhere in the widely extended dominions of Her Majesty has it reached such a magnitude as in India. And in this particular case the difficulty is aggravated by the circumstance that the English, who form a portion of those who are to be subjected to this legislation, are not a permanent body. They go there for a time. Officials, when their term of service has expired, and persons engaged in commercial or agricultural pursuits, when they have made a fortune, return to this country, and, though the English element in India is permanent as belonging to a nation, it is most transitory when we come to consider the individuals who compose it. Such are the circumstances under which we are to legislate, and I regret to say that the recent mutiny has aggravated these difficulties. The unlimited confidence which a few years ago was felt by the European population in the natives of India has given way to feelings of distrust. Formerly there was, at all events, no feeling of antagonism between the higher portion of official persons and the great mass of the population. The latter looked up to the Government as to a protector, and if any feeling of antagonism or jealousy existed it existed only between them and those members of the service or the English settlers who were brought into antagonistic contact with them.

When I heard some time ago that the feeling of antagonism was extending itself lower among the natives and higher among the officers I deeply regretted it, as the most alarming symptom of altered circumstances, which must obviously tend to increase the dangers of our position. I do not wish to dwell on this matter, but it would be folly to shut our eyes to the increasing difficulties of our position in India, and it is an additional reason why we should make the earliest endeavour to put all our institutions on the soundest possible foundations. It is notoriously difficult for any European to make himself intimately acquainted with either the feelings or opinions of the native population, and I was struck the other day by a passage in a letter from one of the oldest Indian servants, Sir Mark Cubbon, whose death we have had recently to regret. He had been in the service for sixty years; he had administered the affairs of Mysore for nearly thirty years; he had been living in the most intimate intercourse with the natives, possessing their love and confidence to an extent seldom obtained by an English officer, and yet he said ' that he was astonished that he had never been able to acquire a sufficient acquaintance with the opinions and feelings of the natives with whom he was in daily communication.' Many of the greatest mistakes into which we have been led have arisen from the circumstance that we have been, not unnaturally, perhaps, for arranging everything according to English ideas. In Bengal we converted the collectors of taxes into the permanent landowners of the country, and left the ryots to their mercy. In Madras, Sir Thomas Munro, from the most benevolent motives, and to avoid the evils of the Bengal settlement, introduced the ryotwarry system. It is now asserted that a more impoverished population than that of Madras does not exist. When I was at the Board of Control it was said that the system of the North-Western provinces was perfect. In consequence of that opinion it was introduced into the newly acquired provinces of Oude. We fancied that we were benefiting the population, and relieving them from the oppression of their chiefs, but in the rebellion the ryots of Oude took part against us and joined their chiefs in the rebellion. Subsequent to the rebellion the Indian Government, profiting by the circumstance, reverted to the old system in Oude, and happily with the greatest success ; and recently at an interview between Lord Canning and the talookdars they expressed their gratification at the restoration of the former system, and the Governor-General justly congratulated them on the fact that tranquillity prevailed in a district which had been so frequently the scene of violence and outrage, and that in the most newly acquired of Her Majesty's Indian dominions confidence existed which was not surpassed in the oldest settlements. The House can hardly be aware of the extraordinary and inherent difficulties in devising a system applicable to the whole of India. It behoves us to be most careful, as a rash step may lead to most dangerous consequences. It is easy to go forward. It is difficult to go back, and I confess I am disposed to err on the side of caution and to profit by the warning of one of the ablest Indian officers, Mountstuart Elphinstone, who said ' Legislation for India should be well considered, gradual, and

slow.' The measure which I propose to introduce
will effect some changes in the executive Government of India. About two years ago the Government thought it right to send to India a distinguished
Member of this House, Mr. Wilson, in order to aid
in putting the finances of that country in a more
satisfactory condition. As far as I can learn, the
changes which Mr. Wilson had the opportunity of
inaugurating, and which have to a considerable
extent been carried out, have gone a great way to
convince the authorities of India of the mistaken
way in which they were proceeding, and to lay
the foundation of a sounder system of finance.
Judging from the accounts which we have received
by the last mail, I believe that a change has come
over the financial affairs of India, and that we
may look forward to a more satisfactory state of
things than has prevailed for many years. There
can be no doubt that the Council of the Governor-
General has suffered serious inconvenience from
the absence of any Member thoroughly acquainted
with the laws and principles of jurisprudence;
and Lord Canning, in one of his dispatches, points
out how desirable it is that a gentleman of the
legal profession, a jurist rather than a technical
lawyer, should be added to the Council. I propose,
therefore, to take powers to send out an additional
member of Council. Although it is not so specified,
it is intended that he should be a lawyer, and I
must endeavour to find a man of high character
and attainments, competent to assist the Governor-
General and his Council in framing laws. The main
change proposed is, however, in the mode in which
laws and regulations are enacted. The history
of legislative power in India is very short. In

1773 the Governor-General in Council was empowered to make regulations for the Government of India, and in 1793 those regulations were collected into a code by Lord Cornwallis. Similar regulations were applied in 1799 and 1801 to Madras and Bombay, and in 1803 they were extended to the North-West Provinces. The territory of Delhi, however, which was nominally under the sovereignty of the Great Mogul, was administered by officers of the Government of India, and with such good effect that in 1815, when Lord Hastings acquired certain provinces, he determined that they should be administered in the same way by Commissioners appointed by the Government. The same system has been applied to the Punjab, Scinde, Pegu, and the various acquisitions made in India since that date. The laws and regulations under which they are administered are framed either by the Governor-General in Council or by the Lieutenant-Governors or Commissioners, as the case may be, and approved by the Governor-General. This different mode of passing ordinances for the two classes of provinces, constitutes the distinction between the regulation and the non-regulation provinces, the former being those subject to the old regulations, and the latter those which are administered in the somewhat irregular manner which, as I have stated, commenced in 1815. There is much difference of opinion as to the legality of the regulations adopted under the latter system, and Sir Barnes Peacock has declared that they are illegal unless passed by the Legislative Council. The Act of 1833 added to the Council of the Governor-General a member whose presence was necessary for the passing of all legislative measures, and put

the whole of the then territory of India under
that body, at the same time withdrawing from
Madras and Bombay the power of making regulations. In that way the whole legislative power
and authority of India were centralized in the
Governor-General and Council, with this additional
member. So matters stood in 1853, but great
complaints had emanated from other parts of
India of the centralization of power at Calcutta.
The practice was then introduced of placing in
the Governor-General's Council members from
different parts of India. The tenour of the evidence
given before the Committee of 1852–3 was to
point out, that the Executive Council alone, even
with the assistance of the legislative member,
was incompetent to perform the increased duties
which were created by the extension of territory.
Mr. M'Leod, a distinguished member of the Civil
Service of India, and who had acted at Calcutta
as one of the Law Commissioners, gave the following evidence before the Committee :

'The Governor-General with four Members of Council,
however highly qualified those individuals may be, is not
altogether a competent Legislature for the great empire
which we have in India. It seems to me very desirable
that, in the Legislative Government of India, there should
be one or more persons having local knowledge and experience of the minor presidencies ; that is entirely wanting
in the Legislative Government as at present constituted.
It appears to me that this is one considerable and manifest
defect. The Governor-General and Council have not
sufficient leisure and previous knowledge to conduct, in
addition to their executive and administrative functions,
the whole duties of legislation for the Indian empire. It
seems to me that it would be advisable to enlarge the
Legislative Council and have representatives of the minor
presidencies in it, without enlarging the Executive Council,
or in any way altering its present constitution.'

Mr. Hill, another eminent Civil Servant, said :

' The mode of carrying out improvements must be by strengthening the hands of the Legislature. . . . It would be a great improvement if, after the preparation of laws by the Executive Government and its officers, when the Legislature met, they had the addition to their number of the Chief Justice and perhaps another judge of the Supreme Court, one or two judges of the Sudder Court, and the Advocate General, or some other competent persons—so that there should be a more numerous deliberative body.'

I quote these two opinions only, because they are so clearly and concisely expressed. In consequence of the general evidence to that effect, I proposed, in 1853, a measure adding to the Council of the Governor-General, when sitting to make laws and regulations, members from the different provinces of India, together with the Chief Justice and another Judge of the Supreme Court of Bengal. My intention was, in accordance with the opinions I have cited, to give to the Council the assistance of local knowledge and legal experience in framing laws. The Council, however, quite contrary to my intention, has become a sort of debating society, or petty parliament. My own view of its duties is expressed in a letter I wrote to Lord Dalhousie in 1853, in which I said :

' I expect the non-official members of your enlarged Legislative Council to be constantly employed as a Committee of Council in working at Calcutta, on the revision of your laws and regulations.'

It was certainly a great mistake that a body of twelve members should have been established with all the forms and functions of a parliament. They have standing orders nearly as numerous as we have ; and their effect has been, as Lord

Canning stated in one of his dispatches, to impede business, cause delay, and to induce a Council, which ought to be regarded as a body for doing practical work, to assume the debating functions of a parliament. In a letter which is among the papers upon the Table of the House, Mr. Grant bears testimony to the success which has attended their labours in framing laws ; and I will quote the words of another able Indian civil servant to the same effect. He says :

' If it be assumed that the enlargement of the Council by the addition of two judges of the Supreme Court and four councillors of the different Presidencies of India was designed only as a means of improving the legislation of the country, the measure must be regarded as a complete success. The Council has effected all that could be expected and may with just pride point to the statutes of the last seven years as a triumphant proof that the intention of Parliament has been fulfilled.'

I think that this is a very satisfactory proof that as far as my intentions—and what I believe were the intentions of the Legislature of this country—are concerned, the objects of the change in the position of the Governor-General's Council, when sitting for legislative purposes, have been most completely fulfilled. I do not wish to say anything against a body the constitution of which I am about to alter, but I think that the general opinion, both in India and England, condemned the action of the Council when it attempted to discharge functions other than those which I have mentioned— when it constituted itself a body for the redress of grievances, and engaged in discussions which led to no practical result. So much has this struck those most competent to form an opinion, that I find that the first Vice-President, Sir

Lawrence Peel, expressed a very decided opinion against it, and says of the Council, in a short memorandum :

'It has no jurisdiction in the nature of that of a grand inquest of the nation. Its functions are purely legislative, and are limited even in that respect. It is not an Anglo-Indian House of Commons for the redress of grievances, to refuse supplies, and so forth.'

These obvious objections were pointed out to me by the Government of India last year, and it was my intention to have introduced a measure upon the subject in the course of that Session. I felt, however, so much difficulty in deciding in what shape the measure should be framed, that I deferred its proposal until the present year ; and Lord Canning, who was very anxious that such a measure should be passed, consented to defer his departure from India in order that he, with his great experience of that country, might introduce the change. The present constitution of the Council for legislative purposes having failed, we have naturally to consider what should be substituted, and in doing so we must advert to the two extreme notions with regard to legislation which prevail in India. The notion of legislation which is entertained by a native is that of a chief or sovereign, who makes what laws he pleases. He has little or no idea of any distinction between the executive and legislative functions of Government. A native chief will assemble his nobles around him in the Durbar, where they freely and frankly express their opinions ; but, having informed himself by their communications, he determines by his own will what shall be done. Among the various proposals which have been made for the government of India is one that the power of legislation should rest entirely on the Executive, but that there should be a consultative body ; that is, that the Governor-General should assemble, from time to time, a considerable number of persons, whose opinions he should hear, but by whose opinions he should not be bound ; and that he should himself consider and decide what measures should be adopted. In the last Session of Parliament Lord Ellenborough developed a scheme approaching this in character in the House of Lords ; but hon. gentlemen will see in the dispatches which have been laid upon the Table, that both Lord Canning considers this impossible, and all the Members of his Government, as well as the Members of the Indian Council, concur in the opinion that, in the present state of feeling in India, it is quite impossible to revert to a state of things in which the Executive Government alone legislated for the country. The opposite extreme is the desire which is natural to Englishmen wherever they be—that they should have a representative body to make the laws by which they are to be governed. I am sure, however, that every one who considers the condition of India will see that it is utterly impossible to constitute such a body in that country. You cannot possibly assemble at any one place in India persons who shall be the real representatives of the various classes of the native population of that empire. It is quite true that when you diminish the area over which legislation is to extend you diminish the difficulty of such a plan. In Ceylon, which is not more extensive than a large collectorate in India, you have a legislative body consisting partly of

Englishmen and partly of natives, and I do not know that the Government has worked unsuccessfully ; but with the extended area with which we have to deal in India, it would be physically impossible to constitute such a body. The natives who are resident in the towns no more represent the resident native population than a highly educated native of London, at the present day, represents a highland chieftain or a feudal baron of half a dozen centuries ago. To talk of a native representation is, therefore, to talk of that which is simply and utterly impossible. Then comes the question to what extent we can have a representation of the English settlers in India. No doubt, it would not be difficult to obtain a representation of their interests ; but I must say that of all governing or legislative bodies, none is so dangerous or so mischievous as one which represents a dominant race ruling over an extended native population. All experience teaches us that, where a dominant race rules another, the mildest form of government is a despotism. It was so in the case of the democratic republics of Greece, and the more aristocratic or autocratic sway of Rome ; and it has been so, I believe, at all times and among all nations in every part of the world. The other day I found in Mr. Mill's book upon *Representative Government* a passage which I will read—not because I go its entire length, but because it expresses in strong terms what I believe is in the main correct. Mr. Mill says :

· ' Now, if there be a fact to which all experience testifies, it is that, when a country holds another in subjection, the individuals of the ruling people who resort to the foreign country to make their fortunes are, of all others, those who most need to be held under powerful restraint. They are always one of the chief difficulties of the Government. Armed with the prestige and filled with the scornful over-bearingness of the conquering nation, they have the feelings inspired by absolute power, without its sense of responsibility.

I cannot, therefore, consent to create a powerful body of such a character. It must be remembered, also, that the natives do not distinguish very clearly between the acts of the Government itself and the acts of those who apparently constitute it, namely, the members of the Legislative Council ; and in one of Lord Canning's dispatches he points out the mischiefs which have on that account risen from publicity. He says that, so far as the English settlers are concerned, publicity is advantageous ; but that, if publicity is to continue, care must be taken to prevent the natives confounding the measures which are adopted with injudicious speeches which may be made in the Legislative Council. I feel it, therefore, necessary to strengthen the hands of the Government, so as to enable them not only by veto to prevent the passing of a law, but to prevent the introduction of any Bill which they think calculated to excite the minds of the native population; repeating the caution which I have before given, I say it behoves us to be cautious and careful in our legislation. I have seen a measure which I myself introduced in 1853, with one view, changed by the mode in which it was carried into execution so as to give it an operation totally different from that which I intended. The mischiefs resulting from that change have been great ; and I am, therefore, anxious that in any measure which I may propose and which the House, I hope, will adopt, we should take care, as far as possible, to avoid the likelihood of misconstruction or misapplication by the Government of India. It is easy at any future time to go farther, but it is difficult to draw back from what we have once agreed to. The dispatches of Lord Canning contain pretty full details of the scheme which he would recommend. Those dispatches have been long under the consideration of the Council of India, and with their concurrence I have framed a measure which embodies the leading suggestions of Lord Canning. I propose that, when the Governor-General's Council meets for the purpose of making laws and regulations, the Governor-General should summon, in addition to the ordinary members of the Council, not less than six nor môre than twelve additional members, of whom one-half at least shall not hold office under Government. These additional members may be either Europeans, persons of European extraction, or natives. Lord Canning strongly recommends that the Council should hold its meetings in different parts of India, for the purpose of obtaining at times the assistance of those native chiefs and noblemen whose attendance at Calcutta would be impossible, or irksome to themselves. I do not propose that the judges *ex officio* shall have seats in the Legislature ; but I do not preclude the Governor-General from summoning one of their number if he chooses. They were useful members of a body meeting as a committee for the purpose of discussing and framing laws, but I think it is inexpedient and incompatible with their functions that they should belong to a body partaking in any degree of a popular character. I propose that the persons nominated should attend all meetings held within

a year. If you compel their attendance for a
longer period you render it very unlikely that any
natives except those resident upon the spot will
attend the meetings of the Council. This also is
recommended by Lord Canning. Hon. gentlemen
will have noticed 'the great success which has
attended the association with us of the Talookdars
of Oude and of the Sirdars in the Punjab in the
duties of administering the revenue, and Lord
Canning has borne testimony to the admirable
manner in which they have performed their
duties. I believe greater advantages will result
from admitting the native chiefs to co-operate
with us for legislative purposes ; they will no
longer feel, as they have hitherto done, that they
are excluded from the management of affairs in
their own country, and nothing, I am persuaded,
will tend more to conciliate to our rule the minds
of natives of high rank. I have no intention of
doing anything to make this Council a debating
society ; I wish, to quote an expression of Sir
Lawrence Peel, to render them a body for making
laws. The Council of the Governor-General, with
these additional members, will have power to pass
laws and regulations affecting the whole of India,
and will have a supreme and concurrent power
with the minor legislative bodies which I propose
to establish in the Presidencies and in other parts
of India. I come now to the power of making
laws which I propose to give the Governors and
Councils of the other Presidencies. Lord Canning
strongly feels that, although great benefits have
resulted from the introduction of members into
his Councils who possess a knowledge of localities
—the interests of which differ widely in different

parts of the country—the change has not been sufficient, in the first place, to overcome the feeling which the other Presidencies entertain against being overridden, as they call it, by the Bengal Council ; or, on the other hand, to overcome the disadvantages of having a body legislating for these Presidencies without acquaintance with local wants and necessities. This must obviously be possessed to a much greater extent by those residing on and nearer the spot. And, therefore, I propose to restore, I may say, to the Presidencies of Madras and Bombay the power of passing laws and enactments on local subjects within their own territories, and that the Governor of the Presidency, in the same manner as the Governor-General, when his council meets to make laws, shall summon a certain number of additional members, to be as before either European or native, and one-half of whom at least shall not be office-holders. It is obviously necessary that these bodies should not be empowered to legislate on subjects which I may call of Indian rather than of local importance. The Indian debt, the customs of the country, the army of India, and other matters, into the details of which it is not necessary that I should enter, belong to a class of subjects which the local Legislatures will be prohibited from entering upon without the sanction of the Governor-General. I propose that Councils rather differently consti- tuted should be established at Bengal; and, if the Governor-General thinks right, as he obviously does from his dispatches, that he shall be empowered hereafter—but not without the sanction of the Secretary of State—to create a Council for the North-West Provinces, or the Punjab, or any other part of India which he may think desirable. It has been represented that the province of Pegu might, perhaps, be constituted into a separate Government, with a Council. I somewhat doubt whether it is at present ripe for such a change ; but, when it has acquired sufficient importance, no doubt the district will be better administered in that way than it is at present. By this means, while we shall attain a general uniformity of legislation, with a sufficient diversity for the differences of each part of India, we shall, I hope, adapt the system to the wants of particular localities. It is quite clear that the public works may be better dealt with by local bodies than by a central authority; but, as each district might be disposed to repudiate liability to maintain its share of the army, on the ground that it would not be first exposed to danger, and as it is highly desirable that the distribution of troops should be in the hands of the central authority, I think that the army, among others, is a subject which should be left to the General Council. The Bill also gives power to the Governor-General in cases of emergency to pass an ordinance having the force of law for a limited period. Questions might arise from the Arms Act, or the press, as to which it would be very injudicious that delay should occur ; and we, therefore, propose to empower the Governor-General on his own authority to pass an ordinance having the force of law, to continue for a period of six months, unless disallowed by the Secretary of State or superseded by an Act of the Legislature. I believe I have now gone through the main provisions of the Bill. They have been carefully considered by the members of the Indian Council men drawn from every part of India, of every profession, and with the most varied experience. The measure has been prepared with their entire concurrence, and it has the approval of most of the persons with whom I have conversed on the subject. All I can say is that every precaution has been taken in the framing of the Bill to make it effectual for the accomplishment of the object which it is designed to achieve. Every one has been consulted whose opinion I thought ought to be taken. It has been carefully considered by the Government in India and the Government at home. I venture therefore, to submit it to the House in the hope that, with such amendments as may be made in it in its progress through Parliament, it may tend to the happiness of India and the prosperity of the Queen's subjects in that portion of Her Majesty's dominions.

The right hon. Baronet concluded by moving for leave to bring in a Bill to amend, in certain respects, the constitution of the Council of the Governor-General of India, and to authorize making laws and regulations for the Presidencies of Fort St. George and Bombay, and for other parts of Her Majesty's Indian territories.

2. *Indian Councils Act*, 1861 (24 & 25 *Victoria, c.* 67)

An Act to make better provision for the Constitution of the Council of the Governor-General of India, and for the Local Government of the several Presidencies and Provinces of India, and for the temporary Government of India in the event of a vacancy in the office of Governor-General. (1 August 1861.)

1. This Act may be cited for all purposes as ' the Indian Councils Act, 1861.'

2. [*Repeal of* 3 & 4 *Will.* 4. *c.* 85, *ss.* 40, 43, 44, 50, 66, 70, *and so much of ss.* 61, 64 *as relates to vacancies in the office of ordinary member of the Council of India ; also* 16 & 17 *Vict. c.* 95, *ss.* 22–4, 26.] All other enactments whatsoever now in force with relation to the Council of the Governor-General of India, or to the Councils of the Governors of the respective Presidencies of Fort Saint George and Bombay, shall, save so far as the same are altered by or are repugnant to this Act, continue in force, and be applicable to the Council of the Governor-General of India and the Councils of the respective Presidencies under this Act.

3. There shall be five ordinary members of the said Council of the Governor-General, three of whom shall from time to time be appointed by the Secretary of State for India in Council, with the concurrence of a majority of members present at a meeting,[1] from among such persons as shall have been, at the time of such appointment, in the service in India of the Crown, or of the Company and the Crown, for at least ten years ; and if the person so appointed shall be in the military service of the Crown he shall not, during his continuance in office as a Member of Council, hold any military command, or be employed in actual military duties, and the remaining two, one of whom shall be a barrister or a member of the Faculty of Advocates in Scotland of not less than five years

---

[1] The power of appointment was given to the Crown by 32 & 33 Vict. c. 97.

standing, shall be appointed from time to time by Her Majesty by Warrant under Her Royal Sign Manual ; and it shall be lawful for the Secretary of State in Council to appoint the Commander-in-Chief of Her Majesty's Forces in India to be an extraordinary member of the said Council, and such extraordinary member of Council shall have rank and precedence at the Council Board next after the Governor-General.

4. The present ordinary members of the Council of the Governor-General of India shall continue to be ordinary members under and for the purposes of this Act; and it shall be lawful for her Majesty on the passing of this Act, to appoint by warrant as aforesaid an ordinary member of Council, to complete the number of five hereby established ; and there shall be paid to such ordinary member, and to all other ordinary members who may be hereafter appointed, such amount of salary as may from time to time be fixed for members of the Council of the Governor-General by the Secretary of State in Council, with the concurrence of a majority of members of Council present at a meeting ; and all enactments of any Act of Parliament or Law of India respecting the Council of the Governor-General of India and the members thereof shall be held to apply to the said Council as constituted by this Act, except so far as they are repealed by or are repugnant to any provisions of this Act.

5. It shall be lawful for the Secretary of State in Council with the concurrence of a majority of members present at a meeting, and for Her Majesty by warrant as aforesaid, respectively, to appoint any person provisionally to succeed to

the office of ordinary member of the Council of the Governor-General, when the same shall become vacant by the death or resignation of the person holding the said office, or on his departure from India with intent to return to Europe, or on any event and contingency expressed in any such provisional appointment, and such appointment again to revoke ; but no persons appointed to succeed provisionally to such office shall be entitled to any authority, salary, or emolument appertaining thereto until he shall be in the actual possession of such office.

6. Whenever the said Governor-General in Council shall declare that it is expedient that the said Governor-General should visit any part of India unaccompanied by his Council, it shall be lawful for the said Governor-General in Council, previously to the departure of the said Governor-General, to nominate some member of the said Council to be president of the said Council, in whom, during the time of such visit, the powers of the said Governor-General in assemblies of the said Council shall be reposed, except that of assenting to or withholding his assent from, or reserving for the signification of Her Majesty's pleasure, any law or regulation, as hereinafter provided ; and it shall be lawful in every such case for the said Governor-General in Council, by an order for that purpose to be made, to authorize the Governor-General alone to exercise all or any of the powers which might be exercised by the said Governor-General in Council in every case in which the said Governor-General may think it expedient to exercise the same, except the power of making laws or regulations.

7. Whenever the Governor-General, or such president so nominated as aforesaid, shall be obliged to absent himself from any meeting of Council (other than meetings for the purpose of making laws and regulations, as hereinafter provided), owing to indisposition or any other cause whatsoever, and shall signify his intended absence to the Council, then and in every such case the senior member for the time being who shall be present at such meeting shall preside thereat, in such manner, and with such full powers and authorities during the time of such meeting, as such Governor-General or president would have had in case he had been present at such meeting : provided always, that no act of Council made at any such meeting shall be valid to any effect whatsoever unless the same shall be signed by such Governor-General or president respectively, if such Governor-General or president shall at the time be resident at the place at which such meeting shall be assembled, and shall not be prevented by such indisposition from signing the same, provided always that in case such Governor-General or president, not being so prevented as aforesaid, shall decline or refuse to sign such act of Council, he, and the several members of Council who shall have signed the same, shall mutually exchange with and communicate in writing to each other the grounds and reasons of their respective opinions, in like manner and subject to such regulations and ultimate responsibility as are by the East India Company Act, 1793, sections forty-seven, forty-eight, forty-nine, fifty, and fifty-one, provided and described in cases where such Governor-General shall, when present, dis-

sent from any measure proposed or agitated in the Council.

8. It shall be lawful for the Governor-General from time to time to make rules and orders for the more convenient transaction of business in the said Council ; and any order made or act done in accordance with such rules and orders (except as hereafter provided respecting laws and regulations) shall be deemed to be the order or act of the Governor-General in Council.

9. The said Council shall from time to time assemble at such place or places as shall be appointed by the Governor-General in Council within the territories of India ; and as often as the said Council shall assemble within either of the Presidencies of Fort Saint George or Bombay, the Governor of such Presidency shall act as an extraordinary member of Council ; and as often as the said Council shall assemble with any other division, province, or territory having a Lieutenant-Governor, such Lieutenant-Governor shall act as an additional councillor at meetings of the Council, for the purpose of making laws and regulations only, in manner hereinafter provided.

10. For the better exercise of the power of making laws and regulations vested in the Governor-General in Council, the Governor-General shall nominate, in addition to the ordinary and extraordinary members above mentioned, and to such Lieutenant-Governor in the case aforesaid, such persons,[1] not less than six nor more than twelve in number, as to him may seem expedient, to be members of Council for the purpose of making laws

---

[1] Not less than ten nor more than sixteen, 55 & 56 Vict. c. 14, s. 1.

and regulations only, and such persons shall not be entitled to sit or vote at any meeting of Council, except at meetings held for such purpose : Provided that not less than one half of the persons so nominated shall be non-official persons, that is, persons, who at the date of such nomination, shall not be in the civil or military service of the Crown in India, and that the seat in Council of any non-official member accepting office under the Crown in India shall be vacated on such acceptance.

11. Every additional member of Council so nominated shall be summoned to all meetings held for the purpose of making laws and regulations, for the term of two years from the date of such nomination.

12. It shall be lawful for any such additional member of Council to resign his office to the Governor-General, and on acceptance of such resignation by the Governor-General such office shall become vacant.

13.[1] On the event of a vacancy occurring by the death, acceptance of office, or resignation, accepted in manner aforesaid, of any such additional member of Council, it shall be lawful for the Governor-General to nominate any person as additional member of Council in his place, who shall exercise the same functions until the termination of the term for which the additional member so dying, accepting office, or resigning was nominated : Provided always that it shall not be lawful for him by such nomination to diminish the proportion of non-official additional members hereinbefore directed to be nominated.

[1] S. 13 repealed by 55 & 56 Vict. c. 14, s. 4.

14. No law or regulation made by the Governor-General in Council, in accordance with the provisions of this Act, shall be deemed invalid by reason only that the proportion of non-official additional members hereby provided was not complete at the date of its introduction to the Council or its enactment.

15. In the absence of the Governor-General and of the president, nominated as aforesaid, the senior ordinary member of the Council present shall preside at meetings of the Council for making laws and regulations ; and the power of making laws and regulations vested in the Governor-General in Council shall be exercised only at meetings of the said Council at which such Governor-General or president, or some ordinary member of Council and six or more members of the said Council (including under the term members of the Council such additional members as aforesaid), shall be present ; and in every case of difference of opinion at meetings of the said Council for making laws and regulations where there shall be an equality of voices, the Governor-General, or in his absence the president, and in the absence of the Governor-General and president such senior ordinary member of Council there presiding, shall have two votes or the casting vote.

16.[1] The Governor-General in Council shall, as soon as conveniently may be, appoint a place and time for the first meeting of the said Council of the Governor-General for making laws and regulations under this Act, and summon thereto as well the additional Councillors nominated by and

[1] S. 16 repealed by 55 & 56 Vict. c. 19. (*S. L. R.*)

under this Act as the other members of such Council; and until such first meeting the powers now vested in the said Governor-General of India in Council of making laws and regulations shall and may be exercised in like manner and by the same members as before the passing of this Act.

17. It shall be lawful for the Governor-General in Council from time to time to appoint all other times and places of meeting of the Council for the purpose of making laws and regulations under the provisions of this Act, and to adjourn, or from time to time to authorize such President, or senior ordinary member of Council in his absence, to adjourn any meeting for the purpose of making laws and regulations from time to time and from place to place.

18. It shall be lawful for the Governor-General in Council to make rules for the conduct of business at meetings of the Council for the purpose of making laws and regulations under the provisions of this Act, prior to the first of such meetings, but such rules may be subsequently amended at meetings for the purpose of making laws or regulations, subject to the assent of the Governor-General; and such rules shall prescribe the mode of promulgation and authentication of such laws and regulations : Provided always that it shall be lawful for the Secretary of State in Council to disallow any such rule, and to render it of no effect.

19. No business shall be transacted at any meeting for the purpose of making laws and regulations, except as last hereinbefore provided, other than the consideration and enactments of measures introduced into the Council for the

purpose of such enactment ; and it shall not be lawful for any member or additional member to make or for the Council to entertain any motion, unless such motion be for leave to introduce some measure as aforesaid into Council, or have reference to some measure actually introduced thereinto : Provided always that it shall not be lawful for any member or additional member to introduce, without the previous sanction of the Governor-General, any measure affecting,—

1st. The Public Debt or Public Revenues of India, or by which any charge would be imposed on such Revenues :

2nd. The religion or religious rites and usages of any class of Her Majesty's subjects in India :

3rd. The discipline or maintenance of any part of Her Majesty's Military or Naval Forces :

4th. The relations of the Government with foreign Princes or States.

20. When any law or regulation has been made by the Council at a meeting for the purpose of making laws and regulations as aforesaid, it shall be lawful for the Governor-General, whether he shall or shall not have been present in Council at the making thereof, to declare that he assents to the same, or that he withholds his assent from the same, or that he reserves the same for the significa-tion of the pleasure of Her Majesty thereon ; no such law or regulation shall have validity until the Governor-General shall have declared his assent to the same, or until (in the case of a law or regulation so reserved as aforesaid) Her Majesty shall have signified her assent to the same to the Governor-General, through the Secretary of

State for India in Council, and such assent shall
have been duly proclaimed by the said Governor-
General.

21. Whenever any such law or regulation has
been assented to by the Governor-General, he
shall transmit to the Secretary of State for India
an authentic copy thereof ; and it shall be lawful
for Her Majesty to signify, through the Secretary
of State for India in Council, her disallowance of
such law ; and such disallowance shall make void
and annul such law from or after the day on which
the Governor-General shall make known, by
proclamation or by signification to his Council,
that he has received the notification of such
disallowance by Her Majesty.

22. The Governor-General in Council shall have
power at meetings for the purpose of making laws
and regulations as aforesaid, and subject to the
provisions herein contained, to make laws and
regulations for repealing, amending, or altering
any laws or regulations whatever, now in force or
hereafter to be in force in the Indian territories
now [or hereafter [1]] under the dominion of Her
Majesty, and to make laws and regulations for all
persons, whether British or native, foreigners or
others, and for all Courts of Justice whatever, and
for all places and things whatever within the said
territories, and for all servants of the Government
of India within the dominions of princes and
states in alliance with Her Majesty ; and the laws
and regulations so to be made by the Governor-
General in Council shall control and supersede
any laws and regulations in anywise repugnant
thereto which shall have been made prior thereto

[1] Words in brackets inserted by 55 & 56 Vict. c. 14 s. 3.

by the Governors of the Presidencies of Fort Saint George and Bombay respectively in Council or the Governor or Lieutenant-Governor in Council of any Presidency or other territory for which a Council may be appointed, with power to make laws and regulations under and by virtue of this Act : Provided always that the said Governor-General in Council shall not have the power of making any laws or regulations which shall repeal or in any way affect any of the provisions of this Act :

Or any of the provisions of the Government of India Act, 1833, and of the Government of India Act, 1854, which after the passing of this Act shall remain in force :

Or any provisions of the Government of India Act, 1858, or of the Government of India Act, 1859 :

Or of any Act enabling the Secretary of State in Council to raise money in the United Kingdom for the Government of India :

Or of the Acts for punishing mutiny and desertion in Her Majesty's Army or in Her Majesty's Indian forces respectively ; but subject to the provision contained in the Government of India Act, 1833, section seventy-three, respecting the Indian Articles of War :

Or any provisions of any Act passed in this present session of Parliament, or hereafter to be passed, in anywise affecting Her Majesty's Indian territories, or the inhabitants thereof :

Or which may affect the authority of Parliament, or the constitution and rights of the East India Company, or any part of the unwritten laws or constitution of the United Kingdom of Great Britain and Ireland, whereon may depend in any degree the allegiance of any persons to the Crown of the United Kingdom, or the sovereignty or dominion of the Crown over any part of the said territories.

23. Notwithstanding anything in this Act contained, it shall be lawful for the Governor-General, in cases of emergency, to make and promulgate from time to time ordinances for the peace and good government of the said territories or of any part thereof, subject however to the restrictions contained in the last preceding section; and every such ordinance shall have like force of law or regulation made by the Governor-General in Council, as by this Act provided, for the space of not more than six months from its promulgation, unless the disallowance of such ordinance by Her Majesty shall be earlier signified to the Governor-General by the Secretary of State for India in Council, or unless such ordinance shall be controlled or superseded by some law or regulation made by the Governor-General in Council at a meeting for the purpose of making laws and regulations as by this Act provided.

24. No law or regulation made by the Governor-General in Council (subject to the power of disallowance by the Crown, as hereinbefore provided), shall be deemed invalid by reason only that it affects the prerogative of the Crown.

25. Whereas doubts have been entertained whether the Governor-General of India, or the Governor-General in India in Council, had the power of making rules, laws, and regulations for the territories known from time to time as ' Non-

regulation Provinces', except at meetings for making laws and regulation in conformity with the provisions of the Government of India Acts, 1833 and 1853, and whether the Governor, or Governor in Council, or Lieutenant-Governor of any Presidency or part of India, had such power in respect of any such territories : Be it enacted, that no rule, law, or regulation which prior to the passing of this Act shall have been made by the Governor-General, or Governor-General in Council, or by any other of the authorities aforesaid, for and in respect of any such Non-regulation Province, shall be deemed invalid only by reason of the same not having been made in conformity with the provisions of the said Acts, or of any other Act of Parliament respecting the constitution and powers of the Council of India or of the Governor-General, or respecting the powers of such Governors, or Governors in Council, or Lieutenant-Governors as aforesaid.

26. It shall be lawful for the Governor-General in Council, or Governor in Council of either of the Presidencies, as the case may be, to grant to an ordinary member of Council leave of absence, under medical certificate, for a period not exceeding six months ; and such member, during his absence, shall retain his office, and shall, on his return and resumption of his duties, receive half his salary for the period of such absence, but, if his absence shall exceed six months, his office shall be vacated.

27. If any vacancy shall happen in the office of an ordinary member of the Council of the Governor-General, or of the Council of either of the Presiden-

cies, when no person provisionally appointed to
succeed thereto shall be then present on the spot,
then, and on every such occasion, such vacancy
shall be supplied by the appointment of the
Governor-General in Council, or the Governor in
Council, as the case may be ; and until a successor
shall arrive, the person so nominated shall execute
the office to which he shall have been appointed,
and shall have all the powers thereof, and shall
have and be entitled to the salary and other
emoluments and advantages appertaining to the
said office during his continuance therein, every
such temporary member of Council foregoing all
salaries and allowances by him held and enjoyed
at the time of his being appointed to such office ;
and if any ordinary member of the Council of the
Governor-General, or of the Council of either of
the Presidencies, shall, by any infirmity or otherwise, be rendered incapable of acting or of attending
to act as such, or if any such member shall be
absent on leave, and if any person shall have been
provisionally appointed as aforesaid, then the
place of such member absent or unable to attend
shall be supplied by such person ; and if no person
provisionally appointed to succeed to the office
shall be then on the spot, the Governor-General
in Council, or Governor in Council, as the case may
be, shall appoint some person to be a temporary
member of Council, and, until the return of the
member so absent or unable to attend, the person
so provisionally appointed by the Secretary of
State in Council, or so appointed by the Governor-
General in Council, or Governor in Council, as the
case may be, shall execute the office to which he
shall have been appointed, and shall have all the

powers thereof, and shall receive half the salary of the member of Council whose place he supplies, and also half the salary of his office under the Government of India, or the Government of either of the Presidencies, as the case may be, if he hold any such office, the remaining half of such last-named salary being at the disposal of the Government of India, or other Government as aforesaid : Provided always that no person shall be appointed a temporary member of the said Council who might not have been appointed as hereinbefore provided to fill the vacancy supplied by such temporary appointment.

28. It shall be lawful for the Governors of the Presidencies of Fort Saint George and Bombay respectively from time to time to make rules and orders for the conduct of business in their Councils, and any order made or act done in accordance with such directions (except as hereinafter provided respecting laws and regulations) shall be deemed to be the order or act of the Governor in Council.

29. For the better exercise of the power of making laws and regulations hereinafter vested in the Governors of the said Presidencies in Council respectively, each of the said Governors shall, in addition to the members whereof his Council now by law consists, or may consist, termed herein ordinary members, nominate to be additional members the Advocate-General of the Presidency, or officer acting in that capacity, and such other persons,[1] not less than four nor more than eight in number, as to him may seem expedient, to be

---

[1] Not less than eight nor more than twenty, besides the Advocate-General of the Presidency or officer acting in that capacity, 55 & 56 Vict. c. 14, s. 1.

members of Council, for the purpose of making laws and regulations only, and such members shall not be entitled to sit or vote at any meeting of Council, except at meetings held for such purpose ; Provided that not less than half of the persons so nominated shall be non-official persons, as hereinbefore described, and that the seat in Council of any non-official member accepting office under the Crown in India shall be vacated on such acceptance.

30. Every additional member of Council so nominated shall be summoned to all meetings held for the purpose of making laws and regulations for the term of two years from the date of such nomination.

31. It shall be lawful for any such additional member of Council to resign his office to the Governor of the Presidency ; and on acceptance of such resignation by the Governor of the Presidency such office shall become vacant.

32.[1] On the event of a vacancy occurring by the death, acceptance of office, or resignation accepted in manner aforesaid, of any such additional member of Council, it shall be lawful for the Governor of the Presidency to summon any person as additional member of Council in his place, who shall exercise the same functions until the termination of the term for which the additional member so dying, accepting office, or resigning was nominated : Provided always that it shall not be lawful for him by such nomination to diminish the proportion of non-official members hereinbefore directed to be nominated.

33. No law or regulation made by any such Governor in Council in accordance with the

---

[1] S. 32 repealed by 55 & 56 Vict. c. 14, s. 4.

provision of this Act shall be deemed invalid by
reason only that the proportion of non-official
additional members hereby established was not
complete at the date of its introduction to the
Council or its enactment.

34. At any meeting of the Council of either of
the said presidencies from which the Governor
shall be absent, the senior civil ordinary member
of Council present shall preside ; and the power
of making laws and regulations hereby vested in
such Governor in Council shall be exercised only
at meetings of such Council at which the Governor,
or some ordinary member of Council, and four or
more members of Council (including under the
term members of Council such additional members
as aforesaid) shall be present; and in any case
of difference of opinion at meetings of any such
Council for making laws and regulations, where
there shall be an equality of voices, the Governor,
or in his absence the senior member then presiding,
shall have two votes or the casting vote.

35.[1] The Governor-General in Council shall, as
soon as conveniently may be, appoint the time for
the first meeting of the Councils of Fort Saint
George and Bombay respectively, for the purpose
of making laws and regulations under this Act,
and the Governors of the said Presidencies respectively shall summon to such meeting as well
the additional councillors appointed by and under
this Act as the ordinary members of the said
Councils.

36. It shall be lawful for every such Governor
to appoint all subsequent times and places of
meeting of his Council for the purpose of making

[1] S. 35 repealed by 55 & 56 Vict. c. 19 (S. L. R.).

laws and regulations under the provisions of this Act, and to adjourn or from time to time to authorize such senior ordinary member of Council in his absence to adjourn any meeting for making laws and regulations from time to time and from place to place.

37. Previously to the first of such meetings of their Councils for the purpose of making laws and regulations under the provisions of this Act, the Governors of the said Presidencies in Council respectively shall make rules for the conduct of business at such meetings, subject to the sanction of the Governor-General in Council; but such rules may be subsequently amended at meetings for the purpose of making laws and regulations, subject to the assent of the Governor : Provided always that it shall be lawful for the Governor-General in Council to disallow any such rule, and render the same of no effect.

38. No business shall be transacted at any meeting of the Council of either of the said Presidencies for the purpose of making laws and regulations (except as last hereinbefore provided) other than the consideration and enactment of measures introduced into such Council for the purpose of such enactment ; and it shall not be lawful for any member or additional member to make, or for the Council to entertain, any motion, unless such motion shall be for leave to introduce some measure as aforesaid into Council, or have reference to some measures actually introduced thereinto : Provided always that it shall not be lawful for any member or additional member to introduce, without the previous sanction of the Governor, any measure affecting the public revenues of the

Presidency, or by which any charge shall be imposed on such revenues.

39. When any law or regulation has been made by any such Council at a meeting for the purpose of making laws and regulations as aforesaid, it shall be lawful for the Governor, whether he shall or shall not have been present in Council at such meeting, to declare that he assents to, or withholds his assent from, the same.

40. The Governor shall transmit forthwith an authentic copy of every law or regulation to which he shall have so declared his assent to the Governor-General, and no such law or regulation shall have validity until the Governor-General shall have assented thereto, and such assent shall have been signified by him to and published by the Governor : Provided always, that in every case where the Governor-General shall withold his assent from any such law or regulation, he shall signify to the Governor in writing his reason for so witholding his assent.

41. Whenever such law or regulation shall have been assented to by the Governor-General, he shall transmit to the Secretary of State for India an authentic copy thereof ; and it shall be lawful for Her Majesty to signify, through the Secretary of State for India in Council, her disallowance of such law or regulation, and such disallowance shall make void and annul such law or regulation from or after the day on which such Governor shall make known by proclamation, or by signification to the Council, that he has received the notification of such disallowance by Her Majesty.

42. The Governor of each of the said Presidencies in Council shall have power at meetings for the

purpose of making laws and regulations as aforesaid, and, subject to the provision herein contained
to make laws and regulations for the peace and
good government of such Presidency, and for
that purpose to repeal and amend any laws and
regulations made prior to the coming into operation
of this Act by an authority in India, so far as they
affect such Presidency : Provided always that
such Governor in Council shall not have the power
of making any laws or regulations which shall in
any way affect any of the provisions of this Act,
or of any other Act of Parliament in force, or
hereafter to be in force, in such Presidency.

43. It shall not be lawful for the Governor
in Council of either of the aforesaid Presidencies,
except with the sanction of the Governor-General,
previously communicated to him, to make regulations or take into consideration any law or
regulation for any of the purposes next hereinafter
mentioned ; that is to say,

1. Affecting the Public Debt in India, or the
   Customs Duties, or any other tax or duty
   now in force and imposed by the authority
   of the Government of India for the general
   purposes of such Government :

2. Regulating any of the current coin, or the
   issue of any bills, notes, or other paper
   currency :

3. Regulating the conveyance of letters by the
   Post Office or messages by the electric
   telegraph within the Presidency :

4. Altering in any way the Penal Code of India,
   as established by Act of the Governor-
   General in Council, No. 42 of 1860 :

5. Affecting the religion or religious rites and

usages of any class of Her Majesty's
subjects in India :

6. Affecting the discipline or maintenance of
any part of Her Majesty's military or
naval forces :

7. Regulating patents or copyright :

8. Affecting the relations of the Government
with foreign princes or states :

Provided always that no law, or provision of
any law or regulation which shall have been made
by any such Governor in Council, and assented to
by the Governor-General as aforesaid, shall be
deemed invalid only by reason of its relating to any
of the purposes comprised in the above list.

44. The Governor-General in Council, so soon
as it shall appear to him expedient, shall, by
proclamation, extend the provisions of this Act
touching the making of laws and regulations for
the peace and good government of the Presidencies
of Fort Saint George and Bombay to the Bengal
Division of the Presidency of Fort William, and
shall specify in such proclamation the period
at which such provisions shall take effect and
the number of councillors whom the Lieutenant-
Governor of the said division may nominate for
his assistance in making laws and regulations ;
and it shall be further lawful for the Governor-
General in Council, from time to time and in his
discretion, by similar proclamation, to extend
the same provisions to the territories known as
the North-Western Provinces and the Punjab
respectively.

45. Whenever such proclamation as aforesaid
shall have been issued regarding the said division
of territories respectively, the Lieutenant-Governor

thereof shall nominate, for his assistance in making laws and regulations, such number of councillors as shall be in such proclamation specified ; provided that not less than one-third of such Councillors shall in every case be non-official persons, as hereinbefore described, and that the nomination of such councillors shall be subject to the sanction of the Governor-General ; and provided further, that at any meeting of any such Council from which the Lieutenant-Governor shall be absent, the member highest in official rank among those who may hold office under the Crown shall preside ; and the power of making laws and regulations shall be exercised only at meetings at which the Lieutenant-Governor or some member holding office as aforesaid, and not less than one-half of the members of Council so summoned as aforesaid, shall be present ; and in any case of difference of opinion at any meetings of such Council for making laws and regulations, where there shall be an equality of voices, the Lieutenant-Governor, or such member highest in official rank as aforesaid then presiding, shall have two votes or the casting vote.

46. It shall be lawful for the Governor-General, by proclamation as aforesaid, to constitute from time to time new provinces for the purposes of this Act, to which the like provisions shall be applicable ; and further to appoint from time to time a Lieutenant-Governor to any Province so constituted as aforesaid, and from time to time to declare and limit the extent of the authority of such Lieutenant-Governor, in like manner as is provided by the Government of India Act, 1854, respecting the Lieutenant-

Governors of Bengal, and the North-Western Provinces.

47. It shall be lawful for the Governor-General in Council, by such proclamation as aforesaid, to fix the limits of any Presidency, Division, Province, or Territory in India for the purposes of this Act, and further by proclamation to divide or alter from time to time the limits of any such Presidency, Division, Province, or Territory for the said purposes : Provided always that any law or regulation made by the Governor or Lieutenant-Governor in Council of any Presidency, Division, Province, or Territory shall continue in force in any part thereof which may be severed therefrom by any such proclamation until superseded by Law or regulation of the Governor-General in Council, or of the Governor or Lieutenant-Governor in Council of the Presidency, Division, Province, or Territory to which such parts may become annexed.

48. It shall be lawful for every such Lieutenant-Governor in Council thus constituted to make laws for the peace and good government of his respective Division, Province, or Territory ; and, except as otherwise hereinbefore specially provided, all the provisions in this Act contained respecting the nomination of additional members for the purpose of making laws and regulations for the Presidencies of Fort Saint George and Bombay, and limiting the power of the Governors in Council of Fort Saint George and Bombay for the purpose of making laws and regulations, and respecting the conduct of business in the meetings of such Councils for that purpose, and respecting the power of the Governor-General to declare or

withhold his assent to laws or regulations made by the Governor in Council of Fort Saint George and Bombay, and respecting the power of Her Majesty to disallow the same, shall apply to Laws or regulations to be so made by any such Lieutenant-Governor in Council.

49. Provided always that no proclamation to be made by the Governor-General in Council under the provisions of this Act for the purpose of constituting any Council for the Presidency, Division, Provinces, or Territories hereinbefore named, or any other Provinces, or for altering the boundaries of any Presidency, Division, Province, or Territory, or constituting any new Province for the purpose of this Act, shall have any force or validity until the sanction of Her Majesty to the same shall have been previously signified by the Secretary of State in Council to the Governor-General.

50. If any vacancy shall happen in the Office of Governor-General of India when no provisional successor shall be in India to supply such vacancy, then and in every such case the Governor of the Presidency of Fort Saint George or the Governor of the Presidency of Bombay who shall have been first appointed to the office of Governor by Her Majesty, shall hold and execute the said office of Governor-General of India and Governor of the Presidency of Fort William in Bengal until a successor shall arrive, or until some person in India shall be duly appointed thereto ; and every such acting Governor-General shall, during the time of his continuing to act as such, have and exercise all rights and powers of Governor-General of India, and shall be entitled to receive the emoluments

and advantages appertaining to the office by him supplied, such acting Governor-General foregoing the salary and allowances appertaining to the office of Governor to which he stands appointed, and such office of Governor shall be supplied for the time during which such Governor shall act as Governor-General, in the manner directed in section sixty-three of the Government of India Act, 1833.

51. If, on such vacancy occurring, it shall appear to the Governor, who by virtue of this Act shall hold and execute the said office of Governor-General, necessary to exercise the powers thereof before he shall have taken his seat in Council, it shall be lawful for him to make known by proclamation his appointment and his intention to assume the said office of Governor-General, and after such proclamation, and thenceforth until he shall repair to the place where the Council may assemble, it shall be lawful for him to exercise alone all or any of the powers which might be exercised by the Governor-General in Council, except the power of making laws and regulations; and all acts done in the exercise of the said powers, except as aforesaid, shall be of the same force and effect as if they had been done by the Governor-General in Council; Provided that all acts done in the said Council after the date of such proclamation, but before the communication thereof to such Council, shall be valid, subject nevertheless to revocation or alteration by such Governor who shall have so assumed the said office of Governor-General; and from the date of the vacancy occurring until such Governor shall have assumed the said office of Governor-General the provisions of section sixty-

two of the Government of India Act, 1833, shall
be and the same are declared to be applicable to
the case.

52. Nothing in this Act contained shall be held
to derogate from or interfere with (except as
hereinbefore expressly provided) the rights vested
in Her Majesty, or the powers of the Secretary of
State for India in Council, in relation to the
government of Her Majesty's Dominions in India,
under any law in force at the date of the passing
of this Act ; and all things which shall be done by
Her Majesty, or by the Secretary of State as aforesaid, in relation to such government, shall have
the same force and validity as if this Act had not
been passed.

53. Wherever any act or thing is by this Act
required or authorized to be done by the Governor-
General or by the Governors of the Presidencies of
Fort Saint George and Bombay in Council, it is
not required that such act or thing should be done
at a meeting for making laws and regulations,
unless where expressly provided.[1]

3. *George Nathaniel Curzon, House of Commons, 28 March, 1892*

I AM glad, sir, at this early period of the Session,
to be able to introduce to the notice of the House
a Bill which, if carried into law, will, I believe, be

---

[1] By 33 & 34 Vict. c. 3 the Governor-General in Council
was authorized to legislate by regulation for such territories as might be defined from time to time by the
Secretary of State in Council.

Legislative Councils were established, under s. 44, in
Bengal in 1862, North-Western Provinces and Oudh in
1886, and Punjab in 1897.

fraught with advantage to the interests of our fellow subjects in India. It is sometimes said, sir, that this House bestows a scant and reluctant concern upon the interests of the millions of India. And yet I am sure that this alleged indifference of the many, if it be true, which I do not altogether accept, is not more than compensated for by the vigilant and uncompromising attention of the few, whilst I have heard it stated on high authority that the greater interference of this House in the government of India might not be a source of unmixed benefit to that country. However that may be, sir, I hope that this Bill will be one that may approve itself to both sections of opinion in this House—both to those hon. members who may not have direct and personal experience of India, and to that smaller section who, either from long residence there or from official experience, are emphatically entitled to speak on Indian questions, and whose interference in our debates is always welcome. And perhaps I may be permitted to take this opportunity of expressing the regret which I am sure has been felt on both sides of the House at the disappearance from among their number of the omnivorous intellect of the late hon. gentleman the member for Kirkcaldy (Sir George Campbell). The object of this Bill which it is my duty to explain to the House is to widen the basis and to expand the functions of government in India ; to give further opportunities than at present exist to the non-official and native elements in Indian society to take part in the work of government, and in this way to lend official recognition to that remarkable development both of political interest and political capacity which has been visible among the higher classes of Indian society since the government of India was taken over by the Crown in 1858. In form this Bill is one to amend the Indian Councils Act of 1861. Legislative powers of some sort or other, but powers of somewhat confused character and conflicting validity, have existed in India for a very long time. They existed under the rule of the old East India Company, dating from the time of the Tudor and Stuart sovereigns ; but the modern legislative system, under which the government of India exists, owes its origin to the viceroyalty of Lord Canning, and the Secretaryship of State of Sir Charles Wood, afterwards Lord Halifax, who in 1861 carried through the House the Indian Councils Act of that year. I may, perhaps, in starting, be permitted to remind the House briefly of the provisions of that Act, as they are the basis on which we are now attempting to proceed. The Act of 1861 constituted three Legislative Councils in India—the Supreme Legislative Council of the Viceroy and the Provincial Legislative Councils of Madras and Bombay. The Supreme Legislative Council of the Viceroy, or, as it is called in the terms of the Act, the Council ' for the purpose of making laws and regulations only ', consists of the Governor-General and his Executive Council, with a minimum of six and a maximum of twelve additional members who are nominated by the Governor-General, and of whom at least one-half must be non-official, whether drawn from the European or the native element. The Legislative Councils of Madras and Bombay are also recruited by a minimum of four and a maximum of eight additional members who are nominated by the

Provincial Governor, and of whom at least one-half must be non-official. Since the passing of that Act, sir, Legislative Councils have been called into existence for Bengal and the North-West Provinces. In Bengal the Council consists of the Lieutenant-Governor and twelve nominated members, and the Council of the North-West Provinces consists of the Lieutenant-Governor and nine Councillors, of whom, in each case, one-third must be non-official. Such is the constitution of the legislative machinery which has existed during the past thirty years. This system has undoubtedly worked well. It has justified itself and the anticipations of its promoters. Operating to a very large extent through the agency of special · committees composed of experienced persons, it has proved to be an efficient instrument for the evolution of laws. The publicity which has attended every stage of its proceedings has had a good effect. A number of native gentlemen of intelligence, capacity, and public spirit have been persuaded to come forward and lend their services to the functions of government, and undoubtedly the standard of merit in these Legislative Councils has stood high. Indeed, I would venture to say that few better legislative machines, with regard to their efficacy for the particular object for which they were constructed, are anywhere in existence, nor can better legislation produced by such bodies be found in any other country. At the same time, these Councils have been subject to restrictions and limitations which were intentionally, and I think wisely, imposed upon them in the first place. The House must recognize that they are in no sense of the term parliamentary bodies. They are deliberative bodies with a comparatively narrow scope, inasmuch as they only assemble for the discussion of the immediate legislation which lies before them, and are not permitted to travel outside that very circumscribed radius. I will take the instance of financial discussion. In these Councils no financial discussion is possible unless there is a proposal for a new tax, and then it can only be in connexion with the immediate legislative proposal before the Council for the time being. Under these circumstances it has been felt that there has been wanting to the Government an opportunity of explaining its policy and of replying to hostile criticism and attack, such as a less restricted system of discussion would provide ; and that at the same time there was wanting an opportunity to the non-official element, to those who may legitimately call themselves the guardians of the public interest, of asking for information, stating their grievances, and becoming acquainted with the policy of the Government. These feelings have been expressed in many memorials which have been addressed over a large number of years to the Government of India by important public bodies and associations in India. They have been further testified to by successive Viceroys. Lord Dufferin, in a speech which he delivered at Calcutta in February 1887, the occasion being the celebration of the Queen's Jubilee, spoke of the desirability of reconstituting the Supreme Legislative Council of the Viceroy on a broader basis, and of enlarging its functions. And in the November of the following year he sent home a dispatch, extracts from which have been published in a parliamentary paper, in which he recommended in the first place a yearly financial discussion in the Supreme Legislative Council of the Budget of the year. And, sir, inasmuch as his words are of very great importance, and will, of course, carry deserved weight in this House, I hope the House will pardon me if I read some portions of it. Lord Dufferin said :

' I do not mean that Votes should be taken in regard to the various items of the Budget, or that the heads of expenditure should be submitted in detail for the examination of the Council, but simply that an opportunity should be given for a full, free, and thorough criticism and examination of the financial policy of the Government. Some such change as this would, I think, be as beneficial to the Indian administration as it would be in accordance with the wishes of the European and native mercantile world of India. At present the Government is exposed to every kind of misapprehension and misrepresentation in regard to its figures and the statement of their results. Were the matter to be gone into thoroughly and exhaustively on the occasion I suggest by independent critics, who, however anxious to detect a flaw and prove the Government wrong, would be masters of their subject and cognizant of the intricacies of Indian administration, the result would be more advantageous to the financial reputation of the Indian Government, as well as more conducive to improve her financial system, than the perfunctory debates of the House of Commons, and the imperfect criticism of Indian finance by some English newspapers.'

In the same dispatch Lord Dufferin expressed the opinion that questions should be asked in the Supreme Legislative Council, subject to certain restrictions, upon matters of domestic as distinguished from matters of Imperial interest. At the end of 1888 Lord Dufferin left India and was succeeded by the eminent statesman who now holds that office. Quite early in his viceroyalty, in a speech delivered in the Legislative Council in March 1889, Lord Lansdowne signified his approbation of the annual discussion of the Budget in the manner suggested, and also of the right of addressing questions to the Government on matters of public interest. Both these proposals were accepted by the Secretary of State in a dispatch dated August 1889, not merely as referring to the Supreme Legislative Council of the Viceroy but also in reference to the Provincial Councils. In the same dispatch my noble friend also signified his desire for an enlargement of the representation of public opinion in India by an addition to the number of members on these Councils by means of an extension of the present system of nomination, and, inasmuch as these changes were found to be impossible without fresh legislation, he also included a draft Bill upon which he invited the opinions of the Government of India and of the several Provincial Governments. These views and other suggestions were received from India, and they were found on the whole to be eminently favourable to the contemplated measure. From these terms sprang the Indian Councils Bill which it is now my privilege to introduce to the notice of this House. Now, a few words as to the parliamentary history of this measure. It has been in no ordinary degree a victim to the vicissitudes of parliamentary exis- tence. Its career up to this point has been one of mingled success and disappointment. It was introduced for the first time in the House of Lords by the Secretary of State in 1890, and a very important discussion—if I may venture humbly to express the opinion, the model of what such a discussion should be—took place on the second reading of the Bill. In Committee a number of important and valuable amendments were intro- duced in it by noble lords who have had experience

in the Government of India, and it passed through
that House. It came down in the same Session to
the House of Commons, but did not succeed in
getting beyond a first reading. In the ensuing
year, 1891, it was again introduced into this House,
and again it fell a victim to that fate which hon.
members, according to their political feelings, will
be disposed to ascribe to the hardships of fortune
or to the immoderate interest displayed by their
opponents in other topics of parliamentary interest.
So much for 1891. This year the present Bill, in
its amended form of 1890, has again been introduced into the House of Lords, and subject to some
speeches implying strong approval from a number
of noble lords it has passed without alteration
through its various stages, and thus it comes about
that it is now my duty to bring it before the House
of Commons. This delay which I have been
describing has naturally been the source of considerable disappointment in India, where there has
been a good deal of murmuring at the tardy arrival
of this long-promised reform, and at the apparent
willingness of this House to postpone the consideration of a non-controversial constitutional change
for India to the perennial and unprofitable discussion of changes of a highly controversial character
for other parts of the Empire nearer home,
which, from the Indian point of view are infini-
tesimally small and unimportant. I think this
disappointment has been a perfectly legitimate
feeling, and it undoubtedly has been felt by the
noble lord the present Viceroy of India, who,
having inaugurated his term of office by signifying
his hearty approval of this Bill, is naturally looking
forward to being able to carry it into execution

before the termination of his period of office. This anxiety has been shared in this House, if I may judge from the numerous questions addressed to my right hon. friend who preceded me in the office I now hold. These feelings of disappointment and interest are; moreover, I believe, shared by those who hold more extreme views, and who, while they regard this Bill as in some respects an inadequate measure, are desirous that it should pass into law. In July of last year the British Committee of the Indian National Congress, who may be supposed to be the representatives of extreme views in India, wrote a letter to the Secretary of State in which occurs the following passage :

' They express the deep regret with which they view the withdrawal by Her Majesty's Minister of the Indian Councils Amendment Bill, and respectfully bring to your notice that bitter disappointment will be caused throughout India by the abandonment for yet another year of any action in a matter of such paramount importance to our Indian fellow citizens.'

In the present year Lord Kimberley, who has himself been Secretary of State for India, has elsewhere expressed himself in the same sense in a paragraph which I propose to read. He says :

' I echo most sincerely the hope that this measure will be pressed by Her Majesty's Government and will pass into law. It is really a misfortune that a measure of this kind should be hung up Session after Session. However important to us may be our domestic legislation, let us not forget that we have an immense responsibility in the Government of that great Empire in India, and that it is not well for us to palter long with questions of this kind. And I am more desirous that this measure should be dealt with, because I have observed, with great pleasure, that in India the tone has much moderated and that very sensible views have been expressed at meetings held in India, and there is now reasonable promise that there will be an agreement as to a tentative and commencing measure on this subject. We must not look for it all at once, but if we can make a beginning, I believe we shall lay the foundation for what may be a real benefit, and a real security to our Indian Empire.'

I hope I may draw from the extracts I have read to the House, and from the expressions of opinion to which I have alluded, the inference that this Bill will be welcomed on both sides of this House, and subject to the expression of opinion by those who hold more advanced views, will as rapidly as possible be passed into law. So much in explanation of the history of the measure and the circumstances under which it falls to my lot to introduce it to this House. Now briefly turning to the Bill itself, I will give an outline of the manner in which it is proposed to carry out the recommendations of successive Viceroys and of the present Secretary of State. The changes which it is proposed to introduce by this Bill are, broadly speaking, three in number. The first is the concession of the privileges of financial criticism both in the Supreme and Provincial Councils; the second, the privilege of interpellation or the right of asking questions; and the third, an addition to the number of members in both classes of Councils. First, as regards the financial discussion. I have already pointed out to the House that under the existing law this is only possible when the Finance Minister proposes a new tax. At other times the Budget in India is circulated in the form of a pamphlet and no discussion can take place upon it at all, and as an illustration of the practical way in which this works, I may mention that during the thirty years since the Councils Act of 1861 there have been sixteen occasions on which new legislation has been called

for and on which discussion has taken place, and
there have been fourteen on which there has been
no discussion at all. In this Bill power will be
given for a regular annual discussion of the Budget
both in the Supreme and Provincial Councils. It
is not contemplated, as the extracts I have read
from the dispatch of Lord Dufferin will show, to
vote the Budget in India item by item in the
manner in which we do it in this House, and to
subject it to all the obstacles and delays which
party ingenuity or loquacity can suggest. That
is not contemplated, but it is proposed to give
opportunities to members of the Councils to indulge
in a full, free and fair criticism of the financial
policy of the Government, and I think all parties
will gain by such a discussion. The Government
will gain, because they will have an opportunity
of explaining their financial policy, of removing
misapprehension, of answering calumny and
attack ; and they will also profit by the criticism
delivered in a public position, and with a due
sense of responsibility, by the most competent
representatives of non-official India. The native
community will gain, because they will have the
opportunity of reviewing the financial situation
independently of the mere accident of legislation
being required for any particular year, and also
because criticism of the financial policy of the
Government, which now finds its bent in anonymous and even scurrilous articles in the newspapers,
will be uttered by responsible persons in a public
position. Lastly, the interests of finance themselves will gain by this increased publicity, and by
the stimulus of a vigorous and instructive scrutiny ;
and the application of the external aid that I have

described cannot have any other result than the promotion of sound and economical administration in India. It is now twenty years since Lord Mayo, that wise and enlightened Viceroy, first proposed the submission of Provincial Budgets to the Provincial Councils. At that time he was over-ruled by the Government at home, which, I believe, was one of the Governments of the right hon. gentleman opposite. However that may be, I hope both sides of the House will now co-operate in introducing this change, which speaks for itself, and requires no further defence from me. The second change introduced by the Bill is the con-cession of the right of interpellation, or of asking questions. That is a system with which we are tolerably familiar and which is sometimes severely attacked in this House. It is not for me to say whether the right is or is not abused, but I have observed that those who denounce the system most savagely when they are its victims, view it with a benevolent regard when they are in a position to become its masters. It is proposed to give to members of both classes of Councils, the Supreme and Provincial Councils, this right of asking questions on matters of public interest. But both this privilege and the one to which I have previously alluded will be subject, under the terms of the Act, to such conditions and restrictions as may be prescribed in rules made by the Governor-General or the Provincial Governors. In answer to the hon. gentleman who cheers somewhat ironically, I may observe that we are not altogether un-familiar with such rules and restrictions in this House, and if they are needed here, where we have, perhaps, the most perfect and highly elaborated system of parliamentary government that has ever been known, how much more will they be needed in India, where parliamentary institutions cannot be said to exist. The merits of this proposal are self-evident. It is desirable in the first place in the interest of the Government, which is at the present moment without the means of making known its policy, or of answering criticism or animadversions, or of silencing calumny, and which has frequently suffered from protracted misapprehension, which it has been powerless to remove ; and it is also desirable in the interests of the public, who, in the absence of correct official information, are apt to be misled, and to entertain erroneous ideas, but who, within the limits dictated by the judgement of the responsible authorities, henceforward have opportunities of making themselves acquainted with the real facts. I hope this liberty may provide a wise and necessary outlet in India for feelings which are now apt to smoulder below the surface because there are no public means for their expression, but which might often be allayed a little if timely information were given from the right quarter. The third proposal is to add to the number of members on these Supreme and Provincial Councils, and I will state the numbers to which, under this Bill, the members will be increased. The Supreme Legislative Council consists at present, in addition to its *ex officio* members, who number seven, of a minimum of six and a maximum of twelve nominated members, of whom half must be non-official. The Bill proposes to raise the minimum to ten and the maximum to sixteen. The Madras and Bombay Councils now consist, independently of their four *ex officio* members, of a minimum of four and a maximum of eight nominated members, of whom half are non-official. In the Bill the minimum is raised to eight and the maximum to twenty. The Council of Bengal consists at present of twelve nominated members, of whom one-third are non-official, and we propose to raise the number to twenty. In the North-West Provinces the number is nine, of which one-third are also non-official, and under the Bill the number will be raised to fifteen. The object of these additions is very easily stated, and will be as easily understood by this House. It is, by extending the area of selection in each case, to add to the strength and representative character of the Councils. The late Mr. Bradlaugh, who at different times introduced two Bills dealing with the reform of the India Councils into this House, proposed in those measures to swell the numbers on these Councils to quite impracticable and unmanageable proportions. Under his first Bill their totals would have amounted to more than two hundred and sixty, and under the second to more than two hundred and thirty. It is within the knowledge of every one who is acquainted with India that the number of persons who are competent and willing to take part in the functions of these Councils is nothing like adequate to supply the extravagant expectations of those Bills.

Mr. SCHWANN : Do the figures just quoted refer to the Councils separately or are they clubbed together ?

Mr. CURZON : I was speaking of the five Councils I have mentioned and the totals for those five Councils. As I was saying, you could not get the number of persons ; but still, the number is

sufficient to justify a not inconsiderable addition
to the present totals. Every year the number of
native gentlemen in India who are both qualified
and willing to take part in the work of Government
is increasing, and every year the advantage of
their co-operation increases in the same ratio.
More especially in the case of the Provincial
Councils it has been found that more effective
means are needed of reinforcing native and non-
official opinion. The Government believe that
this moderate addition which they propose to the
numbers will have the effect which I contemplate,
and at the same time that it will be compatible
with efficiency. This House does not need to be
told by me that the efficiency of a deliberative
body is not necessarily commensurate with its
numerical strength. We have instances in this
country of public bodies prevented from working
well in consequence of the large number of their
members. Over-large bodies do not necessarily
work well. They do not promote economical
administration, but are apt to diffuse their force
in vague and vapid talk. And if this be true of
deliberative bodies in England, it is still more true
of deliberative bodies in a country like India. I
hold in fact that it would be better that competent
men should be left outside than that incompetent
men should be included. Now we will look at the
question of how these additional members are to
be appointed. I notice that the hon. member for
North Manchester (Mr. Schwann) has placed on the
paper an amendment declaring that no reform on
the Indian Councils which does not embody the
elective principle will prove satisfactory. But in
reply I should like to point out that our Bill does

not exclude some such principle, be the method election, or selection, or delegation, or whatever be the particular phrase that you desire to employ. I would, with the permission of the House, read the very important subsection of Clause 1, which deals with that question :

'The Governor-General in Council may from time to time with the approval of the Secretary of State in Council make such regulations as to the conditions under which such nominations (that is the nomination of additional members), or any of them, shall be made by the Governor-General, Governors and Lieutenant-Governors respectively, and shall prescribe the manner in which such regulations should be carried into effect.'

I should say that this clause was introduced into the Bill as an amendment by Lord Northbrook in the House of Lords, and was gladly accepted by the Secretary of State with the avowed object of giving considerable latitude in this respect. Let me call the attention of the hon. member to the fact that Lord Kimberley has thus expressed himself elsewhere on this clause :

'I am bound to say that I can express my own satisfaction because I regard this as to a certain extent an admission of the elective principle.'

On another occasion he said :

'I myself believe that under this clause it will be possible for the Governor-General to make arrangements by which certain persons may be presented to him, having been chosen by election if the Governor-General should find that such a system can properly be established.'

Mr. MacLean (Oldham) : Does the Government accept this view of Lord Kimberley ?

Mr. Curzon : Undoubtedly the opinions expressed by Lord Kimberley are those which are also shared by the Secretary of State. Under this

Act it would be in the power of the Viceroy to invite representative bodies in India to elect or select or delegate representatives of themselves and of their opinions to be nominated to those Houses, and thus by slow degrees, by tentative measures, and in a matter like this measures cannot be otherwise than tentative, we may perhaps approximate in some way to the ideal which the hon. member for North Manchester has in view. With respect to the character of such bodies and associations as those to which I have alluded, I may mention, only as indicating what may be possible, such bodies as the well-known Association of the Zemindars of Bengal, the Chambers of Commerce of India, the municipalities of the great cities, the universities, the British India Association, and perhaps even more important than any, the various great religious denominations in that country. I believe that the House will hold that this method of dealing with the question is a wise method, since it leaves the initiative to those who are necessarily best acquainted with the matter and does not lay down any hard-and-fast rule by which they may find themselves unfortunately bound. I cannot myself conceive anything more unfortunate than that this House should draw up and send out to India a cast-iron elective scheme within the four walls of which the Government would find itself confined, and which, if it proved at some future period inadequate or unsuitable, it would be impossible to alter without coming back to this House and experiencing all the obstacles and delays of parliamentary procedure in this country. But I am well aware that these proposals may not altogether suit those hon. members on

the other side, whose ideas of political progress
have been formed in the breathless atmosphere of
life in the West, and who are perhaps unable to
accommodate their pace to the slow movement of
life in the East. The hon. member (Mr. Schwann),
for instance, is anxious to have the elective principle more clearly defined and more systematically
enforced, and he has placed an amendment on the
paper, in which he asks the House to signify its
opinion that no reform of the Indian Councils
which does not employ the elective principle will
be satisfactory to the Indian people, or will be
compatible with the good government of India.
I venture to say, sir, that this amendment is
vitiated by a twofold fallacy, for while, in the
first place, the hon. member affects to speak on
behalf of the Indian people, he at the same time
entirely ignores the primary conditions of Indian
life. When the hon. member assumes in this House
to be the mouthpiece of the people of India, I must
emphatically decline to accept his credentials in
that capacity. No system of representation that
has ever been devised, no system of representation
that the ingenuity of the hon. member can suggest,
no system of representation that would stand the
test of twenty-four hours' operation, would, in the
most infinitesimal degree, represent the people
of India. Who are the people of India? The
people of India are the voiceless millions who can
neither read nor write their own tongues, who have
no knowledge whatever of English, who are not
perhaps universally aware of the fact that the
English are in their country as rulers. The people
of India are the ryots and the peasants, whose life
is not one of political aspiration, but of mute

penury and toil. The plans and policy of the
Congress Party in India would leave this vast
amorphous residuum absolutely untouched. I do
not desire to speak in any other than terms of
respect of the Congress Party of India. That
party contains a number of intelligent, liberal-
minded, and public-spirited men, who undoubtedly
represent that portion of the Indian people which
has profited by the educational advantages placed
at their doors, and which is more or less imbued
with European ideas ; but as to their relationship
to the people of India, the constituency which the
Congress Party represent cannot be described as
otherwise than a minute and almost microscopic
minority of the total population of India. At the
present time the population of British India is
221,000,000 ; and of that number it has been
calculated that not more than from three to four
per cent. can read or write any one of their native
tongues ; considerably less than one per cent.—
about one-fourth or one-third—can read or write
English. In the Province of Bengal alone, where
the population exceeds 72,000,000, it has been
calculated that the maximum constituency created
by Mr. Bradlaugh's Bill would have only numbered
a total of 870,000. It appears to me that you can
as little judge of the feelings and aspirations of the
people of India from the plans and proposals of
the Congress Party as you can judge of the physical
configuration of a country which is wrapped up
in the mists of early morning, but a few of whose
topmost peaks have been touched by the rising
sun. To propose an elaborate system of representation for a people in this stage of development
would appear to me to be, in the highest degree,

premature and unwise. To describe such a system
as representation of the people of India would be
little better than a farce. The Government assume
the responsibility of stating that, in their opinion,
the time has not come when representative institutions, as we understand the term, can be extended
to India. The idea of representation is alien to the
Indian mind. We have only arrived at it by slow
degrees ourselves, through centuries of conflict
and storm. Nay, it may be said that it is only
within the last twenty-five years that we have
in this country entered into anything like its full
fruition. No doubt we are apt to regard popular
representation as the highest expression of political
equality and political freedom ; but it does not
necessarily so present itself to those who have no
instinctive sense of what political equality is. How
can you predicate political equality of a community
that is sundered into irreconcilable camps—('No!')
—into irreconcilable camps by differences of caste,
of religion, of custom, which hold men fast-bound .
during their lifetime, and the rigour of which is
not abated even beyond the grave ? I notice that
the hon. member has altered the terms of amendment as it was originally placed upon the paper.
At first he spoke of the elective principle as defined
at the meetings of the Indian National Congress.
But those words are now omitted. I think that
that is a prudent omission. For the truth is that
the Indian Congress is not of one mind, and does
not speak with one voice on this matter. In 1890
we had a Bill containing an elaborate system of
electoral colleges and proportional representation,
and overswollen Councils, presented to this House ;
but in the following year this Bill was incontinently

withdrawn, and has never been heard of since. And in that year Mr. Bradlaugh—of whose Parliamentary ability no one could have any doubt—introduced another Bill entirely different, in which he showed such extreme diffidence in himself and in the Indian National Congress, and such confidence in the Indian Government, that, although it contained expressed provisions for a system of election, the means by which that system was to be carried out were left entirely to the discretion of the latter. These ambiguous, fluctuating, and hesitating proposals illustrate the premature and experimental character of every reform hitherto advocated. But while these considerations render it, I believe, impossible so to re-model the Legislative Councils of India as to give them the character of representative chambers, I should be the last to deny the importance of the opinions and the criticism of gentlemen representing the advanced phases of Indian society. At present the sole vent that is available for that body of opinion is in the native Press, and in organized meetings such as the Indian National Congress. Everybody on both sides of the House agrees that this knowledge and activity might be better utilized than it is at present ; and the Government believe that the sub-section of Clause 1 will provide the means by which representatives of the most important sections of native society may be appointed to the Councils, and may have an opportunity of explaining their views with a fuller sense of responsibility than they at present enjoy. If the Government are able at present to go no further it arises from no want of sympathy with the inhabitants of India, but from a sense of the colossal responsibility that rests upon them,

and of the dangers that would accrue from any
rash or imprudent step. This Bill is not, perhaps,
a great, or heroic measure ; but, at the same time,
it does mark a decisive step, and a step in advance.
As such it has been welcomed by every living
Viceroy of India. It was foreshadowed by Lord
Dufferin ; it is earnestly asked for by Lord Lansdowne ; and it has received the emphatic approval
of Lord Northbrook, no less than the approbation
of Lord Ripon. I hope that these facts, and the
explanation which I have given, may commend
this Bill to the sympathy of the House, that it may
be regarded as a useful measure, and may be
exempt from the ordinary Parliamentary obstacles
and delays. There are two main objects which this
House is entitled to require in any new legislation
for India. Firstly, that it should add to, and in no
sense impair, the efficiency of Government ; and,
secondly, that it should also promote the interests
of the governed. It is because I believe this measure
will further both these ends, that I commend it to
the sympathetic attention of the House, and will
conclude by moving that the Bill be now read a
second time.

4. William Ewart Gladstone, House of Commons, 28 March, 1892

I SHOULD wish, if in my power, to curtail this
Debate, so far at any rate as any controversial
element is concerned. I do not speak of the
information, the knowledge and the experience
which may be brought into this Debate by members
competent to enter into an examination of Indian
affairs, but so far as controversy is concerned

I should hope it may be compressed within narrow
limits. We have before us a motion on the part of
the Under Secretary of State for India that this
Bill be now read a second time. We have on the
other hand before us the amendment of my hon.
friend the member for Manchester (Mr. Schwann),
who asks the House by that amendment to
declare that in his opinion

'No reform of the Indian Councils which does not
embody the elective principle will prove satisfactory to
the Indian people or compatible with the good government
of India.'

Well now, sir, I ask myself the question whether
there is between the Bill now before us and the
amendment of my hon. friend such a difference of
opinion or of principle as to make me desirous of
going to an issue in respect of that difference.
Undoubtedly, sir, if I look at the Bill I am disposed
to agree with my hon. friend that taken by itself
its language is unsatisfactory in so far as it is
ambiguous ; but then, sir, I have the advantage
of an authoritative commentary. The hon. gentleman the Under Secretary of State for India has
introduced this Bill to our notice in a very comprehensive and lucid speech. If I were to criticize
any portion of that speech it would be the portion
in which the hon. gentleman addressed himself to
the consideration of the amendment before the
House. It appeared to be his object, or at all
events I thought it was the effect of his language,
to put upon that amendment the most hostile
construction it could bear, whereas I desire to put
on the speeches that we have heard on the Bill not
the most hostile, but the least hostile and the
least controversial construction to which they are

susceptible. Now, sir, while the language of the Bill cannot be said to embody the elective principle, yet, if it is not meant to pave the way for the elective principle, it is in its language very peculiar indeed. It was, I believe, suggested by a nobleman in the House of Lords, friendly to the elective principle, that unless it were intended to leave room for some peculiarities not as yet introduced in the Indian system in the appointment of the members of the Indian Councils under this Bill, it would have been a very singular form of speech to provide, not simply that the Governor-General might nominate, but that he might make regulations as to the conditions under which such nominations, or any of them, might be made either by himself or by the Governor-General in Council. It is quite plain that those who framed that language, and we must assume also those who adopted that language and have sent for our consideration a Bill couched in such language, had in view something beyond mere nomination. Now, sir, I come to the speech of the hon. gentleman the Under Secretary of State for India. That speech appeared to me, I confess, distinctly to embody what is not very different from the assertion of my hon. friend in his amendment, except as to this important point—that the Under Secretary proposes to leave everything to the judgement, the discretion, and the responsibility of the Governor-General of India and the authorities in India ; but, otherwise, apart from limitation, I think I may fairly say what the hon. gentleman the Under Secretary did embody in his speech was the elective principle in the only sense in which he could be expected to embody it. My

construction of that speech is—and I do not
think it admitted of two constructions, especially
considering the reference the hon. gentleman
made to the speeches of Lord Kimberley—my construction of that speech is that it is the intention
of the Government and the intention of the House
of Lords, in which we are now invited to concur,
that a serious effort shall be made to consider
carefully those elements which India in its present
condition may furnish for the introduction into
the Councils of India of the elective principle.
Now, sir, if that effort is seriously to be made, by
whom is it to be made ? I do not think it can be
made by this House, except through the medium
of empowering provisions. The hon. baronet the
member for one of the divisions of Worcester (Sir
R. Temple) has spoken at some period of proposing
a plan of that kind ; and I have observed on more
than one occasion with pleasure, the genuinely
liberal views of the hon. baronet, with respect to
Indian affairs and to the government of the Indian
people ; and were he to produce a plan of that
kind, I have no doubt it would contain a great deal
that was wise, a great deal that was useful, and
a great deal that would be honourable and agree-
able to the spirit of an assembly such as this. But
I doubt if, even under such enlightenment, it would
be well or wise on our part with our imperfect
knowledge, to proceed with the determination of
the particulars of any such plan. The best course
we could take would be to commend to the
authorities of India what is a clear indication of
the principles on which we desire them to proceed.
It is not our business to devise machinery for the
purpose of Indian Government ; it is our business

to give to those who represent Her Majesty in India ample information as to what we believe to be sound principles of government ; and it is of course the function of this House to comment upon any case in which we may think they have failed to give due effect to those principles ; but in the discharge of their high administrative functions, or as to the choice of means, we should leave that in their hands. It would be a great misfortune if, with imperfect information, we were to indicate leanings which might tend to embarrass them in the discharge of the duties of an office so highly responsible. It is quite evident, without any disparagement to the remarks of my hon. friend, that the great question we have before us—the question of real and profound interest—is the question of the introduction of the elective element into the government of India. That question overshadows and absorbs everything else ; it is a question of vital importance, and also, at the same time, a question of great difficulty. Do not let us conceal from ourselves that no more difficult duty has ever been entrusted to a Governor-General than the duty of administering such a Bill as this and giving effect to it in a manner honourable and wise. I am not at all disposed to ask from the Governor-General or the Secretary of State who has communicated with him and shares his responsibilities—I am not at all disposed to ask them at once to produce large and imposing results. What I wish is, that their first steps should be of a nature to be genuine, and whatever amount of scope they give to the elective principle, it shall be real. There are, of course, dangers in the way. There is the danger of subserviency ;

there is another danger, and that is the danger of having persons who represent particular cliques or classes or interests, and who may claim the honour of representing the people of India. The old story of the three tailors of Tooley Street does, after all, embody an important political truth, and it does exhibit a real danger. It is to the Governor-General's wisdom we must trust to do the very best, and to make the most out of the materials at his disposal. What we want is to get at the real heart and mind—at the most upright sentiment and the most enlightened thought, of the people of India. But it is not an easy matter to do this, although, with regard to the view expressed by the Under Secretary of State for India, I think we are justified in being a little more sanguine than he was as to the amount of these materials. The hon. gentleman did not indicate where such materials for the elective element in India are to be found. Undoubtedly, sir, as far as my own prepossessions go, I should look presumptively with the greatest amount of expectation and hope to the municipal bodies and the local authorities in India, in which the elective element is already included. My hon. friend who moved the amendment that is now before the House did valuable service in pointing out the amount of authority that can now be alleged on behalf of the introduction of the elective principle —the authority not merely of men distinguished generally for their political opinions, but of those who have been responsible for the actual administration of India. These men, after carefully examining the matter and divesting themselves of those prejudices which administration is supposed to impart, have given their deliberate sanction to the introduction of this Bill. It is there that I feel we stand on very firm and solid ground, and Her Majesty's Government ought to understand that it will be a most grave and serious disappointment to this House if, after all the assurances we have received from high quarters that some real attempt will be made to bring into operation this great and powerful engine of government, there should not be some result which we can contemplate with satisfaction. I do not speak of its amount. I think it should be judged by its quality rather than by its quantity. In an Asiatic country like India, with its ancient civilization, with its institutions so peculiar, with such diversities of races, religions, and pursuits, with such an enormous extent of country, and such a multitude of human beings, as probably, except in the case of China, never were before comprehended under a single Government, I can well understand the difficulties that confront us in seeking to carry out our task. But, great as the difficulties are, the task is a noble task, and one that will require the utmost prudence and wisdom to carry it to a successful consummation. But we may feel, after the practical assurances we have had from persons of the highest capacity and the greatest responsibility, we may feel justified in expecting something more than a merely nominal beginning in this great and magnificent undertaking. It is not too much to say that this great people—this nation to which we belong—has undoubtedly had committed to it a most peculiar task in the foundation and the government of extraneous territories. But all other parts of the British

Empire present to us a simple problem in comparison with the problem which India presents. Its magnitude and its peculiarities are such as to lift the function of Great Britain in this respect far above all that any other country has ever attempted, and far above all it has itself attempted beyond the sea in any portion of the dependencies of the Empire. I rejoice to think that a great and a real advance has been made, both before and especially since the time of the transfer of the Indian Government to the immediate superintendence of the Executive at home and the supreme authority of the Imperial Legislature. The amount of progress they made has been made by the constant application to the Government of India of the minds of able men acting under a strong sense of duty and also under a strong sense of political responsibility. All that has so far taken place induces us to look forward cheerfully to the future in the expectation that, if there should be a real success in the application, the genuine even though limited application, of the elective principle to that vast community, it will be the accomplishment of a task to which it is difficult to find a parallel in history. In these circumstances I deprecate a division on the amendment of my hon. friend. I see no such difference between the amendment and the language of the Bill as ought to induce my hon. friend to divide the House. If the language of my hon. friend is to receive a perfectly legitimate and not a strained construction, it is only an amplification and not a contradiction of what the speech of the hon. gentleman the Under Secretary implies. I think it would be a great misfortune if the House were to divide on this subject. There is no difference of principle disclosed, because the acceptance of the elective principle by the Under Secretary, though guarded, and necessarily guarded, was, on the whole, not otherwise than a frank acceptance. I do not think there is on the other side of the House any of the jealousy of the introduction of that principle, which, if it existed, would undoubtedly form a strong mark of difference between the two parties. In reality and in substance we have the same object in view, and we are prepared to recommend the employment of the same means to secure that end. If that be so, it would certainly be unfortunate that any division should take place which though the numbers might be unequal (I certainly could not take part in any division hostile or apparently hostile to the Bill) would, after the speech of the Under Secretary, convey a false impression. It is well the people of India should understand the truth —that united views substantially prevail in this House on this matter. My persuasion is that these views are united, and that they are such as likewise tend to the development of an enlightened and so far as circumstances will permit not only of a liberal, but of a free system. While my hon. friend has done service in bringing this matter forward, he has really no substantial quarrel with the declarations of the Government, and I think he would do well to withdraw his amendment and allow this Bill to receive the unanimous assent of the House, in the hope that without serious difficulty it may shortly become law, and fulfil the benevolent purposes with which it has been submitted.

5. *Indian Councils Act.* 1892 (55 & 56 Vict. c. 14)

1. (1) THE number of additional members of Council nominated by the Governor-General under the provisions of section ten of the Indian Councils Act, 1861, shall be such as to him may seem from time to time expedient, but shall not be less than ten nor more than sixteen ; and the number of additional members of Council nominated by the Governors of the Presidencies of Fort St. George and Bombay respectively under the provisions of section twenty-nine of the Indian Councils Act, 1861, shall (besides the advocate general of the Presidency or officer acting in that capacity) be such as to the said Governors respectively may seem from time to time expedient, but shall not be less than eight nor more than twenty.

(2) It shall be lawful for the Governor-General in Council by proclamation from time to time to increase the number of councillors whom the Lieutenant-Governors of the Bengal Division of the Presidency of Fort William and of the North-Western Provinces and Oudh respectively may nominate for their assistance in making laws and regulations : Provided always that not more than twenty shall be nominated for the Bengal Division, and not more than fifteen for the North-Western Provinces and Oudh.

(3) Any person resident in India may be nominated an additional member of Council under sections ten and twenty-nine of the Indian Councils Act, 1861, and this Act, or a member of the Council of the Lieutenant-Governor of any province to which the provisions of the Indian

Councils Act, 1861, touching the making of laws and regulations, have been or are hereafter extended or made applicable.

(4) The Governor-General in Council may from time to time, with the approval of the Secretary of State in Council, make regulations as to the conditions under which such nominations, or any of them, shall be made by the Governor-General, Governors, and Lieutenant-Governors respectively, and prescribe the manner in which such regulations shall be carried into effect.

2. Notwithstanding any provision in the Indian Councils Act, 1861, the Governor-General of India in Council may from time to time make rules authorizing at any meeting of the Governor-General's Council for the purpose of making laws and regulations the discussion of the annual financial statement of the Governor-General in Council and the asking of questions, but under such conditions and restrictions as to subject or otherwise as shall be in the said rules prescribed or declared : And notwithstanding any provisions in the Indian Councils Act, 1861, the Governors in Council of Fort St. George and Bombay respectively, and the Lieutenant-Governor of any province to which the provisions of the Indian Councils Act, 1861, touching the making of laws and regulations, have been or are hereafter extended or made applicable, may from time to time make rules for authorizing at any meeting of their respective councils for the purpose of making laws and regulations the discussion of the annual financial statement of their respective local governments, and the asking of questions, but under such conditions and restrictions, as to subject or

otherwise, as shall in the said rules applicable to such Councils respectively be prescribed or declared. But no member at any such meeting of any Council shall have power to submit or propose any resolution, or to divide the Council in respect of any such financial discussion, or the answer to any question asked under the authority of this Act, or the rules made under this Act :. Provided that any rule made under this Act by a governor in council, or by a lieutenant-governor, shall be submitted for and shall be subject to the sanction of the Governor-General in Council, and any rule made under this Act by the Governor-General in Council shall be submitted for and shall be subject to the sanction of the Secretary of State in Council : Provided also that rules made under this Act shall not be subject to alteration or amendment at meetings for the purpose of making laws and regulations.

3. It is hereby declared that in the twenty-second section of the Indian Councils Act, 1861, it was and is intended that the words ' Indian territories now under the dominion of Her Majesty ' should be read and construed as if the words ' or hereafter ' were and had at the time of the passing of the said Act been inserted next after the word ' now ' ; and further that the Government of India Act, 1833, and the Government of India Act, 1853, respectively, shall be read and construed as if at the date of the enactment thereof respectively it was intended and had been enacted that the said Acts respectively should extend to and include the territories acquired after the dates thereof respectively by the East India Company, and should not be confined to the territories at the dates of the said enactments respectively in

the possession and under the government of the said Company.

4. [Repeal of ss. 13, 32 of the Indian Councils Act, 1861.]

(1) If any additional member of Council, or any member of the council of a lieutenant-governor, appointed under the said Act or this Act, shall be absent from India or unable to attend to the duties of his office for a period of two consecutive months, it shall be lawful for the Governor-General, the Governor, or the Lieutenant-Governor, to whose council such additional member or member may have been nominated (as the case may be) to declare, by a notification published in the Government Gazette, that the seat in Council of such person has become vacant :

(2) In the event of a vacancy occurring by the absence from India, inability to attend to duty, death, acceptance of office, or resignation duly accepted, of any such additional member or member of the council of a Lieutenant-Governor, it shall be lawful for the Governor-General, for the Governor, or for the Lieutenant-Governor, as the case may be, to nominate any person as additional member or member, as the case may be, in his place ; and every member so nominated shall be summoned to all meetings held for the purpose of making laws and regulations for the term of two years from the date of such nomination : Provided always

that it shall not be lawful by such nomination, or by any other nomination made under this Act, to diminish the proportion of non-official members directed by the Indian Councils Act, 1861, to be nominated.

5. The local legislature of any province in India may from time to time, by Acts passed under and subject to the provisions of the Indian Councils Act, 1861, and with the previous sanction of the Governor-General, but not otherwise, repeal or amend as to that province any law or regulation made either before or after the passing of this Act by any authority in India other than that local legislature; Provided that an Act or a provision of an Act made by a local legislature, and subsequently assented to by the Governor-General in pursuance of the Indian Councils Act, 1861, shall not be deemed invalid by reason only of its requiring the previous sanction of the Governor-General under this section.

6. In this Act—

The expression ' local legislature ' means—

(1) The Governor in Council for the purpose of making laws and regulations of the respective provinces of Fort St. George and Bombay ; and

(2) The council for the purpose of making laws and regulations of the Lieutenant-Governor of any province to which the provisions of the Indian Councils Act, 1861, touching the making of laws or regulations have been or are hereafter extended or made applicable :

The expression ' province ' means any presidency,

division, province, or territory over which the powers of any local legislature for the time being extend.

7. Nothing in this Act shall detract from or diminish the powers of the Governor-General in Council at meetings for the purpose of making laws and regulations.

8. This Act may be cited as the Indian Councils Act, 1892, and the Indian Councils Act, 1861, and this Act may be cited together as the Indian Councils Acts, 1861 and 1892.

6. *Viscount Morley of Blackburn. House of Lords, 23 February, 1909*

MY LORDS, I invite the House to take to-day the first definite and operative step in carrying out the policy which I had the honour of stating to your lordships just before Christmas, and which has occupied the active consideration both of the Home Government and of the Government of India, for very nearly, if not even more than, three years. The statement was awaited in India with an expectancy that with time became almost impatience, and it was received in India—and that, after all, is the point to which I looked with the most anxiety—with intense interest and attention and various degrees of approval, from warm enthusiasm to cool assent and acquiescence.

A deputation waited upon the Viceroy a few days after the arrival of my dispatch unique in its comprehensive character ; both the Hindus and the Mahomedans were represented ; it was a remarkable deputation, and they waited upon the Viceroy to offer their expression of gratitude for the scheme which was unfolded before them. Then a few days later at Madras the Congress met, and they, too, expressed their thanks to the Home Government and to the Government of India. Almost at the same time the Moslem League met at Amritsar, and they were warm in their approval of the policy which they took to be foreshadowed in the dispatch, though they found fault with the defects they thought they had discovered in the scheme, and implored the Government, both in India and here, to remedy those defects. So far as I know—and I do beg your lordships to note these details of the reception of our policy in India—there had been no sign in any quarter, save possibly in the irreconcilable camp, of organized hostile opinion among either Indians or Anglo-Indians.

The Indian Civil Service I will speak of very shortly. I will pass them by for the moment. The noble Marquess (Lord Lansdowne) said truly the other night that when I spoke at the end of December I used the words 'formidable and obscure' as describing the situation, and he desired to know whether I thought the situation was still formidable and obscure. I will not drop the words, but I think the situation is less formidable and less obscure. Neither repression on the one hand nor reform on the other could possibly be expected to cut at the roots of anarchical crime in a few weeks, but with unfaltering repression on the one hand and vigour and good faith in reform on the other we all see good reason to hope that we shall weaken, if not destroy, these baleful forces.

There are, I take it, three classes of people that we have to consider in dealing with a scheme of this kind. There are the extremists, who nurse fantastic dreams that some day they will drive us out of India. In this group there are academic extremists and physical force extremists, and I have seen it stated on a certain authority—it cannot be more than guessed—that they do not number, whether academic or physical force extremists, more than one-tenth, I think, or even three per cent., of what are called the educated class in India. The second group nourish no hopes of this sort, but hope for autonomy or self-government of the colonial species and pattern. And then the third section of this classification ask for no more than to be admitted to co-operation in our administration, and to find a free and effective voice in expressing the interests and needs of their people. I believe the effect of the reforms has been, is being, and will be to draw the second class, who hope for colonial autonomy, into the third class, who will be content with being admitted to a fair and full co-operation. A correspondent wrote to me the other day and said :

' We seem to have caught many discontented people on the rebound, and to have given them an excuse for a loyalty which they have badly wanted.'

In spite of all this it is a difficult and critical situation, but by almost universal admission it has lost that tension which strained India two or three months ago, and public feeling is tranquillized, certainly beyond any expectation which either the Viceroy or myself ventured to entertain.

The situation has become, at all events, more hopeful, and I am confident that the atmosphere has changed from being dark and sullen to being hopeful, and I am sure your Lordships will allow me to be confident that nothing will be done at Westminster to cloud that hopeful sky. The noble Marquess the other day said—and I was delighted to hear it—that he, at all events, would give us, with all the reservations that examination of the scheme might demand from him, a whole-hearted support here and his best encouragement to the men in India. I accept that, and I rely upon it and lean upon it, because if anything were done at Westminster, either by delay or otherwise, to show a breach in what ought to be the substantial unity of Parliamentary opinion in face of the Indian situation, it would be a very great disaster. I would venture on the point of delay to say this. Your lordships will not suspect me of having any desire to hurry the Bill, but I remember that when Lord Cross brought in the Bill of 1892 Lord Kimberley, who was so well known and so popular in the House, used this language, which I venture to borrow from him to press upon your lordships to-day :

' I think it almost dangerous to leave a subject of this kind hung up to be perpetually discussed by all manner of persons, and, having once allowed that, at all events, some amendment is necessary in regard to the mode of con-stituting the Legislative Councils, it is incumbent upon the Government and Parliament to pass the Bill which they may think expedient as speedily as possible into law.'

I think the considerations of social order and social urgency in India make that just as useful to be remembered to-day as it was then.

The noble marquess the other day, in a very courteous manner, administered to me an exhortation and an admonition and homily—I had almost said a lecture—as to the propriety of deferring to the man on the spot, and the danger of quarrelling with the man on the spot. I listened with becoming meekness and humility, but then it occurred to me that the language of the noble marquess was not original. Those noble lords who share the bench with him gave deep murmurs of approval to this homily which was administered to me. They had forgotten that they once had a man on the spot, the man there being that eminent and distinguished man whom I may perhaps be allowed to congratulate upon his restoration to health and to his place in this assembly. He said this, which the noble marquess will see is a fair original for his own little discourse; it was said after the noble lord had thrown up the reins :

'What I wish to say to high officers of State and members of Government is this : as far as you can, trust the man on the spot. Do not weary or fret or nag him with your superior wisdom. They claim no immunity from errors of opinion or judgment, but their errors are nothing compared with yours.'

The remonstrance, therefore, of the noble lord (Lord Curzon) to the noble lords sitting near him is identical with that which I have laid to heart from the noble marquess.

The House will pardon me if I for a moment dwell upon what by application is an innuendo conveyed in the admonition of the noble marquess. I have a suspicion that he considered his advice was needed ; he expressed the hope that all who were responsible for administration in India would have all the power for which they had a right to ask. Upon that I can, I think,—though I am half reluctant to do so—completely clear my character, for in December last, shortly before I addressed your lordships, Lord Minto, having observed there was some talk of my interference, telegraphed these words, and desired that I should make use of them whenever I thought fit, having in view my addressing the House :

' I hope you will say from me, in as strong language as you may choose to use, that in all our dealings with sedition I could not be more strongly supported than I have been by you. The question of the control of Indian administration by the Secretary of State, mixed up as it is with the old difficulties of centralization, we may very possibly look at from different points of view, but that has nothing to do with the support the Secretary of State gives to the Viceroy, and which you have given to me in a time of great difficulty and for which I shall always be warmly grateful.'

The Marquess of LANSDOWNE : I think' the noble Viscount will see from the report of my speech that the part he has quoted had reference to measures of repression, and that what I said was that justice should be prompt, that it was undesirable that there should be appeals from one Court to another, or from provincial Governments to the Government in Calcutta, or from the Government at Calcutta to the Secretary of State for India. I did not mean to imply merely the Viceroy, but the men responsible for local government.

Viscount MORLEY OF BLACKBURN : I do not think that when the noble marquess refers to the report of his speech he will find I have misrepresented him. At all events, he will, I am sure, gladly agree that, in dealing with sedition, I have on the whole given all the support the Government of India or anybody else concerned had a right to ask for.

I will now say a word about the Indian Civil Service. Three years ago when we began these operations I felt that a vital element for success was that we should carry the Indian Civil Service with us, and that if we did not do this we should fail. But human nature being what it is, and temperaments varying as they do, it is natural to expect a certain amount of criticism, minute criticism, and observation, and I have had proofs of that, but will content myself with one quotation from a very distinguished member, the Lieutenant-Governor of Bengal, well known to the noble lord opposite. What did he say, addressing the Legislative Council a few weeks ago ? :

'I hold that a solemn duty rests upon the officers of Government in all branches, and more particularly upon the officers of the Civil Service, so to comport themselves in the inception and working of the new measures as to make the task of the people and their leaders easy. It is incumbent upon them loyally to accept the principle that these measures involve the surrender of some portion of the authority and control which they now exercise, and some modifications of the methods of administration. If that task is approached in a grudging or reluctant spirit we shall be sowing the seeds of failure and shall forfeit our claim to receive the friendly co-operation of the representatives of the people. We must be prepared to support, defend, and carry through the administrative policy, and in a certain degree even the executive acts of the Government in the Council, in much the same way as is now prescribed in regard to measures of legislation ; and we must further be prepared to discharge this task without the aid of a standing majority behind us. We will have to resort to the more difficult arts of persuasion and conciliation in the place of the easier methods of autocracy. This is no small demand to make on the resources of a service whose training and traditions have hitherto led its members rather to work for the people than through the people or their representatives. But I am nevertheless confident that the demand will not be made in vain. For more than a hundred years, in the time of the Company and under the rule of the Crown, the Indian Civil Service has never failed to respond to whatever call has been made upon it or to adapt itself to the changing environment of the time. I feel no doubt that officers will be found who possess the natural gifts, the loyalty, the imagination, and the force of character which will be requisite for the conduct of the administration under the more advanced form of government to which we are about to succeed.'

These words I commend to your lordships. They breathe a noble spirit, they admirably express the feeling of a sincere man, and I do not believe anybody who is acquainted with the Service doubts that that spirit, so admirably expressed, will pervade the Service in the admittedly difficult task that now confronts them.

The Bill is a short one, and will speak for itself ; I shall be brief in referring to it, for in December last I made what was practically a second-reading speech. I may point out that there are two rival schools, and that the noble lord opposite (Lord Curzon) may be said to represent one of them. There are two rival schools, one of which believes that better government of India depends on efficiency, and that efficiency is in fact the end of our rule in India. The other school, while not neglecting efficiency, looks also to what is called political concessions. I think I am doing the noble lord no injustice in saying that during his eminent Viceroyalty he did not accept the necessity for political concessions, but trusted to efficiency. I hope it will not be bad taste to say in the noble lord's presence that you will never send to India, and you have never sent to India a Viceroy his superior, if, indeed, his equal, in force of mind, in unsparing remorseless industry, in passionate and devoted interest in all that concerns the well-being of India, with an imagination fired by the grandeur of the political problem

India presents—you never sent a man with more of all these attributes than when you sent Lord Curzon. But splendidly successful as his work was from the point of view of efficiency, he still did leave in India a state of things when we look back—not in consequence of his policy—not completely satisfactory such as would have been the crowning of a brilliant career.

I am as much for efficiency as the noble lord, but I do not believe—and this is the difference between him and myself—that you can have true, solid, endurable efficiency without what are called political concessions. I know risks are pointed out. The late Lord Salisbury, speaking on the last Indian Councils Bill, spoke of the risks of applying occidental machinery in India. Well, we ought to have thought of that before we applied occidental education ; we applied that, and occidental machinery must follow. These Legislative Councils once called into existence, it was inevitable that you would have gradually, in Lord Salisbury's own phrase, to popularize them so as to bring them into harmony with the dominant sentiments of the people in India. The Bill of 1892 admittedly contained the elective principle, and now this Bill extends that principle. The noble lord (Viscount Cross) will remember the Bill of 1892, of which he had charge in the House of Commons. I want the House to be good enough to follow the line taken by Mr. Gladstone, because I base myself on that. There was an amendment moved and there was going to be a division, and Mr. Gladstone begged his friends not to divide, because he said it was very important that we should present a substantial unity to India. This

is upon the question of either House considering
a Bill like the Bill that is now on the Table—a
mere skeleton of a Bill if you like. I see it has been
called vague and sketchy. It cannot be anything
else on the principle explained by Mr. Gladstone :—

' It is the' intention of the Government (that is, the
Conservative Government) that a serious effort shall be
made to consider carefully those elements which India in
its present condition may furnish for the introduction into
the Councils of India of the elective principle. If that
effort is seriously to be made, by whom is it to be made ?
I do not think it can be made by this House, except
through the medium of empowering provisions. The
best course we could take would be to commend to the
authorities of India what is a clear indication of the
principles on which we desire them to proceed. It is not
our business to devise machinery for the purpose of Indian
Government; it is our business to give to those who
represent Her Majesty in India ample information as to
what we believe to be sound principles of Government ;
and it is, of course, the function of this House to comment
upon any case in which we may think they have failed to
give due effect to those principles.'

I only allude to Mr. Gladstone's words in order
to let the House know that I am taking no unusual
course in leaving the bulk of the work, the details
of the work, to the Government of India, and
discussion, therefore, in this House and in Parliament will necessarily be not upon details. But no
doubt it is desirable that some of the heads of the
regulations, rules, and proclamations to be made
by the Government of India under sanction of the
India Office should be more or less placed within
the reach and knowledge of the House so far as
they are complete. The principles of the Bill are
in the Bill and will be affirmed, if your lordships
are pleased to read it a second time, and the
Committee points, important as they are, can well

be dealt with in Committee. The view of Mr. Gladstone was cheerfully accepted by the House then, and I hope it will be accepted by your lordships to-day.

There is one very important chapter in these regulations which I think now on the second reading of the Bill, without waiting for Committee, I ought to say a few words to your lordships about —I mean the Mahomedans. That is a part of the Bill and scheme which has no doubt attracted a great deal of criticism and excited a great deal of feeling in that very important community. We suggested to the Government of India a certain plan. We did not prescribe it, we did not order it, but we suggested and recommended this plan for their consideration—no more than that. It was the plan of a mixed or composite electoral college, in which Mahomedans and Hindus should pool their votes, so to say. The wording of the recommendation in my dispatch was, as I soon discovered, ambiguous—a grievous defect, of which I make bold to hope I am not very often in public business guilty. But, to the best of my belief, under any construction the plan of Hindus and Mahomedans voting together in a mixed and composite electorate would have secured to the Mahomedan electors, wherever they were so minded, the chance of returning their own representatives in their due proportion. The political idea at the bottom of that recommendation which has found so little favour was that such composite action would bring the two great communities more closely together, and this idea of promoting harmony was held by men of very high Indian authority and experience who were among my

advisers at the India Office. But the Mahomedans
protested that the Hindus would elect a pro-Hindu
upon it, just as I suppose in a mixed college of say
seventy-five Catholics and twenty-five Protestants
voting together the Protestants might suspect that
the Catholics voting for the Protestant would
choose what is called a Romanizing Protestant
and as little of a Protestant as they could find.
Suppose the other way. In Ireland there is an
expression, a ' shoneen ' Catholic—that is to say,
a Catholic who, though a Catholic, is too friendly
with English Conservatism and other influences
which the Nationalists dislike. And it might be
said, if there were seventy-five Protestants against
twenty-five Catholics, that the Protestants when
giving a vote in the way of Catholic representation
would return ' shoneens '. I am not going to take
your lordships' time up by arguing this to-day.
With regard to schemes of proportional representation, as Calvin said of another study, ' excessive
study either finds a man mad or makes him so.'
At any rate, the Government of India doubted
whether our plan would work, and we have
abandoned it. I do not think it was a bad plan,
but it is no use, if you are making an earnest
attempt in good faith at a general pacification,
to let parental fondness for a clause interrupt that
good process by sitting obstinately tight.

The Mahomedans demand three things. I had
the pleasure of receiving a deputation from them
and I know very well what is in their minds. They
demand the election of their own representatives
to these councils in all the stages, just as in Cyprus,
where, I think, the Mahomedans vote by themselves. They have nine votes and the non-

Mahomedans have three, or the other way about. So in Bohemia, where the Germans vote alone and have their own register. Therefore we are not without a precedent and a parallel for the idea of a separate register. Secondly, they want a number of seats in excess of their numerical strength. Those two demands we are quite ready and intend to meet in full. There is a third demand that, if there is a Hindu on the Viceroy's Executive Council —a subject on which I will venture to say a little to your lordships before I sit down—there should be two Indian members on the Viceroy's Council and that one should be a Mahomedan. Well, as I told them and as I now tell your lordships, I see no chance whatever of meeting their views in that way to any extent at all.

To go back to the point of the registers, some may be shocked at the idea of a religious register at all, of a register framed on the principle of religious belief. We may wish, we do wish— certainly I do—that it were otherwise. We hope that time, with careful and impartial statesmanship, will make things otherwise. Only let us not forget that the difference between Mahomedanism and Hinduism is not a mere difference of articles of religious faith. It is a difference in life, in tradition, in history, in all the social things as well as articles of belief that constitute a community. Do not let us forget what makes it interesting and even exciting. Do not let us forget that, in talking of Hindus and Mahomedans, we are dealing with and brought face to face with vast historic issues, dealing with some of the very mightiest forces that through all the centuries and ages have moulded the fortunes of great States and the destinies of countless millions of mankind. Thoughts of that kind are what give to Indian politics and to Indian work extraordinary fascination, and at the same time impose the weight of no ordinary burden.

Now I will come to the question which, I think, has excited, certainly in this country, more interest than anything else in the scheme before you— I mean the question of an Indian member on the Viceroy's Executive Council. The noble marquess said here the other day that he hoped an opportunity would be given for discussing it. Whether it is in order or not—I am too little versed in your lordships' procedure to be quite sure—but I am told that the rules of order in this House are of an elastic description and that I shall not be trespassing beyond what is right, if I introduce the point to-night. I thoroughly understand the noble marquess's anxiety for a chance of discussion. It is quite true, and the House should not forget that it is quite true, that this question is in no way whatever touched by the Bill. If this Bill were rejected by Parliament it would be a great and grievous disaster to peace and contentment in India, but it would not prevent the Secretary of State the next morning from advising his Majesty to appoint an Indian Member. The members of the Viceroy's Executive Council are appointed by the Crown.

The noble marquess the other day fell into a slight error, if he will forgive me for saying so. He said that the Government of India had used cautious and tentative words indicating that it would be premature to decide at once this question of the Indian member until after further experience had been gained. I think the noble marquess must have lost his way in the mazes of that enormous blue-book which, as he told us, caused him so much inconvenience and added so much to his excessive luggage during the Christmas holidays. The dispatch, as far as I can discover, is silent altogether on the topic of the Indian member of the Viceroy's Council, and deals only with the Councils of Bombay and Madras and the proposed Councils for the Lieutenant-Governorships.

Perhaps I might be allowed to remind your lordships of the Act of 1833—certainly the most extensive measure of Indian government between Mr. Pitt's famous Act of 1784 and Queen Victoria's assumption of the government of India. There is nothing so important as that Act. It lays down in the broadest way possible the desire of Parliament of that day that there was to be no difference in appointing to offices in India between one race and another, and the covering dispatch wound up by saying that :

'For the future, fitness is to be the criterion of eligibility.'

I need not quote the famous paragraph in the Queen's proclamation of 1858, for every member of the House who takes an interest in India knows that by heart. Now, the noble marquess says that his anxiety is that nothing shall be done to impair the efficiency of the Viceroy's Council. I share that anxiety with all my heart. I hope the noble marquess will do me the justice to remember that in these plans I have gone beyond the Government of India in resolving that a permanent official majority shall remain in the

Viceroy's Council. Lord MacDonnell said the other day :

'I believe you cannot find any individual native gentleman who is enjoying general confidence who would be able to give advice and assistance to the Governor-General in Council.'

It has been my lot to be twice Chief Secretary for Ireland, and I do not believe I can truly say I ever met in Ireland a single individual native gentleman who ' enjoyed general confidence '. And yet I received at Dublin Castle most excellent and competent advice. Therefore I will accept that statement from the noble lord. The question is whether there is no one of the 300 millions of the population of India who is competent to be the officially constituted adviser of the Governor-General in Council in the administration of Indian affairs. You make an Indian a Judge of the High Court, and Indians have even been acting Chief Justices. As to capacity who can deny that they have distinguished themselves as administrators of native States, where far more demand is made on their resources, intellectual and moral ? It is said that the presence of an Indian member would cause restraint in the language of discussion. For a year and a half I have had two Indians at the Council of India, and I have never found the slightest restraint whatever.

Then there is the question, What are you going to do about the Hindu and the Mahomedan ? When Indians were first admitted to the High Courts, for a long time the Hindus were more fit and competent than the Mahomedans ; but now I am told the Mahomedans have their full share, The same sort of operation would go on in quinquennial periods between Hindus and Mahomedans. Opinion amongst the great Anglo-Indian officers now at home is divided, but I know at least one, not, I think, behind even Lord MacDonnell in experience or mental grasp, who is strongly in favour of this proposal. One circumstance which cannot but strike your lordships as remarkable is the comparative absence of hostile criticism of this idea by the Anglo-Indian Press, and, as I am told, in Calcutta society. I was apprehensive at one time that it might be otherwise. I should like to give a concrete illustration. The noble marquess opposite said the other day that there was going to be a vacancy in one of the posts on the Viceroy's Executive Council—namely, the legal member's time would soon be up. Now, suppose there were in Calcutta an Indian lawyer of large practice and great experience in his profession—a man of unstained professional and personal repute, in close touch with European society and much respected, and the actual holder of important legal office. Am I to say to that man : ' In spite of all these excellent circumstances to your credit, in spite of your undisputed fitness, in spite of the emphatic declaration of 1833 that fitness is to be the criterion of eligibility, in spite of that noble promise in Queen Victoria's proclamation of 1858 —a promise of which every Englishman ought to be for ever proud if he tries to adhere to it, and rather ashamed if he tries to betray or mock it — in spite of all this, usage and prejudice are so strong that I dare not appoint you, but must appoint instead some stranger to India from Lincoln's Inn or the Temple ? ' Is there one of your lordships who would envy the Secretary of State who had to hold language of that kind to a meritorious candidate, one of the King's equal subjects ? I put it to your lordships in that concrete way. These abstract general arguments are slippery. I do not say there is no force in them, but there are deeper questions at issue to which Lord Minto and myself attach the greatest importance. My lords, I thank you for listening to me, and I beg to move the Second Reading.

7. *Lord Courtney of Penwith, House of Lords, 24 February, 1909*

I DEPRECATE the division of the politicians of India into the three classes mentioned yesterday. I deprecate the habit of thinking of them in that fashion. I trust that the general effect of what my noble friend the Secretary of State has done will be a great reduction in the number of irre- concilables, though some, of course, will continue to exist—they exist everywhere—and the develop- ment of constitutional methods of procedure. I deprecate entirely pronouncements as to what may or may not be the outcome of all these changes in the distant future. It has taken a long time to come about, but my noble friend said last night and said truly, that what he is proposing to-day is the development of what Mr. James Mill wrote in 1833, and of what the Queen said in her proclamation to the people of India in 1858. It is a mere form of evolution of the principle that fitness is the sole qualification for office, and that no discrimination should be made, as far as possible, in respect of race and creed. What is proposed now is the development of what was said then.

Yet it is probably true that Mr. Mill did not conceive then what is being proposed now, nor can we now say what will be the development fifty years hence of the beginnings we are making to-day.

I see no reason whatever for laying down the maxim that Colonial self-government can never, under any circumstances, come to pass in India. When we consider what has been done in the last thirty years in Japan and observe the movement in China, is it not rash to declare what may be the ultimate form of government fifty years hence in India ? We have had government for the people in India. It is impossible to carry that on without proceeding to government through the people of India. By and by you will come more and more to government by the people. If it is done cautiously, as I have no doubt it will be done, there is no necessity to trouble much about the ultimate goal. There must be great changes, there will be great changes, and the mass of the people of India will be associated more and more with every branch of the administration and government of India from the highest to the lowest. I am content to watch and wait, and, if the act done to-day is good, to support it thoroughly, leaving to the future the working out of one of the greatest problems that ever befell statesmen or nation—the problem of gradually moderating the government of a whole subject people by an imported handful of persons of another race, another creed, and another training. It is wonderful, under such conditions, that the problem has been so successfully met as it had been up to this time. Not a few of the people of India think that the creed of the governing race is an impiety, that their lives are bestial, and their touch an abomination. We have to work all that down, and we shall only do it by great toleration of their ideals and by not attempting to circumscribe to-day what may come to pass hereafter.

8. *Indian Councils Act, 1909 (9 Edward 7, Chapter 4)*

BE it enacted by the King's most excellent Majesty, by and with the advice and consent of the Lords Spiritual and Temporal, and Commons, in this present Parliament assembled, and by the authority of the same, as follows :

1. (1) The additional members of the councils for the purpose of making laws and regulations (hereinafter referred to as Legislative Councils) of the Governor-General and of the Governors of Fort Saint George and Bombay, and the members of the Legislative Councils already constituted, or which may hereafter be constituted, of the several Lieutenant-Governors of Provinces, instead of being all nominated by the Governor-General, Governor, or Lieutenant-Governor in manner provided by the Indian Councils Acts, 1861, and 1892, shall include members so nominated and also members elected in accordance with regulations made under this Act, and references in those Acts to the members so nominated and their nomination shall be constructed as including references to the members so elected and their election.

(2) The number of additional members or

members so nominated and elected, the number of such members required to constitute a quorum, the term of office of such members and the manner of filling up casual vacancies occurring by reason of absence from India, inability to attend to duty, death; acceptance of office, or resignation duly accepted, or otherwise, shall, in the case of each such council, be such as may be prescribed by regulations made under this Act :

Provided that the aggregate number of members so nominated and elected shall not, in the case of any Legislative Council mentioned in the first column of the first schedule to this Act, exceed the number specified in the second column of that schedule.

2. (1) The number of ordinary members of the councils of the Governors of Fort Saint George and Bombay shall be such number not exceeding four as the Secretary of State in Council may from time to time direct, of whom two at least shall be persons who at the time of their appointment have been in the service of the Crown in India for at least twelve years.

(2) If at any meeting of either of such councils there is an equality of votes on any question, the Governor or other person presiding shall have two votes or the casting vote.

3. (1) It shall be lawful for the Governor-General in Council, with the approval of the Secretary of State in Council, by proclamation, to create a council in the Bengal Division of the Presidency of Fort William for the purpose of assisting the Lieutenant-General in the executive government of the Province, and by such proclamation—

(a) To make provision for determining what shall be the number (not exceeding four) and qualifications of the members of the council ; and

(b) to make provision for the appointment of temporary or acting members of the council during the absence of any member from illness or otherwise, and for the procedure to be adopted in case of a difference of opinion between a Lieutenant-Governor and his council, and in the case of equality of votes, and in the case of a Lieutenant-Governor being obliged to absent himself from his council from indisposition or any other cause.

(2) It shall be lawful for the Governor-General in Council, with the like approval, by a like proclamation to create a council in any other province under a Lieutenant-Governor in the executive government of the province : Provided that before any such proclamation is made a draft thereof shall be laid before each House of Parliament for not less than sixty days during the session of Parliament, and, if before the expiration of that time an address is presented to His Majesty by either House of Parliament against the draft or any part thereof, no further proceedings shall be taken thereon, without prejudice to the making of any new draft.

(3) Where any such proclamation has been made with respect to any province the Lieutenant-Governor may, with the consent of the Governor-General in Council, from time to time make rules and orders for the more convenient transaction of business in his council, and any order made or

act done in accordance with the rules and orders so made shall be deemed to be an act or order of the Lieutenant-Governor in Council.

(4) Every member of any such council shall be appointed by the Governor-General, with the approval of His Majesty, and shall, as such, be a member of the Legislative Council of the Lieutenant-Governor, in addition to the members nominated by the Lieutenant-Governor and elected under the provisions of this Act.

4. The Governor-General, and the Governors of Fort Saint George and Bombay, and the Lieutenant-Governor of every province respectively, shall appoint a member of their respective councils to be Vice-President thereof, and, for the purpose of temporarily holding and executing the office of Governor-General or Governor of Fort Saint George or Bombay and of presiding at meetings of Council in the absence of the Governor-General, Governor, or Lieutenant-Governor, the Vice-President so appointed shall be deemed to be the senior member of Council and the member highest in rank, and the Indian Councils Act, 1861, and sections sixty-two and sixty-three of the Government of India Act, 1833, shall have effect accordingly.

5. (1) Notwithstanding anything in the Indian Councils Act, 1861, the Governor-General in Council, the Governors in Council of Fort Saint George and Bombay respectively, and the Lieutenant-Governor or Lieutenant-Governor in Council of every province, shall make rules authorizing at any meeting of their respective legislative councils the discussion of the annual financial statement of the Governor-General in Council or of their respective local governments,

as the case may be, and of any matter of general public interest, and the asking of questions, under such conditions and restrictions as may be prescribed in the rules applicable to the several councils.

(2) Such rules as aforesaid may provide for the appointment of a member of any such council to preside at any such discussion in the place of the Governor-General, Governor, or Lieutenant-Governor, as the case may be, and of any Vice-President.

(3) Rules under this section, where made by a Governor in Council, or by a Lieutenant-Governor or a Lieutenant-Governor in Council, shall be subject to the sanction of the Governor-General in Council, and where made by the Governor-General in Council shall be subject to the sanction of the Secretary of State in Council, and shall not be subject to alteration or amendment by the Legislative Council of the Governor-General, Governor, or Lieutenant-Governor.

6. The Governor-General in Council shall, subject to the approval of the Secretary of State in Council, make regulations as to the conditions under which and manner in which persons resident in India may be nominated or elected as members of the Legislative Councils of the Governor-General, Governors, and Lieutenant-Governors, and as to the qualifications for being, and for being nominated or elected, a member of any such council, and as to any other matter for which regulations are authorized to be made under this Act, and also as to the manner in which those regulations are to be carried into effect. Regulations under this. section shall not be subject to alteration or amendment by the Legislative Council of the Governor-General.

7. All proclamations, regulations, and rules made under this Act, other than rules made by a Lieutenant-Governor for the more convenient transaction of business in his Council, shall be laid before both Houses of Parliament as soon as may be after they are made.

8. (1) This Act may be cited as the Indian Councils Act, 1909, and shall be construed with the Indian Councils Acts, 1861 and 1892, and those Acts, the Indian Councils Act, 1869, the Indian Councils Act, 1871, the Indian Councils Act, 1874, the Indian Councils Act, 1904, and this Act may be cited together as the Indian Councils Acts, 1861 to 1909.

(2) This Act shall come into operation on such date or dates as the Governor-General in Council, with the approval of the Secretary of State in Council, may appoint, and different dates may be appointed for different purposes and provisions of this Act and for different councils.

On the date appointed for the coming into operation of this Act as respects any Legislative Council, all the nominated members of the council then in office shall go out of office, but may, if otherwise qualified, be renominated or be elected in accordance with the provisions of this Act.

(3) The enactments mentioned in the Second Schedule to this Act are hereby repealed to the extent mentioned in the third column of that schedule.

SCHEDULES

FIRST SCHEDULE

*Maximum Numbers of Nominated and Elected Members
of Legislative Councils*

Legislative Council.	*Maximum Number.*
Legislative Council of the Governor-General .	60
Legislative Council of the Governor of Fort Saint George	50
Legislative Council of the Governor of Bombay	50
Legislative Council of the Lieutenant-Governor of the Bengal Division of the Presidency of Fort William	50
Legislative Council of the Lieutenant-Governor of the United Provinces of Agra and Oudh	50
Legislative Council of the Lieutenant-Governor of the Province of Eastern Bengal and Assam	50
Legislative Council of the Lieutenant-Governor of the Province of the Punjab . .	30
Legislative Council of the Lieutenant-Governor of the Province of Burma . . .	30
Legislative Council of the Lieutenant-Governor of any Province which may hereafter be constituted	30

SECOND SCHEDULE

Enactments Repealed

Session and Chapter.	*Short Title.*	*Extent of Repeal.*
24 & 25 Vict. c. 67.	The Indian Councils Act, 1861.	In section ten, the words 'Not less than six nor more than twelve in number'. In section eleven, the words 'for the term of two years from the date of such nomination'. In section fifteen, the words from 'and the power of making laws and regulations' to 'shall be present'. In section twenty-nine, the words 'not less than four nor more than eight in number'. In section thirty, the words 'for the term of two years from the date of such nomination'. In section thirty-four, the words from 'and the power of making laws and regulations' to 'shall be present'. In section forty-five, the words from 'and the power of making laws and regulations' to 'shall be present'.
55 & 56 Vict. c. 14.	The Indian Councils Act, 1892.	Sections one and two. In section four, the words 'appointed under the said Act or this Act' and paragraph (2).

III

THE WAR AND RESPONSIBLE GOVERNMENT IN INDIA, 1914–21

1. *G. K. Gokhale's Political Testament,* 1915

THE grant of Provincial Autonomy foreshadowed in the Delhi Dispatch would be a fitting concession to make to the people of India at the close of the War. This will involve the twofold operation of freeing the Provincial Governments on one side from the greater part of the control which is at present exercised over them by the Government of India and the Secretary of State in connexion with the internal administration of the country and substituting on the other, in place of the control so removed, the control of the representatives of tax-payers through Provincial Legislative Councils. I indicate below in brief outline the form of administration that should be set up in different provinces to carry out this idea.

Each province should have :

1. A Governor appointed from England at the head of the administration.
2. A Cabinet or Executive Council of six members, three of whom should be Englishmen and three Indians with the following portfolios :
   (a) Home (including law and justice).
   (b) Finance.
   (c) Agriculture, irrigation, and public works.
   (d) Education.
   (e) Local self-government (including sanitation and medical relief).
   (f) Industries and commerce.

While members of the Indian Civil Service should

be eligible for appointment to the Executive
Council, no place in the Council should be reserved
for them, the best men available being taken, both
English and Indian.

3. A Legislative Council of between seventy-five
and a hundred members, of whom not less than
four-fifths should be elected by different constituencies and interests. Thus in the Bombay
Presidency, roughly speaking, each district should
return two members, one representing municipalities and the other district and Taluk Boards.
The city of Bombay should have about ten members allotted to it. Bodies in the Mofussil like
the Karachi Chamber, Ahmedabad mill-owners,
Deccan Sardars, should have a member each.
Then there would be the special representation of
Mahomedans, and here and there a member may
have to be given to communities like the Lingayats,
where they are strong. There should be no nominated non-official members, except as experts.
A few official members may be added by the
Governor as experts or to assist in representing
the Executive Government.

4. The relations between the Executive Government and the Legislative Council so constituted
should be roughly similar to those between the
Imperial Government and the Reichstag in Ger-
many. The Council will have to pass all provincial
legislation and its assent will be necessary to
additions to or changes in provincial taxation.
The Budget too will have to come to it for discussion;
and its resolutions in connexion with it, as also on
questions of general administration, will have to
be given effect to, unless vetoed by the Governor.
More frequent meetings or longer continuous

sittings will also have to be provided for. But the members of the Executive Government shall not depend, individually or collectively, on the support of a majority of the Councils for holding their offices.

5. The Provincial Government, so reconstituted and working under the control of the Legislative Council as outlined above, should have complete charge of the internal administration of the province and it should have virtually independent financial powers, the present financial relations between it and the Government of India being largely revised,—and to some extent even reversed. The revenue under salt, customs, tributes, railway, post, telegraph, and Mint should belong exclusively to the Government of India, the services being Imperial; while that under land revenue, including irrigation, excise, forests, assessed taxes, stamps, and registration should belong to the Provincial Government, the services being provincial. As under this division, the revenue falling to the Provincial Government will be in excess of its existing requirements, and that assigned to the Government of India will fall short of its present expenditure, the Provincial Government should be required to make an annual contribution to the Government of India, fixed for periods of five years at a time. Subject to this arrangement the Imperial and the Provincial Governments should develop their separate systems of finance, the Provincial Governments being given powers of taxation and borrowing within certain limits.

Such a scheme of Provincial Autonomy will be incomplete unless it is accompanied by (a) a liberalizing of the present form of district administration

| and (*b*) a great extension of local self-government. For (*a*) it will be necessary to abolish the Commissionerships of divisions except where special reasons may exist for their being maintained as in Sind, and to associate small District Councils, partly elected and partly nominated, with the Collector for whom most of the present powers of the Commissioners could then be transferred,—the functions of the Councils being advisory to begin with. For (*b*) Village Panchayats, partly elected and partly nominated, should be created for villages and groups of villages; and Municipal Boards in towns and Taluk Boards in Talukas should be made wholly elected bodies, the Provincial Government reserving to itself and exercising stringent powers of control. A portion of the excise revenue should be made over to those bodies so that they may have adequate resources at their disposal for the due performance of their duties. The district being too large an area for efficient local self-government by an honorary agency, the functions of the District Boards should be strictly limited and the Collector should continue to be its ex-officio President.

THE GOVERNMENT OF INDIA

1. The provinces being thus rendered practically autonomous, the Constitution of the Executive Council or the Cabinet of the Viceroy will have to be correspondingly altered. At present there are four members in that Council with portfolios which concern the internal administration of the country —namely, home, agriculture, education, and industries and commerce. As all internal administration will now be made over to Provincial Governments and the Government of India will only

retain in its hands nominal control to be exercised on very rare occasions, one member to be called member for the interior should suffice in place of these four. It will, however, be necessary to create certain other portfolios, and I would have the Council consist of the following six members (at least two of whom shall always be Indians).

(a) Interior, (b) finance, (c) law, (d) defence, (e) communications (railways, post and telegraph), and (f) foreign.

(a) The Legislative Council of the Viceroy should be styled the Legislative Assembly of India. Its members should be raised to about one hundred to begin with and its power enlarged, but the principle of an official majority (for which perhaps it will suffice to substitute a nominated majority) should for the present be maintained, until sufficient experience has. been gathered of the working of autonomous arrangements for provinces. This will give the Government of India a reserve power in connexion with Provincial administration to be exercised in emergencies. Thus, if a Provincial Legislative Council persistently decline to pass legislation which the Government regard to be essential in the vital interests of the province, it could be passed by the Government of India in its Legislative Assembly over the head of the province. Such occasions would be extremely rare, but the reserve power will give a sense of security to the authorities and will induce them to enter on the great experiment of Provincial Autonomy with greater readiness. Subject to this principle of an official or nominated majority being for the present maintained, the Assembly should have increased opportunities of influencing the policy of the

Government by discussion, questions connected with the army and navy (to be now created) being placed on a level with other questions. In fiscal matters the Government of India so constituted should be freed from the control of the Secretary of State, whose control in other matters too should be largely reduced, his Council being abolished and his position steadily approximated to that of the Secretary of State for the Colonies.

Commissions in the army and navy must now be given to Indians, with proper facilities for military and naval instruction.

German East Africa, if conquered from the Germans, should be reserved for Indian colonization and should be handed over to the Government of India.

2. *Memorandum as to post-war Reforms, signed by 19 Elected Members of the Indian Legislative Council, October 1916*

THERE is no doubt that the termination of the War will see a great advance in the ideals of government all over the civilized world, and especially in the British Empire, which entered into the struggle in defence of the liberties of weak and small nationalities and is pouring forth its richest blood and treasure in upholding the cause of justice and humanity in the international relations of the world. India has borne her part in this struggle and cannot remain unaffected by the new spirit of change for a better state of things. Expectations have been raised in this country and hopes held out that after the War the problems of Indian administration will be looked at from a new angle of vision. The people of India have good reasons to be grateful to England for the great progress in her material resources and the widening of her intellectual and political outlook under British rule, and for the steady, if slow, advance up to date.

Commencing with the Charter Act of India of 1833 up to 1909, the Government of India was conducted by a bureaucracy almost entirely non-Indian in its composition and not responsible to the people of India. The reforms of 1909 for the first time introduced an Indian element in the direction of affairs in the administration of India. This element was of a very limited character. The Indian people accepted it as an indication on the part of the Government of a desire to admit the Indians into the inner counsels of the Indian Empire so far as the Legislative Councils are concerned. The numbers of non-official members were enlarged with increased facilities for debate and interpellation. The Supreme Legislative Council retained an absolute official majority, and in the Provincial Legislative councils, where a non-official majority was allowed, such a majority included nominated members and the European representatives; and in measures largely affecting the people, whether of legislation or taxation, by which Europeans were not directly affected, the Europeans would naturally support the Government, and the nominated members, being nominees of Government, would be inclined to take the same side. Past experience has shown that this has actually happened on various occasions. The non-official majorities, therefore, in the Provincial Councils have proved largely illusory and give no real power to the representatives of the people.

The Legislative Councils, whether supreme or provincial, are at present nothing but advisory bodies, without any power of effective control over the Government, Imperial or Provincial.

The people or their representatives are practically as little associated with the real government of the country as they were before the reforms, except for the introduction of the Indian members in the Executive Councils, where again the nomination rests entirely with the Government, the people having no voice in the selection of the Indian members. The object which the Government had in view in introducing the reforms of 1909 was, as expressed by the Prime Minister in his speech in the House of Commons on the second reading of the India Councils Bill on 1 April 1909, that it was most desirable in the circumstances to give to the people of India the feeling that these Legislative Councils are not mere automatons, the wires of which were pulled by the official hierarchy. This object, it is submitted, has not been attained.

Apart from this question of the constitution of the Legislative and Executive Councils, the people labour under certain grave disabilities which not only prevent the utilization but also lead to the wastage of what is best in them and are positively derogatory to their sense of national self-respect. The Arms Act, which excludes from its operation Europeans and Anglo-Indians and applies only to the pure natives of the country, the disqualification of Indians for forming or joining Volunteer Corps and their exclusion from the commissioned ranks of the army, are disabilities which are looked upon with an irritating sense of racial differentiation. It would be bad enough if these were mere disabilities. Restrictions and prohibitions regarding the possession and use of arms have tended to emasculate the civil population in India and expose them to serious danger. The position of Indians in India is practically this, that they have no real part or share in the direction of the government of the country and are placed under very great and galling disabilities, from which the other members of the British Empire are exempt and which have reduced them to a state of utter help-lessness.

The existence, moreover, of the system of in-dentured emigration gives to the British Colonies and the outside world the impression that Indians as a whole are no better than indentured coolies who are looked upon as very little, if at all, above the slaves. The present state of things makes the Indians feel that, though theoretically they are equal subjects of the King, they hold a very in-ferior position in the British Empire. Other Asiatic races also hold the same, if not a worse, view about India and her status in the Empire. Humiliating as this position of inferiority is to the Indian mind, it is almost unbearable to the youth of India whose outlook is broadened by education and travel in foreign parts, where they come in contact with other free races.

In the face of these grievances and disabilities, what has sustained the people is the hope and faith inspired by the promises and assurances of fair and equal treatment which have been held out from time to time by our Sovereigns and British statesmen of high standing. In the crisis we are now going through, the Indian people have sunk domestic differences between themselves and the

Government, and have faithfully and loyally stood by the Empire. The Indian soldiers were eager to go to the battlefields of Europe, not as mercenary troops but as free citizens of the British Empire which required their services, and her civilian population was animated by one desire, namely, to stand by England in the hour of her need. Peace and tranquillity reigned throughout India when she was practically denuded of British and Indian troops. The Prime Minister of England, while voicing the sentiments of the English people in regard to India's part in this Great War, spoke of Indians as the joint and equal custodians of one common interest and future. India does not claim any reward for her loyalty, but she has a right to expect that the want of confidence on the part of Government, to which she not unnaturally ascribes her present, should now be a thing of the past, and that she should no longer occupy a position of subordination *but one of comradeship*. This would assure the people that England is ready and willing to help them to attain self-government under the ægis of the British Crown and thus discharge the noble mission which she has undertaken and to which she has so often given voluntary expression through her rulers and statesmen.

What is wanted is not merely good government or efficient administration, *but government that is acceptable to the people, because it is responsible to them*. This is what, India understands, would constitute the changed angle of vision. If, after the termination of the War, the position of India practically remains what it was before, and there is no material change in it, it will undoubtedly cause bitter disappointment and great discontent in the country, and the beneficent efforts of participation in common danger overcome by common effort will soon disappear, leaving no record behind save the painful memory of unrealized expectations. We feel sure that the Government is also alive to the situation and is contemplating a measure of reform in the administration of the country.

We feel that we should avail ourselves of this opportunity to offer to the Government our humble suggestions as to the lines on which these reforms should proceed. They must, in our opinion, go to the root of the matter. They must give to the people real and effective participation in the government of the country and also remove those irritating disabilities as regards the possession of arms and a military career which indicate want of confidence in the people and place them in a position of inferiority and helplessness. Under the first head we would take the liberty to suggest the following measures for consideration and adoption :

1. In all the Executive Councils, Provincial and Imperial, half the number of members should be Indians. The European element in the Executive Councils should, as far as possible, be nominated from the ranks of men trained and educated in the public life of England, so that India may have the benefit of a wider outlook and larger experience of the outside world. It is not absolutely essential that the members of the Executive Councils, Indians or Europeans, should have experience of actual administration ; for, as in the case of Ministers in England, the assistance of the permanent officials of the department is always available to them. As regards Indians we venture to say that a sufficient number of qualified Indians,

who can worthily fill the office of members of the Executive Council and hold portfolios, is always available. Our short experience in this direction has shown how Indians like Sir S. P. Sinha, Sir Syed Ali Imam, the late Mr. Krishnaswami Iyer, Sir Shams-ul-Huda, and Sir Sankaran Nair have maintained a high level of administrative ability in the discharge of their duties. Moreover, it is well known that the native states, where Indians have opportunities, have produced renowned administrators like Sir Salar Jung, Sir T. Madhav Rao, Sir Seshadri Iyer, Dewan Bahadur Ragunath Rao, not to mention the present administrators in the various native states of India. The statutory obligation now existing, that three of the members of the Supreme Executive Council shall be selected from the public services in India, and similar provisions with regard to Provincial Councils, should be removed. The elected representatives of the people should have a voice in the selection of the Indian members of the Executive Councils and for that purpose a principle of election should be adopted.

2. All the Legislative Councils in India should have a substantial majority of elected representatives. We feel that they will watch and safeguard the interests of the masses and the agricultural population, with whom they are in closer touch than any European officer, however sympathetic, can possibly be. The proceedings of the various Legislative Councils, the Indian National Congress and the Moslem League bear ample testimony to the solicitude of the educated Indians for the welfare of the masses and their acquaintance with their wants and wishes. The franchise should be

broadened and extended directly to the people, Mahomedans or Hindus, wherever they are in a minority, being given proper and adequate representation, having regard to their numerical strength and position.

3. The total number of the members of the Supreme Council should be not less than one hundred and fifty, and of the Provincial Councils not less than one hundred for the major provinces and not less than sixty to seventy-five for the minor provinces.

4. The Budget should be passed in the shape of money bills, fiscal autonomy being conceded to India.

5. The Imperial Legislative Council should have power to legislate on all matters and to discuss and pass resolutions relating to all matters of Indian administration, and the Provincial Councils should have similar powers with regard to provincial administrations, save and except that the direction of military affairs, of foreign relations, declarations of war, the making of peace and the entering into treaties other than commercial, should be vested in the Government of India. As a safeguard, the Governor-General-in-Council, or the Governor-in-Council, as the case may be, should have the right of veto, but subject to certain conditions and limitations.

6. The Council of the Secretary of State should be abolished. The Secretary of State should, as far as possible, hold in relation to the Government of India a position similar to that which the Secretary of State for the Colonies holds in relation to the colonies. The Secretary of State should be assisted by two permanent under-Secretaries, one of whom

should be an Indian. The salaries of the Secretary and the under-Secretaries should be placed on the British estimates.

7. In any scheme of Imperial federation, India should be given, through her chosen representatives, a place similar to that of the self-governing dominions.

8. The Provincial Governments should be made autonomous as stated in the Government of India's dispatch, dated 25 August 1911.

9. The United Provinces as well as the other major provinces should have a Governor brought from the United Kingdom with an Executive Council.

10. A full measure of local self-government should be immediately granted.

11. The right to carry arms should be granted to Indians on the same conditions as to Europeans.

12. Indians should be allowed to enlist as volunteers and units of a territorial army established in India.

13. Commissions in the army should be given to Indian youths under conditions similar to those applicable to Europeans.

3. *Scheme of Reforms passed at the 31st session of the Indian National Congress held at Lucknow on 29 December, 1916, and adopted by the All-India Moslem League at its Meeting on 31 December, 1916*

I.—PROVINCIAL LEGISLATIVE COUNCILS

1. PROVINCIAL Legislative Councils shall consist of four-fifths elected and of one-fifth nominated members.

2. Their strength shall be not less than one

hundred and twenty-five members in the Major Provinces, and from fifty to seventy-five in the Minor Provinces.

3. The members of Councils should be elected directly by the people on as broad a franchise as possible.

4. Adequate provision should be made for the representation of important minorities by election, and that the Mahomedans should be represented through special electorates on the Provincial Legislative Council.

Punjab—One half of the elected Indian members.
United Provinces—30 per cent.   ,,   ,,
Bengal—40 per cent.   ,,   ,,
Behar—25 per cent.   ,,   ,,
Central Provinces—15 per cent.   ,,   ,,
Madras—15 per cent.   ,,   ,,
Bombay—One-third   ,,   ,,

Provided that Mahomedans shall not participate in any of the other elections to the Legislative Councils.

Provided further that no Bill, nor any clause thereof, nor a resolution introduced by a non-official member affecting one or the other community, which question is to be determined by the members of that community in the Legislative Council concerned, shall be proceeded with, if three-fourths of the members of that community in the particular Council, Imperial or Provincial, oppose the bill or any clause thereof or the resolution.

5. The head of the Provincial Government should not be the President of the Legislative Council, but the Council should have the right of electing its President.

6. The right of asking supplementary questions

should not be restricted to the member putting the original question but should be allowed to be exercised by any other member.

7. (a) Except customs, post, telegraph, mint, salt, opium, railways, army and navy, and tributes from Indian States, all other sources of revenue should be provincial.

(b) There should be no divided heads of revenue. The Government of India should be provided with fixed contributions from the Provincial Governments, such fixed contributions being liable to revision when extraordinary and unforeseen contingencies render such revision necessary.

(c) The Provincial Council should have full authority to deal with all matters affecting the internal administration of the province, including the power to raise loans, to impose and alter taxation and to vote on the Budget. All items of expenditure and all proposals concerning ways and means for raising the necessary revenue should be embodied in Bills and submitted to the Provincial Council for adoption.

(d) Resolutions on all matters within the purview of the Provincial Government should be allowed for discussion in accordance with rules made in that behalf by the Council itself.

(e) A resolution passed by the Legislative Council shall be binding on the Executive Government, unless vetoed by the Governor in Council, provided however that if the resolution is again passed by the Council after an interval of not less than one year, it must be given effect to.

(f) A motion for adjournment may be brought forward for the discussion of a definite matter of urgent public importance if supported by not less than one-eighth of the members present.

8. Any special meeting of the Council may be summoned on a requisition by not less than one-eighth of the members.

9. A Bill, other than a Money Bill, may be introduced in Council in accordance with the rules made in that behalf by the Council itself, and the consent of the Government should not be required therefor.

10. All Bills passed by Provincial Legislatures shall have to receive the assent of the Governor before they become law, but may be vetoed by the Governor-General.

11. The terms of office of the members shall be five years.

II.—Provincial Governments

1. The head of every Provincial Government shall be a Governor who shall not ordinarily belong to the Indian Civil Service or any of the permanent services.

2. There shall be in every Province an Executive Council which, with the Governor, shall constitute the Executive Government of the Province.

3. Members of the Indian Civil Service shall not ordinarily be appointed to the Executive Councils.

4. Not less than one-half of the members of Executive Council shall consist of Indians to be elected by the elected members of the Provincial Legislative Council.

5. The term of office of the members shall be five years.

III.—Imperial Legislative Council

1. The strength of the Imperial Legislative Council shall be one hundred and fifty.

2. Four-fifths of the members shall be elected.

3. The franchise for the Imperial Legislative Council should be widened as far as possible on the lines of the Mahomedan electorates, and the elected members of the Provincial Legislative Councils should also form an electorate for the return of members to the Imperial Legislative Council.

4. The President of the Council shall be elected by the Council itself.

5. The right of asking supplementary questions shall not be restricted to the member putting the original question but should be allowed to be exercised by any other member.

6. Any special meeting of the Council may be summoned on a requisition by not less than one-eighth of the members.

7. A Bill, other than a Money Bill, may be introduced in Council in accordance with rules made in that behalf by the Council itself, and the consent of the Executive Government should not be required therefor.

8. All Bills passed by the Council shall have to receive the assent of the Governor-General before they become law.

9. All financial proposals relating to sources of income and items of expenditure shall be embodied in Bills. Every such Bill and the Budget as a whole shall be submitted for the vote of the Imperial Legislative Council.

10. The term of office of members shall be five years.

11. The matters mentioned hereinbelow shall be exclusively under the control of the Imperial Legislative Council:

(a) Matters in regard to which uniform legislation for the whole of India is desirable.

(*b*) Provincial legislation in so far as it may affect inter-provincial fiscal relations.

(*c*) Questions affecting purely Imperial revenue, excepting tributes from Indian States.

(*d*) Questions affecting purely Imperial expenditure, except that no resolution of the Imperial Legislative Council shall be binding on the Governor-General in Council in respect of military charges for the defence of the country.

(*e*) The right of revising Indian tariffs and customs-duties, of imposing, altering, or removing any tax or cess, modifying the existing system of currency and banking, and granting any aids or bounties to any or all deserving and nascent industries of the country.

(*f*) Resolutions on all matters relating to the administration of the country as a whole.

12. A resolution passed by the Legislative Council should be binding on the Executive Government, unless vetoed by the Governor-General in Council : provided, however, that, if the resolution is again passed by the Council after an interval of not less than one year, it must be given effect to.

13. A motion for adjournment may be brought forward for the discussion of a definite matter of urgent public importance, if supported by not less than one-eighth of the members present.

14. The Crown may exercise its power of veto in regard to a Bill passed by a Provincial Legislative Council or by the Imperial Legislative Council within twelve months from the date on which it is passed, and the Bill shall cease to have effect as from the date on which the fact of such veto is made known to the Legislative Council concerned.

15. The Imperial Legislative Council shall have no power to interfere with the Government of India's direction of the military affairs and the foreign and political relations of India, including the declaration of war, the making of peace and the entering into treaties.

IV.—THE GOVERNMENT OF INDIA

1. The Governor-General of India will be the head of the Government of India.

2. He will have an Executive Council, half of whom shall be Indians.

3. The Indian members should be elected by the elected members of the Imperial Legislative Council.

4. Members of the Indian Civil Service shall not ordinarily be appointed to the Executive Council of the Governor-General.

5. The power of making all appointments in the Imperial Civil Services shall vest in the Government of India as constituted under this scheme, and subject to any laws that may be made by the Imperial Legislative Council.

6. The Government of India shall not ordinarily interfere in the local affairs of a province, and powers not specifically given to a Provincial Government shall be deemed to be vested in the former. The authority of the Government of India will ordinarily be limited to general supervision and superintendence over the Provincial Governments.

7. In legislative and administrative matters, the Government of India, as constituted under this scheme, shall, as far as possible, be independent of the Secretary of State.

8. A system of independent audit of the accounts of the Government of India should be instituted.

V.—THE SECRETARY OF STATE IN COUNCIL

1. The Council of the Secretary of State for India should be abolished.

2. The salary of the Secretary of State should be placed on the British Estimates.

3. The Secretary of State should, as far as possible, occupy the same position in relation to the Government of India as the Secretary of State for the Colonies in relation to the Governments of the self-governing Dominions. •

4. The Secretary of State for India should be assisted by two permanent under-secretaries, one of whom should always be an Indian.

VI.—MILITARY AND OTHER MATTERS OF POLICY

1. The military and naval services of His Majesty, both in their commissioned and non-commissioned ranks, should be thrown open to Indians and adequate provision should be made for their selection, training and instruction in India.

2. Indians should be allowed to enlist as volunteers.

3. Indians should be placed on a footing of equality in respect of status and rights of citizenship with other subjects of His Majesty the King throughout the Empire.

4. The Executive Officers in India shall have no judicial powers entrusted to them, and the judiciary in every province shall be placed under the highest Court of that province.

4. *Resolutions VII, IX, and XXII of the Imperial War Conference, April 1917*

VII

REPRESENTATION OF INDIA AT FUTURE IMPERIAL CONFERENCES

(Eighth Day ; Friday, April 13th.)

That the Imperial War Conference desires to place on record its view that the Resolution of the Imperial Conference of 20th April 1907 should be modified to permit of India being fully represented at all future Imperial Conferences, and that the necessary steps should be taken to secure the assent of the various Governments in order that the next Imperial Conference may be summoned and constituted accordingly.

IX

CONSTITUTION OF THE EMPIRE

(Ninth Day ; Monday, April 16th.)

The Imperial War Conference are of opinion that the readjustment of the constitutional relations of the component parts of the Empire is too important and intricate a subject to be dealt with during the War, and that it should form the subject of a special Imperial Conference to be summoned as soon as possible after the cessation of hostilities.

They deem it their duty, however, to place on record their view that any such readjustment, while thoroughly preserving all existing powers of self-government and complete control of domestic affairs, should be based upon a full recognition of

the Dominions as autonomous nations of an
Imperial Commonwealth, and of India as an important portion of the same, should recognize the
right of the Dominions and India to an adequate
voice in foreign policy and in foreign relations, and
should provide effective arrangements for continuous consultation in all important matters of
common Imperial concern, and for such necessary
concerted action, founded on consultation, as the
several Governments may determine.

XXII

RECIPROCITY OF TREATMENT BETWEEN INDIA AND THE SELF-GOVERNING DOMINIONS

(Fifteenth day ; Friday, April 27th.)

That the Imperial War Conference, having
examined the Memorandum on the position of
Indians in the Self-governing Dominions presented
by the Indian representatives to the Conference,
accepts the principle of reciprocity of treatment
between India and the Dominions and recommends
the Memorandum to the favourable consideration
of the Governments concerned.

5. *Edwin S. Montagu, House of Commons, 20 August, 1917*

The policy of His Majesty's Government, with
which the Government of India are in complete
accord, is that of increasing the association of
Indians in every branch of the administration and
the gradual development of self-governing institutions with a view to the progressive realization
of responsible government in India as an integral
part of the British Empire. They have decided

that substantial steps in this direction should be taken as soon as possible, and that it is of the highest importance as a preliminary to considering what these steps should be that there should be a free and informal exchange of opinion between those in authority at home and in India. His Majesty's Government have accordingly decided, with His Majesty's approval, that I should accept the Viceroy's invitation to proceed to India to discuss these matters with the Viceroy and the Government of India, to consider with the Viceroy the views of local governments, and to receive with him the suggestions of representative bodies and others.

I would add that progress in this policy can only be achieved by successive stages. The British Government and the Government of India, on whom the responsibility lies for the welfare and advancement of the Indian peoples, must be judges of the time and measure of each advance, and they must be guided by the co-operation received from those upon whom new opportunities of service will thus be conferred and by the extent to which it is found that confidence can be reposed in their sense of responsibility.

Ample opportunity will be afforded for public discussion of the proposals which will be submitted in due course to Parliament.

6. *Imperial War Conference, 24 July, 1918*

CHAIRMAN : Mr. Hughes cannot come this morning, and Sir Robert Borden is away. The first subject on the agenda is reciprocity of treatment between India and the Dominions, on which there is a Memorandum by Sir Satyendra Sinha, which has been circulated, and also a draft Resolution, which I understand is the result of a meeting at the India Office. Shall I read the draft Resolution as the basis of discussion ?

Sir S. P. SINHA : As you please, sir.

CHAIRMAN : The Resolution is as follows :

' The Imperial War Conference is of opinion that effect should now be given to the principle of reciprocity approved by Resolution XXII of the Imperial War Conference, 1917. In pursuance of that Resolution it is agreed that :

' 1. It is an inherent function of the Governments of the several communities of the British Commonwealth, including India, that each should enjoy complete control of the composition of its own population by means of restriction on immigration from any of the other communities.

' 2. British citizens domiciled in any British country, including India, should be admitted into any other British country for visits, for the purpose of pleasure or commerce, including temporary residence for the purpose of education. The conditions of such visits should be regulated on the principle of reciprocity, as follows :

' (a) The right of the Government of India is recognized to enact laws which shall have the effect of subjecting British citizens domiciled in any other British country to the same conditions in visiting India as those imposed on Indians desiring to visit such country.

' (b) Such right of visit or temporary residence shall, in each individual case, be embodied in a passport or written permit issued by the country of domicile and subject to *visé* there by an officer appointed by, and acting on behalf of, the country to be visited, if such country so desires.

' (c) Such right shall not extend to a visit or temporary residence for labour purposes or to permanent settlement.

' 3. Indians already permanently domiciled in the other British countries should be allowed to bring in their wives and minor children on condition (a) that not more than one wife and her children shall be admitted for each such Indian, and (b) that each individual so admitted shall be certified by the Government of India as being the lawful wife or child of such Indian.

' 4. The Conference recommends the ' other questions covered by the memoranda presented this year and last year to the Conference by the representatives of India, in so far as not dealt with in the foregoing paragraphs of this Resolution, to the various Governments concerned, with a view to early consideration.'

Sir S. P. SINHA : Mr. Long, I am desired by my colleague, the Maharaja of Patiala, who is unfortunately prevented from being present to-day, to express his entire concurrence in what I am going to say to the Conference. I also regret exceedingly the absence of Sir Robert Borden, because I wanted to express in his presence my deep feeling of gratitude for the generous and sympathetic spirit in which he has treated the whole question, both last year and this year. I desire to express my gratitude to him for the very great assistance he has rendered, to which I think the satisfactory solution which has been reached is very largely due—that is, if the Conference accepts the Resolution which I have the honour to propose.

Sir, the position of Indian immigrants in the Colonies has been the cause of great difficulties, both in the Dominions themselves and particularly in my own country, India. As long ago as 1897, the late Mr. Joseph Chamberlain, in addressing the Conference of Colonial Premiers, made a stirring appeal on behalf of the Indians who had emigrated to the Dominions. The same appeal was made in 1907 by Mr. Asquith, and in 1911. During all this time India was not represented at the Conference, and it is only due to the India Office here to say that they did all they could to assist us. In 1911 the Marquess of Crewe, as Secretary of State for India, presented a Memorandum to the Conference, which is printed in the proceedings for that year,[1] and I cannot do better than just read one of the passages from that Memorandum, which shows the nature of the difficulties which had arisen and the solutions which had been proposed on behalf of the Secretary of State. The Memorandum presented by the Secretary of State says this [2] :

‘ It does not appear to have been thoroughly considered that each Dominion owes responsibility to the rest of the Empire for ensuring that its domestic policy shall not unnecessarily create embarrassment in the administration of India.

‘ It is difficult for statesmen who have seen Indians represented only by manual labourers and petty traders to realise the importance to

[1] P. 272 of [Cd. 5746—1].   [2] P. 277 of [Cd. 5746—1].

F 3

the Empire as a whole of a country with some three hundred million inhabitants, possessing ancient civilizations of a very high order, which has furnished and furnishes some of the finest military material in the world to the Imperial forces, and which offers the fullest opportunities to financial and commercial enterprise. It is difficult to convey to those who do not know India the intense and natural resentment felt by veterans of the Indian Army, who have seen active service and won medals under the British flag, and who have been treated by their British officers with the consideration and courtesy to which their character entitles them, when (as has actually happened) they find themselves described as 'coolies', and treated with contemptuous severity in parts of the British Empire. Matters like this are, of course, very largely beyond the power of any Government to control, but popular misunderstandings are such a fruitful source of mischief that it seems worth while to put on record the grave fact that a radically false conception of the real position of India is undoubtedly rife in many parts of the Empire.

'The immigration difficulty, however, has, on the whole, been met by a series of statutes which succeed in preventing Asiatic influx. without the use of differential or insulting language. It is accepted that the Dominions shall not admit as permanent residents people whose mode of life is inconsistent with their own political and social ideals.

'But the admission of temporary visitors, to which this objection does not apply, has not yet been satisfactorily settled. If the question were not so grave, it would be seen to be ludicrous that regulations framed with an eye to coolies should affect ruling princes who are in subordinate alliance with His Majesty, and have placed their troops at his disposal, members of the Privy Council of the Empire, or gentlemen who have the honour to be His Majesty's own Aides-de-Camp. It is, of course, true that no persons of such distinguished position would, in fact, be turned back if he visited one of the Dominions. But these Indian gentlemen are known to entertain very strongly the feeling that, while they can move freely in the best society of any European capital, they could not set foot in some of the Dominions without undergoing vexatious catechisms from petty officials. At the same time, the highest posts in the Imperial services in India are open to subjects of His Majesty from the Dominions.

'The efforts of the British Government to create and foster a sense of citizenship in India have, within the last few years, undoubtedly been hampered by the feeling of soreness caused by the general attitude of the Dominions towards the peoples of India. The loyalty of the great mass of Indians to the Throne is a very conspicuous fact, and it is noteworthy that this feeling is sincerely entertained by many Indian critics of the details of British administration. The recent constitutional changes have given the people of the country increased association with the Government, and have at the same time afforded Indians greater opportunities of bringing to the direct notice of

Government their views on the wider question of
the place of India in the Empire. The gravity of
the friction between Indians and the Dominions
lies in this, that on the Colonial question, and on
that alone, are united the seditious agitators and
the absolutely loyal representatives of moderate
Indian opinion.'

This, sir, was in 1911, three years before the war ;
and if the position was correctly described then,
you will conceive with how much greater strength
the same observations apply to the present position
as between India and the Dominions. Of course,
since 1911, so far as South Africa is concerned,
many practical grievances which then existed
have, I gratefully acknowledge, been removed,
but there are still many others outstanding.
Those are referred to in the Memorandum which
has been circulated to the Conference, and I trust
my friends, Mr. Burton and General Smuts, to
whose statemanship South Africa, including all its
inhabitants, owes so much, will be able, on their
return to their own country, in process of time to
remove all, or at any rate some, of the grievances to
which I refer. I recognise that it is a matter of time.
I recognise their desire to remove those grievances,
in so far as they are grievances, and I appreciate
the difficulties of getting any legislation through
their own Parliaments for that purpose ; but at
the same time I hope the matter will not be lost
sight of, and that an early consideration will be
given to matters which have not been the subject
of agreement between us on this occasion.

But, sir, so far as the outstanding difficulty of
India is concerned, I am happy to think that the
Resolution which I now propose before the

Conference, if accepted, will get rid of that which
has caused the greatest amount of trouble both
in Canada and in India.   There are now about
4,000 or 5,000—I think nearer 4,000 than 5,000—
Indians in the Dominion of Canada, mostly in
British Columbia, I think—in fact, all in British
Columbia ; and the great difficulty of their position
—a difficulty which is appreciated in India — is
that these men are not allowed to take their wives
and children with them.   Now the Resolution, in
paragraph 3, removes this difficulty—that is to say,
if it is accepted and given effect to—and I consider
that that will cause the greatest satisfaction to my
countrymen, and particularly to that great
community of Sikhs who have furnished the
largest number of soldiers during this war, and to
whom these 4,000 men in Canada belong.

The principle of reciprocity, which was accepted
by the Conference on the last occasion, is again
referred to with approval, and effect is to be given
to it immediately as regards some of the most
urgent matters concerned.

I have read from Lord Crewe's Memorandum, sir,
the ludicrous position which now exists with regard to Indians of position visiting the Dominions.
That position will be altogether altered if the
Conference accepts the second part of the Resolution which I propose—namely, that ' British
citizens domiciled in any British country, including India, should be admitted into any other
British country for visits ', and that the system of
passports now in existence be continued, which
would prevent any influx of undesirable labour
population.

I think that, as the whole matter has been before

the Conference so long, it would not be right for
me to take up the time of the Conference further. I
venture to think that if this Resolution is accepted,
it will solve many of the most acute difficulties
which have arisen between the Dominions and
India ; and, speaking for India, I can assure you
that it will cause the greatest satisfaction, and will
help us to allay the agitation which, particularly
at a time like this, is a source of grave embarrassment. That is all I have to say, sir.

Mr. ROWELL : There are just one or two observations I should like to make, Mr. Chairman. May
I say how sincerely Sir Robert Borden regrets that
he could not be here this morning for this question.
He has personally taken a very keen interest in
the question, and I am sure he will appreciate the
very kind references which the representatives of
India have made to his endeavour to find a solution
of the difficulties which have existed for many years
between India and the Dominions in connection with
this very important problem.

The Resolution as submitted is accepted by
Canada. We have had several conferences, and
the terms of the Resolution represent an understanding arrived at by India and the Dominions.
We look upon it as a matter of importance that
the principle applied in the first paragraph of
the Resolution should be frankly recognized by all
the communities within the British Commonwealth. We recognize that there are distinctions
in racial characteristics, and in other matters,
which make it necessary that, while we fully
recognize the principle of reciprocity, each should
exercise full control over its own population. The
other paragraphs of the Resolution give effect to

the proposals which have been discussed before the Committee set up by the Conference for the purpose, and give effect in such a way as I am sure we all hope will meet the general approval of the citizens of the Dominions and of India, as well as of the other portions of the Empire. We are glad to be able to remove the grounds of objection which India has felt, particularly with reference to the liberty of the Indians resident in Canada to bring their wives and minor children to Canada ; but it was felt that this matter could not be dealt with except as part of the whole problem, and it is in connexion with the solution of the whole problem that this forms an important part.

I think the number of Sikhs in Canada is not quite so large as Sir Satyendra has mentioned. While there was this number at one time, I think a number have returned to India, and the number is not now large. I am sure we all appreciate the splendid qualities which the Sikhs have shown in this war, and the magnificent contribution which that portion of India particularly has given to the fighting forces of the Empire, and I am sure it would have been a matter of gratification to us all if Sir Robert Borden could have been here when this important matter was being dealt with by the Conference. I am also confident that the effect of this Resolution will be to draw together the Dominions and India into closer bonds of sympathy, and to cement the bonds that bind our whole Empire together as a unit for great national purposes—for those great, humane, and Imperial purposes for which our Empire exists.

CHAIRMAN : Mr. Cook, do you desire to say anything on this ?

Mr. COOK : No, I think not, sir.

Mr. MASSEY : I am very glad that this solution of the difficulty has been arrived at. So far as New Zealand is concerned, there is no serious trouble. We have very, very few Indians in New Zealand, and, so far as I know, the people of India have never shown any tendency to emigrate to New Zealand. I simply state the fact—I am not able to explain the reason. The objections, I understand, have come mostly from Canada and South Africa, and I am very glad indeed, from what has been said, to learn that those objections have been removed. Of course, we shall have the administration of the law in so far as it does apply to New Zealand, but I do not anticipate any difficulty there, and I think what has been done to-day not only removes the present difficulties, such as they are, but will prevent serious difficulty occurring in the future. I value the Resolution on that account really more than on any other. Though New Zealand, as I have said, is not seriously interested in this matter—I have no doubt if Indians had come to New Zealand in considerable numbers, objections would have been raised, and it would have been the duty of the Government to take the matter in hand. That, however, has not taken place.

I should like to learn from Sir Satyendra Sinha whether this will affect Fiji in any way. Fiji is a neighbour of ours, and most of our sugar is produced there. It is not refined there, but is sent to Auckland for refining purposes. I understand a very large number—I am not going into details, but I believe about 60,000 Indians—are employed in Fiji at the present time in the production of sugar. I simply ask the question because the point is likely to be raised as to whether it will affect them.

Sir S. P. SINHA. In no way.

Mr. MASSEY : I am very glad to hear it. I hope as far as Fiji labour is concerned that even in Fiji some satisfactory solution of the difficulty will be arrived at in connexion with that Dependency of the Empire. I know there is a little friction— not serious, but a little—but as far as I can understand the position—I do not profess to know the whole details—the difficulties are not insurmountable.

Sir S. P. SINHA : The difficulties are of a different nature. I hope they have been practically solved.

Mr. MASSEY : That is all I wish to say, sir.

Mr. BURTON : The matters which were raised by Sir Satyendra Sinha and the Maharaja in connexion with this question present, I suppose, some of the most difficult and delicate problems which we have had to deal with, and which it is our duty as statesmen to attempt to solve satisfactorily if the British Empire is to remain a healthy organization. I am sure we all feel, as far as we are concerned—I have told Sir Satyendra myself that my own attitude has been, and I am sure it is the attitude of my colleagues—sympathetic towards the Indian position generally. There are, of course, difficulties, and it would be idle to disguise the fact that many of these difficulties are of substantial importance, which have to be faced in dealing with this matter. But I do not despair of satisfactory solutions being arrived at.

Sir Satyendra Sinha has been good enough to refer to the attitude adopted by Canada and ourselves in discussing this matter in Committee, and I think it is only right from our point of view to add that the possibility of our arriving at a satisfactory solution on this occasion has been due very largely indeed to the reasonable and moderate attitude which the Indian representatives themselves have adopted. But for that, of course, the difficulties would have been ever so much greater. As far as we are concerned, it is only fair to say—and it is the truth—that we have found that the Indians in our midst in South Africa, who form in some parts a very substantial portion of the population, are good, law-abiding, quiet citizens, and it is our duty to see, as he himself expressed it, that they are treated as human beings, with feelings like our own, and in a proper manner.

As to the details, I need not go into all of them. Paragraph No. 3 embodies, as a matter of fact, the present law of the Union of South Africa. That is our position there, so that our agreement as to that is no concession. I pointed out to Sir Satyendra when we were in Committee, that in some of these points which he brought up as affecting South Africa, I thought in all probability, if he were in a position to investigate some of them himself, he would find that perhaps the complaints had been somewhat exaggerated. I cannot help feeling that that is the case, but I will not go into these matters now. As far as we are concerned in South Africa, we are in agreement with this Resolution, and also with the proposal referring the Memorandum to the consideration of our Government, and we will give it the most sympathetic consideration that we can, certainly.

Mr. LLOYD : This is not a matter which directly

affects Newfoundland, but I should like to express my satisfaction that some solution has been found, and also to express the feelings which have already been given utterance to by South Africa with regard to the reasonable and moderate attitude of India.

Sir JOSEPH WARD : Mr. Long, this is a development in connexion with the Empire that I regard as one of the very greatest importance. At the last Conference we made a move in the direction of meeting the wishes of India, and this Resolution now, embodying the results arrived at by the Committee which has been inquiring into this matter, carries the matter, I think rightly so, a good deal further. I think it is a move in the right direction. The underlying recognition of the right of the overseas communities to control their own populations within or coming to their own territories is one as to which no recommendation from this Conference, if it were made in the opposite direction to their wishes, could have the least effect within any portion of the British Empire. It is laying down a foundation upon which I regard the whole of these proposals as being based.

The important factor in connexion with it is this. All our countries, at all events New Zealand, have in the past, from causes or reasons one need not specially refer to, viewed with some concern the possibility of large numbers of Indians coming to them and becoming factors that would disturb, interfere with, or change the course of employment. I am of the opinion that that first proposal submitted is one that would be agreed to by every reasonable person in our country and would meet with their approval.

I take the opportunity of saying that sub-clause (c) of the second paragraph of this draft Resolution —' Such right shall not extend to a visit or temporary residence for labour purposes or to permanent settlement '—completely meets the position that otherwise there would be difficulties about accepting it, and I assume the Indian representatives are just as familiar with those difficulties as we are.

Upon the question of the introduction—although I have nothing to do with it as a representative here—of the wives of these men who have been admitted into Canada, that is, in my opinion, not only a wise thing to do, but on the highest grounds possible—moral grounds—it seems to be a legitimate corollary to what the Canadian Dominion have done with regard to the 4,000 or 5,000 men who are there.

I want to say with regard to the Memorandum [1] which has been placed before us by the Indian representative on those several matters, that as far as I am concerned I have read the Memorandum very carefully this morning, and I shall be glad, at the proper time, to give the matters referred to the fullest consideration in our country.

Mr. MONTAGU : Mr. Long, may I just detain the Conference one minute to express, on behalf of the Government of India and my colleagues, our gratitude for the way in which this resolution has been received at this meeting of the Conference. Sir Joseph Ward has rightly said that this Resolution takes the question a good deal further. I emphasize that by way of caution, and I hope I shall not be charged with ingratitude when I say

[1] See pp. 215–18 of [Cd. 9177].

that it would not be fair to the Conference to regard this Resolution as a solution of all outstanding questions. Many of them can only be cured by time. Many of them, as Mr. Burton has said, require careful study. But I feel sure that the spirit in which the Resolution has been met, and the whole attitude which the representatives of the various Dominions have taken towards it, will prove to India that as matters progress, and as time advances, there is every prospect that Indians throughout the Empire will be treated not only as human beings, but will have all the rights and privileges of British citizens.

Mr. Cook : Mr. Long, may I just say one word, lest my silence should be misunderstood. As my friends know, I attended the Committee meeting yesterday, and concurred in these proposals, and the reason I do not occupy the time of the Conference is because there is nothing specifically relating to Australia in them. That is to say, many of the things referred to in this Memorandum are concessions which have already been agreed to in Australia very many years ago, even with regard to the bringing of the wives and minor children. I do not think there is any trouble in Australia about that. Whatever the technical difficulties may be, I do not think there is any trouble occurring along those lines. At any rate, I am one of those who believe that when we admit a man to our shores we should admit his wife also and his family, and, if we are not prepared to admit his wife and family, we have no right to admit him. It seems to me that is among the elementary things. I concur entirely with the proposal in that respect, but that being the only outstanding

feature of the proposal which can in the remotest
degree affect Australia, I will not take up time in
discussing the matter, but agree cordially with
what has been suggested and what has been done.
I think we owe a great debt of gratitude to India
for the attitude she has taken since this war began.
That is the feeling in Australia through and through
—one of the most profound and cordial appreciation of the attitude of India in regard to this war.

Mr. MASSEY : It is the feeling all over the Empire.

CHAIRMAN : Perhaps I may be allowed to say
a word in putting the Resolution. It will only be
a very brief one. Last year the Conference was
specially marked by the addition to our councils
of the representatives of India, and I think we all
feel that that made the Conference more complete
and more real than it ever claimed to be before.
This year sees another steady step forward, and
I am bound to say that I think, having followed
these proceedings very closely—I had the privilege
to be present at the meeting which the Prime
Minister of Canada was good enough to summon
last year, when Sir Satyendra put the general case
before us, and I think you will agree that that was
a very useful meeting and started us in the direction
which has been consistently followed since—I think
this steady advance is due, as has been said, not
only to the wise, moderate, and extremely able
line taken by Sir Satyendra and his colleagues—
last year it was Sir James Meston and the Maharaja
of Bikanir who represented India with him, while
this year it is the Maharaja of Patiala—but also
to the very statesmanlike view which has been
taken of their responsibilities by those who speak
on behalf of the great self-governing Dominions

of the Empire. And certainly I rejoice more than I can say to see this evidence of the steady progress of the Empire along these lines which have been always followed in the past, and which, I believe, have made the Empire what it is—the recognition of fundamental principles, and a steady refusal to deny to any citizen of the Empire the privileges of Empire simply because of the accident of birth or locality. I regard this as a very important decision. On behalf of the Conference, I may perhaps be allowed to offer my congratulations to those who represent India and the Dominions upon this very considerable step in the development of our Empire. May I put the Resolution ?

Mr. ROWELL : May I add one word ? It is simply that I desire to associate Canada and myself with the remarks which Mr. Burton made with reference to the very reasonable and statesmanlike attitude of the representatives of India in dealing with this matter. The Resolution which embodies the understanding arrived at is, perhaps, the best evidence of our appreciation.

CHAIRMAN : I ought to say that Sir Robert Borden sent me a communication yesterday, expressing a great desire that this should be taken when he was present, and we did our best so to arrange matters ; but I need not point out to the Conference that, unless we are able to take the subjects as they are put down, it is almost impossible to get our business properly forward, or to complete it, within the time at our disposal.

Mr. MASSEY : I hope we shall finish this week.

CHAIRMAN : That is what we are working for, of course. May I put this to the Conference ?

[*The Resolution was carried unanimously.*]

7. Government of India Notification, July 1918

THE Government of India have had under consideration for some time past proposals for grant of commissions to Indians. Expression was given to their views by the Viceroy in his speech at the War Conference at Delhi, and these views were at once communicated to His Majesty's Government, but the latter's preoccupation with other matters has delayed their reply. This reply has now been received, and is to the effect that His Majesty the King-Emperor has decided to grant :

1. A certain number of substantive King's commissions in the Indian Army to selected Indian officers who have specially distinguished themselves in the present war.

2. A certain number of King's Commissions conferring honorary rank in the Indian Army on selected Indian officers who have rendered distinguished service not necessarily during the present war, and who, owing to age or lack of educational qualifications, are not eligible for substantive King's Commissions. Such honorary commissions will carry with them special advantages in respect of pay and pension.

3. A certain number of temporary but substantive King's commissions in the Indian army to selected candidates nominated partly from civil life and partly from the Army.

Those selected from civil life will be nominated by the Viceroy on the recommendation of the Commander-in-Chief and local governments and political administrations concerned. They must be between the ages of nineteen and twenty-five, and will be drawn from gentlemen who have rendered good service to Government, and more especially those who have actively assisted in recruitment during the present war.

Those selected from the Army must also be between the ages of nineteen and twenty-five, and will be nominated by the Viceroy, on the recommendation of the Commander-in-Chief and general officers in whose commands they are serving. Preference will be shown to officers or non-commissioned officers who have displayed special aptitude as leaders and instructors.

No candidate will be eligible for nomination unless he is medically fit and has passed a qualifying examination as a test of his general education. The standard required of civilian candidates will be that prescribed for the diploma of one of the Chiefs' colleges ; a school-leaving certificate recognized by a local government ; the matriculation examination of an incorporated university ; or any higher examination. Holders of such certificates will be exempted from the qualifying examination referred to above. The standard of the qualifying examination demanded of military candidates will be prescribed by the Commander-in-Chief.

Candidates selected for nomination will be required to join a school of instruction. Their *status* while under military training will be that of cadets. The length of the course will depend on the attainments of the cadets. It will usually be not less than a year. No cadet will be granted a commission unless reported fit in all respects for employment as an officer on active service. On completion of the school course, candidates who qualify for commissions will be posted to Indian regiments as temporary second lieutenants, and will be subject to the same regulations and enjoy the same *status* as British officers of the same rank. On the termination of the war temporary officers appointed under this scheme who have proved themselves efficient in every respect, and who desire to make the army their profession, will be considered for permanent commissions. The remainder will be retired on a gratuity, with permission to wear the uniform of the rank held at the time of retirement.

CADETSHIPS AT SANDHURST

The Government of India have also decided, with the approval of the Secretary of State for India, to nominate ten Indian gentlemen annually during the war for cadetships at the Royal Military College, Sandhurst. Candidates will be nominated by the Viceroy, on the recommendation of the Commander-in-Chief and local governments or political administrations concerned. No candidate will be eligible for nomination unless he is medically fit and has passed a qualifying examination, which will be held in Simla. This examination will include an oral examination similar to that required by the Admiralty in the case of candidates for the Naval College at Osborne, designed as a test of general intelligence. A syllabus of the qualifying examination will be published at an early date. The general standard required will be that prescribed for candidates for temporary commissions.

The payment of fees for the education of cadets at Sandhurst is in abeyance during the war. Parents and guardians are required, however, to contribute towards the cost of uniform, books, recreation, &c.,

and a pocket-money allowance not exceeding £50 a year to be paid through the college authorities is also usually necessary. While at Sandhurst, Indian cadets will be treated in precisely the same way as British cadets, and, after passing the qualifying examination on the termination of the course, will, if found suitable in all respects, be granted permanent King's commissions in the Indian Army.

8. Report on Indian Constitutional Reforms by Edwin S. Montagu and Lord Chelmsford, 1918

EXTENT OF THE ADVANCE PROPOSED IN LOCAL BODIES

188. LET us now consider the principles on which our proposals are based. We have surveyed the existing position ; we have discussed the conditions of the problem : and the goal to which we wish to move is clear. What course are we to set across the intervening space ? It follows from our premises, and it is also recognized in the announcement of August 20, that the steps are to be gradual and the advance tested at each stage. Consistently with these requirements a substantial step is to be taken at once. If our reasoning is sound, this can be done only by giving from the outset some measure of responsibility to representatives chosen by an electorate. There are obviously three levels at which it is possible to give it—in the sphere of local bodies, in the provinces, and in the Government of India. Of certain other levels which have been suggested, intermediate between the first and second of these, we shall speak in due course. Also,

since no man can serve two masters, in proportion as control by an electorate is admitted at each level, control by superior authority must be simultaneously relaxed. If our plans are to be soundly laid, they must take account of actual conditions. It follows that the process cannot go on at one and the same pace on all levels. The Secretary of State's relaxation of control over the Government of India will be retarded, if for no other reason, by the paramount need for securing Imperial interests ; the Government of India have the fundamental duty to discharge of maintaining India's defence ; the basic obligation of provincial governments is to secure law and order. As we go upwards, the importance of the retarding factors increases ; and it follows that popular growth must be more rapid and extensive in the lower levels than in the higher. Let us state the proposition in another way. The functions of government can be arranged in an ascending scale of urgency, ranging from those which concern the comfort and well-being of the individual to those which secure the existence of the State. The individual understands best the matters which concern him and of which he has experience ; and he is likely to handle best the things which he best understands. Our predecessors perceived this before us, and placed such matters to some extent under popular control. Our aim should be to bring them entirely under such control. This brings us to our first formula :

There should be, as far as possible, complete popular control in local bodies and the largest possible independence for them of outside control (1).

In Provincial Governments

189. When we come to the provincial governments the position is different. Our objective is the realization of responsible government. We understand this to mean first, that the members of the executive government should be responsible to, because capable of being changed by, their constituents; and, secondly, that these constituents should exercise their power through the agency of their representatives in the assembly. These two conditions imply in their completeness that there exist constituencies based on a franchise broad enough to represent the interests of the general population, and capable of exercising an intelligent choice in the selection of their representatives; and, secondarily, that it is recognized as the constitutional practice that the executive government retains office only so long as it commands the support of a majority in the assembly. But in India these conditions are as yet wanting. The provincial areas and interests involved are immense, indeed are on what would elsewhere be regarded as a national scale. The amount of administrative experience available is small; electoral experience is almost entirely lacking. There must be a period of political education, which can only be achieved through the gradual but expanding exercise of responsibility. The considerations of which we took account in chapter VI forbid us immediately to hand over complete responsibility. We must proceed therefore by transferring responsibility for certain functions of government while reserving control over others. From this starting-point we look for a steady approach to the transfer

of complete responsibility. We may put our
second formula thus :

*The provinces are the domain in which the earlier
steps towards the progressive realization of responsible
government should be taken. Some measure of responsibility should be given at once, and our aim is to give
complete responsibility as soon as conditions permit.
This involves at once giving the provinces the largest
measure of independence, legislative, administrative,
and financial, of the Government of India which is
compatible with the due discharge by the latter of its
own responsibilities* (2).

In the Government of India

190. But, as we shall see, any attempt to establish equilibrium between the official and popular
forces in government inevitably introduces additional complexity into the administration. For
such hybrid arrangements precedents are wanting ;
their working must be experimental, and will
depend on factors that are yet largely unknown.
We are not prepared, without experience of their
results, to effect like changes in the Government of
India. Nevertheless, it is desirable to make the
Indian Legislative Council more truly representative of Indian opinion, and to give that opinion
greater opportunities of acting on the Government.
While, therefore, we cannot commend to Parliament a similar and simultaneous advance both in
the provinces and in the Government of India, we
are led to the following proposition :

*The Government of India must remain wholly
responsible to Parliament, and, saving such responsibility, its authority in essential matters must remain
indisputable, pending experience of the effect of the*

changes now to be introduced in the provinces. In the meantime the Indian Legislative Council should be enlarged and made more representative and its opportunities of influencing Government increased (3).

In England

191. Further, the partial control of the executive in the provinces by the legislature, and the increasing influence of the legislature upon the executive in the Government of India will make it necessary that the superior control over all governments in India which is now exercised by the authorities at home must be in corresponding measure abated : for otherwise the executive governments in India will be subjected to pressure from different sources which will wholly paralyse their liberty of action, and also the different pressures may be exercised in opposite directions. We may put this proposition briefly as follows :

In proportion as the foregoing changes take effect, control of Parliament and the Secretary of State over the Government of India and provincial governments must be relaxed (4).

Local Self-government

192. We have been told that, inasmuch as local self-government has not yet been made a reality in most parts of India, we should content ourselves with such reforms as will give it reality, and should await their result before attempting anything more ambitious, on the principle that children learn to walk by learning first to crawl. We regard this solution as outside the range of practical politics ; for it is in the councils that the Morley-Minto reforms have already brought matters to an issue ;

and Indian hopes and aspirations have been aroused to such a pitch that it is idle to imagine that they will now be appeased by merely making over to them the management of urban and rural boards. Moreover, the development of the country has reached a stage at which the conditions justify an advance in the wider sphere of government; and at which indeed government without the co-operation of the people will become increasingly difficult. On the other hand, few of the political associations that addressed us seemed adequately to appreciate the importance of local affairs, or the magnitude of the advance which our recommendation involves. But the point has been made time and time again by their own most prominent leaders. It is by taking part in the management of local affairs that aptitude for handling the problems of government will most readily be acquired. This applies to those who administer, but even more to those who judge of the administration. Among the clever men who come to the front in provincial politics, there will be some who will address themselves without more difficulty, and indeed with more interest and zeal, to the problems of government than to those of municipal or district board administration. But the unskilled elector, who has hitherto concerned himself neither with one nor the other, can learn to judge of things afar off only by accustoming himself to judge first of things near at hand. This is why it is of the utmost importance to the constitutional progress of the country that every effort should be made in local bodies to extend the franchise, · to arouse interest in elections, and to develop local committees, so that education in citizenship may as far as possible be extended,, and everywhere begin in a practical manner. If our proposals for changes on the higher levels are to be a success, there must be no hesitation or paltering about changes in local bodies. Responsible institutions will not be stably-rooted until they become broad-based ; and far-sighted Indian politicians will find no field into which their energies can be more profitably thrown than in developing the boroughs and communes of their country.

PROVINCIAL EXECUTIVE
COUNCIL GOVERNMENT

214. Let us now explain how we contemplate in future that the executive governments of the provinces shall be constituted. As we have seen, three provinces are now governed by a Governor and an executive council of three members, of whom one is in practice an Indian and two are usually appointed from the Indian Civil Service, although the law says only that they must be qualified by twelve years' service under the Crown in India. One province, Bihar and Orissa, is administered by a Lieutenant-Governor with a Council of three constituted in the same way. The remaining five provinces, that is to say, the three Lieutenant-Governorships of the United Provinces, the Punjab and Burma and the two Chief Commissionerships of the Central Provinces and Assam, are under the administration of a single official head. We find throughout India a very general desire for the extension of council government. There is a belief that when the administration centres in a single man, the pressure of work

inevitably results in some matters of importance being disposed of, in his name but without personal reference to him, by secretaries to Government. There is also a feeling that collective decisions, which are the result of bringing together different points of view, are more likely to be judicious and well-weighed than those of a single mind. But above all council government is valued by Indians, because of the opportunity it affords for taking an Indian element into the administration itself. To our minds, however, there is an over-riding reason of greater importance than any of these. The retention of the administration of a province in the hands of a single man precludes the possibility of giving it a responsible character. Our first proposition, therefore, is that in all these provinces single-headed administration must cease and be replaced by collective administration.

THE STRUCTURE OF THE EXECUTIVE

215. In determining the structure of the executive we have to bear in mind the duties with which it will be charged. We start with the two postulates that complete responsibility for the government cannot be given immediately without inviting a breakdown, and that some responsibility must be given at once if our scheme is 'to have any value. We have defined responsibility as consisting primarily in amenability to constituents, and in the second place in amenability to an assembly. We do not believe that there is any way of satisfying these governing conditions other than by making a division of the functions of the provincial government, between those which may be made over to popular control and those which for the present

must remain in official hands. The principles and methods of such division and also the difficulties which it presents we shall discuss hereafter. For the moment let us assume that such division has been made, and that certain heads of business are retained under official and certain others made over to popular control. We may call these the ' reserved ' and ' transferred ' subjects respectively. It then follows that for the management of each of these two categories there must be some form of executive body, with a legislative organ in harmony with it, and if friction and disunion are to be avoided it is also highly desirable that the two parts of the executive should be harmonized. We have considered the various means open to us of satisfying these exacting requirements.

OUR OWN PROPOSALS

218. We propose therefore that in each province the executive government should consist of two parts. One part would comprise the head of the province and an executive council of two members. In all provinces the head of the government would be known as Governor, though this common designation would not imply any equality of emoluments or status, both of which would continue to be regulated by the existing distinctions, which seem to us generally suitable. One of the two executive councillors would in practice be a European qualified by long official experience, and the other would be an Indian. It has been urged that the latter should be an elected member of the provincial legislative council. It is unreasonable that choice should be so limited. It should be open to the Governor to recommend whom he wishes.

In making his nominations, the Governor should be free to take into consideration the names of persons who had won distinction whether in the legislative council or any other field. The Governor in Council would have charge of the reserved subjects. The other part of the government would consist of one member or more than one member, according to the number and importance of the transferred subjects chosen by the Governor from the elected members of the legislative council. They would be known as ministers. They would be members of the executive government but not members of the executive council ; and they would be appointed for the lifetime of the legislative council, and if re-elected to that body would be re-eligible for appointment as members of the executive. As we have said, they would not hold office at the will of the legislature but at that of their constituents. We make no recommendation in regard to pay. This is a matter which may be disposed of subsequently.

RELATION OF THE GOVERNOR TO MINISTERS

219. The portfolios dealing with the transferred subjects would be committed to the ministers, and on these subjects the ministers, together with the Governor, would form the administration. On such subjects their decisions would be final, subject only to the Governor's advice and control. We do not contemplate that from the outset the Governor should occupy the position of a purely constitutional Governor who is bound to accept the decisions of his ministers. Our hope and intention is that the ministers will gladly avail themselves of the Governor's trained advice upon administrative

questions, while on his part he will be willing to meet their wishes to the furthest possible extent in cases where he realizes that they have the support of popular opinion. We reserve to him a power of control, because we regard him as generally responsible for his administration, but we should expect him to refuse assent to the proposals of his ministers only when the consequences of acquiescence would clearly be serious. Also we do not think that he should accept without hesitation and discussion proposals which are clearly seen to be the result of inexperience. But we do not intend that he should be in a position to refuse assent at discretion to all his ministers' proposals. We recommend that for the guidance of Governors in relation to their ministers, and indeed on other matters also, an instrument of instructions be issued to them on appointment by the Secretary of State in Council.

PROVINCIAL LEGISLATURES

COMPOSITION OF THE COUNCILS

225. We will now explain how we intend that the provincial legislatures of the future shall be constituted. We propose there shall be in each province an enlarged legislative council, differing in size and composition from province to province, with a substantial elected majority, elected by direct election on a broad franchise, with such communal and special representation as may be necessary.

STANDING COMMITTEES

235. Our next proposal is intended to familiarize other elected members of the legislative council, besides ministers, with the processes of administra-

tion ; and also to make the relations between the executive and legislative more intimate. We propose that to each department or group of departments, whether it is placed under a member of the executive council or under a minister, there should be attached a standing committee elected by the legislative council from among their own members. Their functions would be advisory. They would not have any administrative control of departments. It would be open to the Government to refuse information when it would be inconsistent with the public interest to furnish it. We do not intend that all questions raised in the course of day-to-day administration should be referred to them; but that they should see, discuss, and record for the consideration of Government their opinions upon all questions of policy, all new schemes involving expenditure above a fixed limit, and all annual reports upon the working of the departments. If the recommendations of the standing committee were not accepted by Government, it would, subject of course to the obligation of respecting confidence, be open to any of its members to move a resolution in the legislative council in the ordinary way. The member of the executive council or minister concerned with the subject-matter should preside over the committee, and as an exception to the rule that it should be wholly non-official, the heads of the departments concerned, whether sitting in the legislative council or not, should also be full members of it with the right to vote.

CONTROL OF BUSINESS

236. Bearing in mind the facts that the legislative councils will in future be larger bodies and will contain a certain number of members unversed in discussion, we feel the importance of maintaining such standards of business as will prevent any lowering of the council's repute. The conduct of business in a large deliberative body is a task that calls for experience which cannot be looked for at the outset in an elected member. We consider therefore that the Governor should remain the President of the legislative council, but inasmuch as it is not desirable that he should always preside, he should retain the power to appoint a Vice-President. He should not be formally limited in his selection, but we suggest that for some time to come it will be expedient that the Vice-President should be chosen from the official members.

Power to make its own rules of business is a normal attribute of a legislative body. But a simple and satisfactory procedure is of the essence of successful working ; and it is advisable to avoid the risk that inexperience may lead to needless complication or other defect in the rules. We think therefore that the existing rules of procedure should, for the time being, continue in force, but that they should be liable to modification by the legislative council with the sanction of the Governor.

One or two points in connection with the rules require notice. Any member of the legislative council and not merely the asker of the original question should, we think, have power to put supplementary questions. Power should be retained in the Governor's hands to disallow questions, the mere putting of which would be detrimental to the public interests. If a question is not objectionable in itself but cannot be answered without harm to the public interests, the Governor should not disallow the question, but his Government should refuse to answer it on that ground. We have not considered in what respect existing restrictions upon the moving of resolutions should be modified; but here also it seems inevitable that some discretionary power of disallowance should remain in the Governor's hands.

EFFECT OF RESOLUTIONS

237. We do not propose that resolutions, whether on reserved or transferred subjects, should be binding. The Congress-League proposal to give them such authority is open to the objections which we have already pointed out. If a member of the legislative council wishes the Government to be constrained to take action in a particular direction, it will often be open to him to bring in a Bill to effect his purpose; and when ministers become, as we intend they should, accountable to the legislative council, the council will have full means of controlling their administration by refusing them supplies or by means of votes of censure, the carrying of which may in accordance with established constitutional practice, involve their quitting office.

DIVISION OF THE FUNCTIONS OF GOVERNMENT

238. It is time to show how we propose that the sphere of business to be made over to the control of the popular element in the Government should

be demarcated. We assumed in paragraphs 212 and 213 above that the entire field of provincial administration will be marked off from that of the Government of India. We assumed further that in each province certain definite subjects should be transferred for the purpose of administration by the ministers. All subjects not so transferred will be reserved to the hands of the Governor in Council. The list of transferred subjects will of course vary in each province ; indeed, it is by variation that our scheme will be adjusted to varying local conditions. It will also be susceptible of modification at subsequent stages. The determination of the list for each province will be a matter for careful investigation, for which reason we have not attempted to undertake it now. We could only have done so if after settling the general principles on which the lists should be framed we had made a prolonged tour in India and had discussed with the government and people of each province the special conditions of its own case. This work should, we suggest, be entrusted to another special committee similar in composition to, but possibly smaller in size than, the one which we have already proposed to constitute for the purpose of dealing with franchises and constituencies. It may be said that such a task can be appropriately undertaken only when our main proposals are approved. We find it difficult, however, to believe that any transitional scheme can be devised which will dispense with the necessity for some such demarcation ; and for this reason we should like to see the committee constituted as soon as possible. It should meet and confer with the other committee which is to deal with franchises, because the extent to which responsibility can be transferred is related to the nature and extent of the electorate which will be available in any particular province. The committee's first business will be to consider what are the services to be appropriated to the provinces, all others remaining with the Government of India. We suggest that it will find that some matters are of wholly provincial concern, and that others are primarily provincial, but that in respect of them some statutory restrictions upon the discretion of provincial governments may be necessary. Other matters again may be provincial in character so far as administration goes, while there may be good reasons for keeping the right of legislation in respect of them in the hands of the Government of India. The list so compiled will define the corpus of the material to which our scheme is to be applied. In the second place the committee will consider which of the provincial subjects should be transferred ; and what limitations must be placed upon the ministers' complete control of them. Their guiding principle should be to include in the transferred list those departments which afford most opportunity for local knowledge and social service, those in which Indians have shown themselves to be keenly interested, those in which mistakes which may occur (though serious) would not be irremediable, and those which stand most in need of development. In pursuance of this principle we should not expect to find that departments primarily concerned with the maintenance of law and order were transferred. Nor should we expect the transfer of matters which vitally affect the well-being of the masses who may not be adequately represented in the new councils, such for example as questions of land revenue or tenant rights. As an illustration of the kind of matters which we think might be treated as provincial and those which might be regarded as transferred, we have presented two specimen lists in an appendix to this report. We know that our lists cannot be exhaustive ; they will not be suitable to all provinces ; they may not be exactly suitable to any province ; but they will serve at all events to illustrate our intentions if not also as a starting-point for the deliberations of the committee. Our lists are in the main mere categories of subjects. But we have mentioned by way of illustration some of the limitations which it will be necessary to impose or maintain. In dealing with each subject the powers of the provincial legislatures to alter Government of India Acts on that subject will have to be carefully considered. We have indicated in paragraph 240 below certain other reservations which seem to us necessary. On the publication of this report we should like to see the lists discussed in the provincial councils and considered by the provincial governments, so that the committee may have ready at hand considered criticisms upon the applicability of our suggestions to the circumstances of each particular province.

SETTLEMENT OF DISPUTES

239. We realize that no demarcation of subjects can be decisive in the sense of leaving open no matter for controversy. Cases may arise in which it is open to doubt into which category a particular administrative question falls. There will be other cases in which two or more aspects of one and the

same transaction belong to different categories. There must therefore be an authority to decide in such cases which portion of the Government has jurisdiction. Such a matter should be considered by the entire Government, but its decision must in the last resort lie definitely and finally with the Governor. We do not intend that the course of administration should be held up while his decision is challenged either in the law courts or by an appeal to the Government of India.

POWERS OF INTERVENTION

240. Further, inasmuch as administration is a living business and its corpus cannot be dissected with the precision of an autopsy, we must, even in the case of matters ordinarily made over to non-official control, secure the right of re-entry either to the official executive government of the province, or to the Government of India in cases where their interests are essentially affected. For instance, the central Government must have the power, for reasons which will be readily apparent in every case, of intervening effectively, whether by legislation or administrative action, in matters such as those affecting defence, or foreign or political relations, or foreign trade, or the tariff ; or which give rise to questions affecting the interests of more than one province ; or which concern the interests of all-India services, even if serving under provincial governments. Similarly the ,Governor in executive council must have power to intervene with full effect in matters which concern law and order, or which raise religious or racial issues, or to protect the interests of existing services. We do not claim that this list of reserva-

tions is exhaustive or definitive ; we look to the committee to assist in making it so. Our aim must be to secure to the official executive the power of protecting effectually whatever functions are still reserved to it and to the Government of India, of intervening in all cases in which the action of the non-official executive or council affects them to their serious prejudice. For otherwise the official Government which is still responsible to Parliament may be unable to discharge its responsibility properly.

MEANS OF SECURING THE AFFIRMATIVE POWER OF LEGISLATION

247. We now turn to a consideration of the work of the legislative councils. Assuming that they have been reconstituted with elective majorities, and that the reserved and transferred subjects have been demarcated in the way suggested, let us consider how the executive government is to be enabled to secure the passing of such legislation or such supplies as it considers absolutely necessary in respect of the reserved services. For we must make some such provision if we are going to hold it responsible for the government of the province.

Now in respect of legislation there are several possibilities. We might leave it to the Government of India to pass the laws which a provincial government has failed to carry in the Indian legislature where, as we shall show, we intend to leave it in a position to pass the laws which it deems essential : or we might leave it to the Governor-General, or preferably perhaps to the Governor-General in Council, to make and promulgate ordinances, having effect either for a specified period, or else

until such time as the life of the provincial legislative council which refused the desired legislation
was cut short or expired, and a new council was
elected in its place : or we might arm the provincial
government, with a similar power of ordinance-
making. We shall explain why we reject all these
alternatives.

Our Proposals. Grand Committees

252. Because, as we shall show in paragraph
258, we have decided not to recommend the institution of second chambers in the provinces we
cannot apply to the provinces the scheme which
we propose hereafter for the Government of India ;
and we must turn to some form of unicameral
arrangements. The solution which we propose is
as follows. For the purpose of enabling the provincial government to get through its legislation
on reserved subjects, we propose that the head of
the Government should have power to certify that
a Bill dealing with a reserved subject is a measure
' essential to the discharge of his responsibility
for the peace or tranquillity of the province or of
any part thereof, or for the discharge of his responsibility for the reserved subjects '. In employing
these words we are not assuming the function of
a parliamentary draughtsman : we merely mean to
indicate that words will be needed to show that
this exceptional procedure will be used only when
the Government feels that its legislation is necessary if peace and tranquillity are to be secured, or
more generally if it is properly to discharge its
responsibility for the reserved subjects even if no
question of maintaining order arises. It will be
seen hereafter that we propose similar procedure

for controlling non-official bills, amendments, and clauses, and for controlling budget allotments on reserved subjects. In these cases also we shall speak of certification as indicating that the Governor was using the exceptional procedure in the circumstances described above. Such a certificate as we have described would not be given without strong reason ; and we suggest that the reasons justifying recourse to it might be included in the instructions to Governors which the India Office should issue ; for instance, we think that the Governor should not certify a Bill if he thought its enactment could safely be left to the legislative council. The effect of the Governor's certificate when published with the Bill will be to initiate the procedure which we now describe. The Bill will be read and its general principles discussed in the full legislative council. It will at this stage be open to the council by a majority vote to request the Governor to refer to the Government of India, whose decision on the point shall be final, the question whether the certified Bill deals with a reserved subject. If no such reference is made, or if the Government of India decide that the certificate has been properly given, the Bill will then be automatically referred to a grand committee of the council. Its composition should reproduce as nearly as possible the proportion of the various elements in the larger body. Our first intention was that the grand committee in each province should be a microcosm of the existing council. But we find that the existence of communal and special electorates makes it difficult to secure to all of these their due representation on a smaller body without at the same time sacrificing the representation of the interests represented by the general electorates, to which it is our special intention to give a greater voice in the councils than heretofore. Accordingly, we propose that the grand committee in every council should be constituted so as to comprise from forty to fifty per cent. of its strength. It should be chosen for each Bill, partly by election by ballot, and partly by nomination. The Governor should have power to nominate a bare majority exclusive of himself. Of the members so nominated not more than two-thirds should be officials, and the elected element should be elected *ad hoc* by the elected members of the council on the system of the transferable vote. It is clear that the composition of the grand committee ought to vary with the subject-matter of the particular Bill ; and we believe that the council and the Governor between them can be trusted to ensure that whether by election or nomination all the interests affected by the Bill are properly represented. It may be objected that such a grand committee so composed offers the official executive no absolute guarantee that its measure will get through. We agree that this is the case ; but there is no such guarantee at present. In a grand committee of forty members there could be fourteen officials, and we consider that no great harm will ensue if Government defers legislative projects which are opposed by the whole elected element and for which it cannot secure the support of six out of the seven members whom the Governor has it in his power to select from the whole body of the non-official members in the council.

UPPER HOUSES

258. At this point we may explain that we have considered the feasibility of establishing a bicameral system in the provinces. Its advocates urge that in creating upper houses we should follow the system which generally prevails in countries where popular government has firmly established itself. We might also expect that the representation of minority interests would become more effective in an upper house than in a single composite chamber, because minority representatives sitting in a chamber of their own might feel themselves freer to defend the interests which they represented than if they sat together with other elements in a lower house. We might secure men for the upper houses who would not seek election or even accept nomination to a composite assembly, where the majority of members were of a different status from themselves; and so the second chamber might develop a conservative character which would be a valuable check on the possibly too radical proclivities of a lower house. But we see very serious practical objections to the idea. In many provinces it would be impossible to secure a sufficient number of suitable members for two houses. We apprehend also that a second chamber representing mainly landed and moneyed interests might prove too effective a barrier against legislation which affected such interests. Again, the presence of large landed proprietors in the second chamber might have the unfortunate result of discouraging other members of the same class from seeking the votes of the electorate. We think that the delay involved in passing legislation through

two houses would make the system far too cumbrous to contemplate for the business of provincial legislation. We have decided for the present therefore against bicameral institutions for the provinces. At the same time we bear in mind that as provincial councils approach more closely to parliamentary forms the need for revising chambers may be the more felt ; and we think that the question should be further considered by the periodic commission which we propose hereafter.

THE GOVERNOR-GENERAL'S EXECUTIVE COUNCIL

271. We have explained already how the executive council of the Governor-General is constituted and how portfolios are allotted in it. Its changed relations with provincial governments will in themselves materially affect the volume of work coming before the departments, and for this reason alone some redistribution will be necessary. We would therefore abolish such statutory restrictions as now exist in respect of the appointment of members of the Governor-General's Council, so as to give greater elasticity both in respect of the size of the Government and the distribution of work. If it is desired to retain Parliamentary control over these matters, they might be embodied in statutory orders to be laid before Parliament.

INCREASE IN INDIAN ELEMENT

272. Further we propose to increase the Indian element in the executive council. We do not think it necessary to argue the expediency of enabling the wishes of India to be further represented in the Cabinet of the country. The decision of Lord Morley and Lord Minto to appoint one Indian

member to the council marked an important stage in India's political development ; and has proved of value in enabling the Government to have first-hand acquaintance with Indian opinion. In recommending a second appointment we are only pursuing the policy already determined upon in respect of the public services. There exists of course at present no racial prescription in the Statute nor do we propose that any should be introduced. There is even no 'formal guarantee that any appointment shall be made on the grounds of race. The appointment of Indian members will be made in the future, as in the past, as a matter of practice by the Crown on the recommendation of the Secretary of State ; and we suggest the appointment of another Indian member as soon as may be.

THE INDIAN LEGISLATIVE ASSEMBLY

273. We now come to the changes required in the Indian Legislative Council. Its existing composition we have already explained. No argument is needed to show that under present conditions twenty-seven elected members, many of them returned by small class electorates, cannot adequately represent the interests of the entire country in the supreme assembly. Indeed no council, the composition of which is conditioned by the necessity of maintaining an official majority, could possibly serve that purpose. We recommend therefore that the strength of the legislative council, to be known in future as the legislative assembly of India, should be raised to a total strength of about one hundred members, so as to be far more truly representative of British India. We propose that two-

thirds of this total should be returned by election ; and that one-third should be nominated by the Governor-General, of which third not less than a third again should be non-officials selected with the object of representing minority or special interests. We have decided not to present to His Majesty's Government a complete scheme for the election of the elected representatives ; our discussions have shown us that we have not the data on which to arrive at any sound conclusions. Some special representation, we think, there must be, as · for European and Indian commerce, and also for the large landlords. There should be also communal representation for Muhammadans in most provinces and also for Sikhs in the Punjab. There is no difficulty about direct election in the case of special constituencies. It is in respect of the general or residuary electorate, including therein the communal electorates for Muhammadans and Sikhs, that complexities present themselves. Our decided preference is for a system of direct electorates, but the immensity of the country makes it difficult, it may be impossible, to form constituencies of reasonable size in which candidates will be able to get into direct touch with the electorates. Moreover there is the further difficulty (which, however, presents itself in any system of constituencies) of the inequalities of wealth existing between the different communities. If constituencies are to be approximately even in size, it may be necessary to concede a special franchise to the Muhammadans, who, taken as a whole, are poorer than the Hindus : and this means giving a vote to some Muhammadans who would not be entitled to vote if they were Hindus. That is an undesirable anomaly, to which we should prefer the anomaly of unequal constituencies; but on our present information we find it impossible to say how great the practical difficulties of variation in size might be. Similar problems will present themselves in respect of constituencies for the elections to provincial councils. It is obviously desirable to deal on uniform lines with the electoral arrangements both in the provincial and Indian councils. As regards the former, we have already recommended the appointment of a special committee to investigate questions of franchises and electorates; and to that body we would therefore also commit the task of determining the electorates and constituencies for the Indian Legislative Assembly. They may find it wholly impracticable to arrange for direct election. In that case they will consider the various possible systems of indirect election. We are fully aware of the objections attaching to all forms of indirect election; but if the difficulties of direct election compel us to have recourse to indirect, we incline to think that election by non-official members of provincial councils is likely to prove far more acceptable to Indian opinion, and, in spite of the smallness of the electoral bodies, certainly not open in practice to greater objection than any of other alternative methods which have been from time to time proposed.

For reasons similar to those which we have given in the case of the provincial legislative councils, we recommend that members of the Indian Legislative Assembly should not be designated ' Honourable ', but should be entitled to affix the letters M.L.A. to their names.

REPRESENTATION OF THE PROVINCES

274. The suggestion we have made for the number of elected members was based on the calculation, that the three presidencies would be represented by eleven members each—the United Provinces by ten, the Punjab and Bihar and Orissa by seven each, the Central Provinces by five, Burma by three, and Assam by two. We also think that in view of the importance of the Delhi province as the Imperial enclave and the seat of the central Government, it should be represented by a member.

NOMINATED MEMBERS

275. In respect of the non-official members to be nominated by the Governor-General, we advise that no hard-and-fast rule should be laid down. These seats should be regarded as a reserve in his hands for the purpose of adjusting inequalities and supplementing defects in representation. Nominations should not be made until the results of all the elections are known; and then they should be made after informal consultation with the heads of provinces. The maximum number of nominated officials will be two-ninths of the whole, and it will rest with the Governor-General to determine whether he requires to appoint up to this maximum. The officials will, however, include the executive members of council, sitting not by appointment but ex-officio; and also some representation from the provinces. It may therefore not be possible for secretaries to the Government of India to continue to sit in the assembly; this may in itself be of advantage as decreasing the dislocation of administrative business during the session. It

may, however, be necessary to allow the secretary to speak and vote on behalf of the member when occasion demands. But for this purpose we think that a preferable alternative may be to appoint members of the Assembly, not necessarily elected nor even non-official, to positions analogous to those of Parliamentary Under-Secretaries in England ; and we advise that power be taken to make such appointments. We attach importance to the further proposal that official members of the Assembly, other than members of the executive government, should be allowed a free right of speech and vote, except when the Government decides that their support is necessary. We think that this change of procedure will affect the tone of discussions very beneficially. We think that, for the reasons which we have given already in support of a similar recommendation in respect of the provincial councils, the President of the Legislative Assembly should be nominated by the Governor-General. We do not propose that his choice should be formally limited, but it seems necessary that, at any rate for the present, the President should be designated from among the official members.

MEANS OF SECURING THE AFFIRMATIVE POWER OF LEGISLATION

276. We began with the fundamental proposition that the capacity of the Government of India to obtain its will in all essential matters must be unimpaired. The institution of an assembly with a large elected majority confronts us with the problem, as in the case of the provinces, of enabling the executive government to secure its essential

legislation and its supplies. Here also we have examined several possible expedients. In this instance there can be no question of relying on legislation by superior authority. The only superior authority is Parliament, and Parliament is too far off and notoriously too preoccupied and not suitably constituted to pass laws for the domestic needs of India. It is true that the Governor-General has the power of making temporary ordinances for certain emergent purposes. We propose that this power should be retained : its utility has been strikingly demonstrated during the present war. It merely provides, however, a means of issuing decrees after private discussion in the executive council, and without opportunities for public debate or criticism : and normally it should be used only in rare emergencies. It would be unsuitable for our purpose. What we seek is some means, for use on special occasions, of placing on the Statute book, after full publicity and discussion, permanent measures to which the majority of members in the Legislative Assembly may be unwilling to assent. We seek deliberately, when the purpose justifies us, to depart from popular methods of legislation, and it is obvious that no device which conforms to those methods can possibly serve our purpose. For this purpose we have come to the conclusion that we should employ the method now familiar to Indian institutions of maintaining such a number of votes, upon which the Government can in all circumstances rely, as to ensure the passage of the legislation that it requires. It is here alone, and only (as will be seen hereafter) for use in cases where it is obviously necessary, that we propose to perpetuate the official *bloc.* We are seeking to provide for a period of transition ; for which purpose no novel expedient, such as multiplying the value of official votes or calling in officials who have not taken part in the argument to record their votes, or of passing measures automatically after discussion, would be as easily understood or as acceptable as the continuance in modified form of the present system.

The Council of State

277. One suggestion which we considered was that we should follow the plan adopted in the provinces, and institute grand committees to which the Government's essential Bills should be referred. But the conditions of Indian legislation are different from those of provincial. Matters are more important, the Government's responsibility to Parliament is closer, and the affirmative power must be more decisively used. We feel also that there are advantages, both direct and incidental, in setting up a separate constitutional body, in which Government will be able to command a majority. We do not propose to institute a complete bicameral system, but to create a second chamber, known as the Council of State, which shall take its part in ordinary legislative business and shall be the final legislative authority in matters which the Government regards as essential. The Council of State will be composed of fifty members, exclusive of the Governor-General, who would be President, with power to appoint a Vice-President who would normally take his place : not more than twenty-five will be officials, including the members of the executive council, and four would be non-officials nominated by the Governor-General. Official

members would be eligible for nomination to both the legislative assembly and the Council of State. There would be twenty-one elected members, of whom fifteen will be returned by the non-official members of the provincial legislative councils, each council returning two members, other than those of Burma, the Central Provinces and Assam, which will return one member each. Elected members returned to the Council of State would vacate any seats they occupied on the provincial council or the legislative assembly. The remaining six elected members are intended to supplement the representation which the Muhammadans and the landed classes will otherwise secure ; and also to provide for the representation of chambers of commerce. Each of these three interests should, we suggest, return two members directly to the Council of State. Bearing in mind the fact that among the members of the provincial legislative councils who will elect to the fifteen seats there will be a proportion of Muhammadans, and assuming that in each of the bigger provinces each elector will be able as now to give both his votes to one candidate, we estimate that the composition of the Council of State should comprise at least six Muhammadans whether sitting by direct or indirect election or by the Governor-General's nomination. Moreover it is desirable that the four seats to be filled by direct election should be used so as to ensure that the Muhammadan and landed members should as far as possible be representative of the whole of India. Deficiencies may occur in this respect in any one council, but they should be corrected in elections to the subsequent council. For this reason the regulations for elections to the

four seats should be framed by the Governor-
General in Council in such way as to enable him
to decide, after consideration of the results of the
indirect elections, from what part of India or
possibly in what manner from India generally the
seats should be filled.

LEGISLATIVE PROCEDURE. GOVERNMENT BILLS

279. Let us now explain how this legislative
machinery will work. It will make for clearness
to deal separately with Government Bills and Bills
introduced by non-official members. A Government Bill will ordinarily be introduced and carried
through all the usual stages in the legislative
assembly. It will then go in the ordinary course to
the Council of State, and if there amended in any
way which the Assembly is not willing to accept,
it will be submitted to a joint session of both
Houses, by whose decision its ultimate fate will
be decided. This will be the ordinary course of
legislation. But it might well happen that amendments made by the Council of State were such as
to be essential in the view of the Government if
the purpose with which the Bill was originally
introduced was to be achieved, and in this case
the Governor-General in Council would certify that
the amendments were essential to the interests of
peace, order, or good government. The Assembly
would then not have power to reject or modify
these amendments, nor would they be open to
revision in a joint session.

We have to provide for two other possibilities.
Cases may occur in which the legislative assembly
refuses leave to the introduction of a Bill or throws
out a Bill which the Government regarded as

necessary. For such a contingency we would provide that if leave to introduce a Government Bill is refused, or if the Bill is thrown out at any stage, the Government should have the power, on the certificate of the Governor-General in Council that the Bill is essential to the interests of peace, order, or good government, to refer it *de novo* to the Council of State ; and if the Bill, after being taken in all its stages through the Council of State, was passed by that body, it would become law without further reference to the Assembly. Further, there may be cases when the consideration of a measure by both chambers would take too long if the emergency which called for the measure is to be met. Such a contingency should rarely arise ; but we advise that in cases of emergency, so certified by the Governor-General in Council, it should be open to the Government to introduce a Bill in the Council of State, and upon its being passed there merely to report it to the Assembly.

FISCAL LEGISLATION. EFFECT OF RESOLUTIONS

284. Fiscal legislation will, of course, be subject to the procedure which we have recommended in respect of Government Bills. The budget will be introduced in the Legislative Assembly, but the Assembly will not vote it. Resolutions upon budget matters and upon all other questions, whether moved in the Assembly or in the Council of State, will continue to be advisory in character. We have already given our reasons for holding that it is not feasible to give resolutions a legal sanction. But since resolutions will no longer be defeated in the Assembly by the vote of an official majority, they will, if carried, stand on record as the

considered opinion of a body which is at all events more representative than the Legislative Council which it displaced. That in itself will mean that the significance of resolutions will be enhanced ; there will be a heavier responsibility upon those who pass them, because of their added weight ; and the Government's responsibility for not taking action upon them will also be heavier. It will be therefore incumbent on Government to oppose resolutions which it regards as prejudicial with all the force and earnestness that it can command in the hope of convincing the Assembly of their undesirability. There must, however, remain to the Government power not to give effect to any resolution which it cannot reconcile with its responsibility for the peace, order, and good government of the country.

Position of the States

297. Although compared with the British provinces the states are thinly populated, they comprise among them some of the fairest portions of India. The striking differences in their size, importance, and geographical distribution, are due partly to variations of policy, partly to historical events which no Government could control. Wherever consolidating forces were at work before the British advance occurred, we find that large units of territory were constituted into States : wherever disorder or other disintegrating factors were at work longer, as in Bombay and Central India, we find a large number of fragmentary territories. ' Political as well as physical geography bears witness to the stress of the destructive forces through which a country has passed.' The policy of the British

Government towards the states has changed from time to time, passing from the original plan of non-intervention in all matters beyond its own ring-fence to the policy of ' subordinate isolation ' initiated by Lord Hastings ; which in its turn gave way before the existing conception of the relation between the states and the Government of India, which may be described as one of union and co-operation on their part with the paramount power. In spite of the varieties and complexities of treaties, engagements, and *sanads*, the general position as regards the rights and obligations of the native states can be summed up in a few words. The states are guaranteed security from without ; the paramount power acts for them in relation to foreign powers and other states, and it intervenes when the internal peace of their territories is seriously threatened. On the other hand the states' relations to foreign powers are those of the paramount power ; they share the obligation for the common defence ; and they are under a general responsibility for the good government and welfare of their territories. .

Effects of the War

298. Now let us consider what factors have been at work to bring the ruling princes into closer relations with the Government of India. Foremost is the war. No words of ours are needed to make known the services to the Empire which the states have rendered. They were a profound surprise and disappointment to the enemy ; and a cause of delight and pride to those who knew beforehand the princes' devotion to the Crown. With one accord the rulers of the native states in India

rallied to fight for the Empire when war was declared; they offered their personal services and the resources of their states. Imperial service troops from over a score of states have fought in various fields, and many with great gallantry and honour. The princes have helped lavishly with men and horses, material and money, and some of them have in person served in France and elsewhere. They have shown that our quarrel is their quarrel; and they have both learned and taught the lesson of their own indissoluble connection with the Empire, and their immense value as part of the polity of India.

A COUNCIL OF PRINCES

306. We have explained how, on various occasions in recent years, the princes have met in conference at the invitation of the Viceroy. These conferences have been of great value in assisting in the formulation of the Government's policy on important matters like minority administration and succession, and in promoting interest in such questions as scientific agriculture and commercial and agricultural statistics. The meetings have given the princes the opportunity of informing the Government as to their sentiments and wishes, of broadening their outlook, of conferring with one another and with the Government. But although the meetings have in the last few years been regular, they depend upon the invitation of the Viceroy; and our first proposal is to replace them by the institution of a Council of Princes. We wish to call into existence a permanent consultative body. There are questions which affect the states generally, and other questions which are of concern

either to the Empire as a whole, or to British India and the states in common, upon which we conceive that the opinion of such a body would be of the utmost value. The Viceroy would refer such questions to the Council, and we should have the advantage of their considered opinion. We think it is all-important that the meetings should be regular, and that ordinarily the Council should meet once a year to discuss agenda approved by the Viceroy. Any member of the Council or the Council as a whole might request the Viceroy to include in the agenda any subject on which discussion was desired. If questions of sufficient importance arose in the intervals between the annual meetings, the princes might suggest to the Viceroy that an extraordinary meeting should be held. We contemplate that the Viceroy should be President and should as a rule preside, but that in his absence one of the princes should be Chairman. The rules of business would be framed by the Viceroy after consultation with the princes, who might perhaps from time to time suggest modifications in the rules. We believe that most of the princes desire to see such a Council created, although some of the most eminent among them have not taken part in the conferences in 1916 and 1917. The direct transaction of business between the Government of India and any state would of course not be affected by the institution of the Council. We have used the name ' Council of Princes ' to describe the body which we desire to see instituted. We have had difficulty, however, in finding a name appropriate to such a unique assembly. We wish to avoid a designation associated with other institutions, and to find one which will connote the real position of this body of rulers with the representative of the King-Emperor as Chairman. From both these points of view the terms Council or Chamber or House of Princes are open to criticism. There is much to be said in favour of an Indian name for an Indian body which, from the circumstances of the case, would exist nowhere else ; but it would be necessary to choose one not peculiarly associated historically either with Hindus or with Muhammadans. While therefore we have adopted the term Council for temporary purposes, we hope that discussion may produce some happier alternative.

Standing Committee of the Council

307. It has been represented to us that difficulties have occurred in the past by reason of the fact that the political department comes to decisions affecting the native states without being in a position to avail itself of the advice of those who are in a position to know from their own personal experience or the history of their states the right course to pursue. On matters of custom and usage in particular we feel that such advice would be of great value, and would help to ensure sound decisions. Our second proposal therefore is that the Council of Princes should be invited annually to appoint a small standing committee, to which the Viceroy or the political department might refer such matters. We need hardly say that no reference affecting any individual state would be made to the committee without the concurrence of its ruler. The Council of Princes might appoint to the standing committee not only princes but also dewans or ministers, who were willing to place

their services at the disposal of the Viceroy when called upon for advice. This machinery is based on the principle of consultation, which in so many matters underlies our recommendations in regard to British India.

THE PUBLIC SERVICES

THE CASE FOR INCREASING THE INDIAN ELEMENT

313. In the forefront of the announcement of August 20 the policy of the increasing association of Indians in every branch of the administration was definitely placed. It has not been necessary for us—nor indeed would it have been possible—to go into this large question in detail in the time available for our inquiry. We have already seen that Lord Hardinge's Government were anxious to increase the number of Indians in the public services, and that a Royal Commission was appointed in 1912 to examine and report on the existing limitations in the employment of Indians. The commission made an exhaustive inquiry into the whole subject, in the course of which it visited every province in India, and its report is now being examined by the Government of India and the local governments with a view to formulating their recommendations with all possible dispatch. The report must form the basis of the action now to be taken, but in view of the altered circumstances we think that it will be necessary to amplify its conclusions in some important respects. The report was signed only a few months after the outbreak of war and its publication was deferred in the hope that the war would not be prolonged. When written it might have satisfied moderate

Indian opinion, but when published two years later it was criticized as wholly disappointing. Our inquiry has since given us ample opportunity of judging the importance which Indian opinion attaches to this question. While we take account of this attitude, a factor which carries more weight with us is that since the report was signed an entirely new policy towards Indian government has been adopted, which must be very largely dependent for success on the extent to which it is found possible to introduce Indians into every branch of the administration. It is a great weakness of public life in India to-day that it contains so few men who have found opportunity for practical experience of the problems of administration. Although there are distinguished exceptions, principally among the dewans of native states, most Indian public men have not had an opportunity of grappling with the difficulties of administration, nor of testing their theories by putting them into practice. Administrative experience not only sobers the judgement and teaches appreciation of the practical difficulties in the way of the wholesale introduction of reforms, however attractive, and the attainment of theoretical ideals, but by training an increasing number of men in the details of day-to-day business it will eventually provide India with public men versed in the whole art of government. If responsible government is to be established in India, there will be a far greater need than is even dreamt of at present for persons to take part in public affairs in the legislative assemblies and elsewhere; and for this reason the more Indians we can employ in the public services the better. Moreover it would lessen the burden of imperial responsibilities if a body of capable Indian administrators could be produced. We regard it as necessary therefore that recruitment of a largely increased proportion of Indians should be begun at once. The personnel of a service cannot be altered in a day : it must be a long and steady process ; if, therefore the services are to be substantially Indian in personnel by the time that India is ripe for responsible government, no time should be lost in increasing the proportion of Indian recruits.

LIMITATIONS TO THIS PROCESS

314. At the same time we must take note of certain limitations to the policy of change. The characteristics which we have learned to associate with the Indian public services must as far as possible be maintained ; and the leaven of officers possessed of them should be strong enough to assure and develop them in the service as a whole. The qualities of courage, leadership, decision, fixity of purpose, detached judgement, and integrity in her public servants will be as necessary as ever to India. There must be no such sudden swamping of any service with any new element that its whole character suffers a rapid alteration. As practical men we must also recognize that there are essential differences between the various services and that it is possible to increase the employment of Indians in some more than in others. The solution lies therefore in recruiting year by year such a number of Indians as the existing members of the service will be able to train in an adequate manner and to inspire with the spirit of the whole. Again it is important that there should be so far as possible

an even distribution of Europeans and Indians, not indeed between one service and another, but at least between the different grades of the same service. Apart from other considerations this is a reason for exercising caution in filling up the large number of vacancies which have resulted from short recruitment during the last four years. We must also remember how greatly conditions vary between the provinces. In arriving at any percentage to be applied to certain services we should take into account the fact that in some provinces the admissible percentage will probably be much lower than what seems possible for the service as a whole, with the result that the percentage in other provinces must be much higher. If the Indian Civil Service be taken as an example, and if, for the sake of argument, the recommendation of the commission is accepted that recruitment for twenty-five per cent. of the superior posts be made in India, then to attain an all-round percentage of twenty-five the proportion in say Bombay, Bengal, and Madras will have to be considerably more than twenty-five per cent., because in Burma certainly and probably also in the Punjab it will be much less. Indeed it seems self-evident that the actual percentage for the whole of a service can only be worked out with special regard to the conditions of each province. Lastly it would be unwise to create a demand in excess of the supply. At present the number of candidates of higher quality than those who are now forthcoming for the provincial services is strictly limited, and, though the opening of the more attractive services may be expected to stimulate the supply, it will still be necessary, if the present quality of the services is not to be unduly impaired, to take special steps to see that recruits are of a satisfactory standard.

REMOVAL OF RACIAL DISTINCTIONS

315. Subject to these governing conditions we will now put forward certain principles on which we suggest that the action to be now taken should be based. First, we would remove from the regulations the few remaining distinctions that are based on race, and would make appointments to all branches of the public service without racial discrimination.

INSTITUTION OF RECRUITMENT IN INDIA

316. Next we consider that for all the public services, for which there is recruitment in England open to Europeans and Indians alike, there must be a system of appointment in India. It is obvious that we cannot rely on the present method of recruitment in England to supply a sufficiency of Indian candidates. That system must be supplemented in some way or other : and we propose to supplement it by fixing a definite percentage of recruitment to be made in India. This seems to us to be the only practical method of obtaining the increased Indian element in the services which we desire. We do not suggest that it will be possible to dispense with training in Europe for some of the principal services. It will be necessary to make arrangements to send for training in England the candidates selected in India, but as to this we anticipate no difficulty.

FUTURE POSITION OF THE EUROPEAN SERVICES

323. We have already touched more than once on the question of the future of the European services in India ; but the importance of the subject justifies us in returning to it. Do the changes which we propose point to the gradual, possibly the rapid, extrusión of the Englishman with all the consequences that may follow therefrom ? Is it conceivable that India's only surviving connexion with the empire will be found in the presence of British troops for the purpose of defending her borders ? We may say at once that the last contingency cannot be contemplated. We cannot imagine that Indian self-respect or British commonsense would assent for a moment to such a proposition. At least so long as the empire is charged with the defence of India, a substantial element of Englishmen must remain and must be secured both in her Government apd in her public services. But that is not the practical or the immediate question before us. What we have had to bear in mind is how our reforms may react on the position and the numbers of Europeans in the Indian services. We are making over certain functions to popular control, and in respect of these—and they will be an increasing number— English commissioners, magistrates, doctors, and engineers will be required to carry out the policy of Indian ministers. Simultaneously we are opening the door of the services more widely to Indians, and thereby necessarily affecting the cohesion of the service. Some people have been so much impressed by the undoubted difference of view

between the services and educated Indians, and by the anticipated effects of a larger Indian element in the services that they apprehend that this may result in increasing pressure to get rid of Englishmen, and increasing reluctance on the part of Englishmen to give their further services to India under the new conditions. This danger is one which we have anxiously considered. We are certain that the English members of the services will continue to be as necessary as ever to India. They may be diminished in numbers; but they must not fall off in quality. Higher qualifications than ever will be required of them if they are to help India along her difficult journey to self-government. We have, therefore, taken thought to improve the conditions of the services, and to secure them from attack. But we sincerely hope that our protection will not be needed. There was a time in Indian politics when service opinion and Indian opinion often found themselves in alliance against other points of view. Our reforms will, we believe, do away with the factors which worked a change in those relations. With the removal of disabilities, and the opening of opportunity there is no reason why relations between educated Indians and the services should not improve. In the reservations which we propose there is nothing to arouse hostility. No reasonable man should cavil at safeguards which are imposed in order to gain time for processes of growth to occur. If our own judgement has been too cautious we have provided means for correcting it, and of adjusting future progress to the results attained.

THE INDIAN CIVIL SERVICE

326. Of the Indian Civil Service in particular we have something further to say. Its past record we might well leave to speak for itself. But all the more because of the vehement and sometimes malignant abuse to which the service is exposed, it is not out of place to pay our tribute to energies finely dedicated to the well-being of India. This abuse is partly due to the fact that on the personnel of the service, which is at once the parent and the mainstay of the existing system, has fallen much of the odium which would more justly be directed against the impersonal system itself. Partly it is due also, we think, to the tradition of the service, dating from days when it had no vocal criticism to meet, which imposes silence on the individual officer while the order of things that he represents is attacked and calumniated. Now the position of the Indian Civil Servant, as we have already said, is not analogous to that of the civil servant at home. He takes his place in the legislative and executive councils; he assists in the formulation of policy. But when his doings are attacked he remains except for a few official and rather formal spokesmen in the legislative councils mute. This gives him in the eyes of educated Indians a certain intangible superiority of position, a cold invulnerability, which makes sympathetic relations between them impossible. We do not think this condition of silence can altogether be maintained. With coming changes there must be a greater liberty of action to the European public servant in India to defend his position when attacked. He ought not to leave the task of political education solely to

the politicians. He also must explain and persuade, and argue and refute. We believe he will do it quite effectively. The matter is, however, by no means free from difficulty; there are obvious limitations to the discretion which can be granted; and these will be considered by the Government of India.

MILITARY VALUE OF ECONOMIC DEVELOPMENT

337. These are political considerations peculiar to India itself. But both on economic and military grounds imperial interests also demand that the natural resources of India should henceforth be better utilized. We cannot measure the access of strength which an industrialized India will bring to the power of the empire; but we are sure that it will be welcome after the war. Mere traders with an outlook of less than a generation ahead may be disposed to regard each new source of manufacture as a possible curtailment of their established sources of profit. But each new acquisition of wealth increases the purchasing power of the whole, and changes in the configuration of trade that disturb individuals must be accompanied by a total increase in its value which is to the good of the whole. Meanwhile the War has thrown a strong light on the military importance of economic development. We know that the possibility of sea communications being temporarily interrupted forces us to rely on India as an ordnance base for protective operations in Eastern theatres of war. Nowadays the products of an industrially developed community coincide so nearly in kind though not in quantity with the catalogue of munitions of war that the develop-

ment of India's natural resources becomes a matter of almost military necessity. We believe that this consideration also is not a matter of indifference to India's political leaders ; and that they are anxious to see India self-supporting in respect of military requirements.

DIFFICULTIES AND POTENTIALITIES

338. We are agreed therefore that there must be a definite change of view ; and that the Government must admit and shoulder its responsibility for furthering the industrial development of the country. The difficulties by this time are well known. In the past and partly as a result of recent *swadeshi* experiences, India's capital has not generally been readily available ; among some communities at least there is apparent distaste for practical training, and a comparative weakness of mutual trust ; skilled labour is lacking, and, although labour is plentiful, education is needed to inculcate a higher standard of living and so to secure a continuous supply ; there is a dearth of technical institutions ; there is also a want of practical information about the commercial potentialities of India's war products. Though these are serious difficulties they are not insuperable ; but they will be overcome only if the State comes forward boldly as guide and helper. On the other hand there are good grounds for hope. India has great natural resources, mineral and vegetable. She has furnished supplies of manganese, tungsten, mica, jute, copra, lac, &c., for use in the War. She has abundant coal, even if its geographical distribution is uneven ; she has also in her large rivers ample means of creating water-power. There is good

reason for believing that she will greatly increase
her output of oil. Her forest wealth is immense,
and much of it only awaits the introduction of
modern means of transport, a bolder investment
of capital, and the employment of extra staff;
while the patient and laborious work of conserva-
tion that has been steadily proceeding, joined with
modern scientific methods of improving supplies
and increasing output, will yield a rich harvest in
future. We have been assured that Indian capital
will be forthcoming once it is realized that it can
be invested with security and profit in India ; a
purpose that will be furthered by the provision
of increased facilities for banking and credit.
Labour, though abundant, is handicapped by still
pursuing uneconomical methods, and its output
would be greatly increased by the extended use of
machinery. We have no doubt that there is an
immense scope for the application of scientific
methods. Conditions are ripe for the development
of new and for the revival of old industries on
European lines ; and the real enthusiasm for
industries, which is not confined to the ambitions
of a few individuals but rests on the general desire
to see Indian capital and labour applied jointly
to the good of the country, seems to us of the
happiest augury.

FISCAL POLICY

341. Connected intimately with the matter of
industries is the question of the Indian tariff. This
subject was excluded from the deliberations of the
Industrial Commission now sitting because it was
not desirable at that juncture to raise any question
of the modification of India's fiscal policy ; but

its exclusion was none the less the object of some legitimate criticism in India. The changes which we propose in the Government of India will still leave the settlement of India's tariff in the hands of a Government amenable to Parliament and the Secretary of State ; but, inasmuch as the tariff reacts on many matters which will henceforth come more and more under Indian control, we think it well that we should put forward for the information of His Majesty's Government the views of educated Indians upon this subject. We have no 'immediate proposals to make ; we are anxious merely that any decisions which may hereafter be taken should be taken with full appreciation of educated Indian opinion.

DESIRE FOR A PROTECTIVE TARIFF

342. The theoretical free trader, we believe, hardly exists in India at present. As was shown by the debates in the Indian Legislative Council in March 1913, educated Indian opinion ardently desires a tariff. It rightly wishes to find another substantial base than that of the land for Indian revenues, and it turns to a tariff to provide one. Desiring industries which will give him Indian-made clothes to wear and Indian-made articles to use, the educated Indian looks to the example of other countries which have relied on tariffs, and seizes on the admission of even free traders that for the nourishment of nascent industries a tariff is permissible. We do not know whether he pauses to reflect that these industries will be largely financed by foreign capital attracted by the tariff, although we have evidence that he has not learned to appreciate the advantages of foreign capital.

But whatever economic fallacy underlies his reasoning, these are his firm beliefs ; and though he may be willing to concede the possibility that he is wrong, he will not readily concede that it is our business to decide the matter for him. He believes that as long as we continue to decide for him we shall decide in the interests of England and not according to his wishes ; and he points to the debate in the House of Commons on the differentiation of the cotton excise in support of his contention. So long as the people who refuse India protection are interested in manufactures with which India might compete, Indian opinion cannot bring itself to believe that the refusal is disinterested or dictated by care for the best interests of India. This real and keen desire for fiscal autonomy does not mean that educated opinion in India is unmindful of imperial obligations. On the contrary, it feels proud of, and assured by, India's connexion with the empire, and does not desire a severance that would mean cutting the ties of loyalty to the Crown, the assumption of new and very heavy responsibilities, and a loss of standing in the world's affairs. Educated Indians recognize that they are great gainers by the Imperial connexion, and they are willing to accept its drawbacks. They recognize that the question of a tariff may be mainly, but is not wholly, a matter of domestic politics.

9. *Edwin S. Montagu, House of Commons, 5 June, 1919*

I BEG to move, 'That the Bill be now read a second time'. The House having now somewhat approximated, but by no means reached its ordinary aspect on Indian Debates, I rise to discharge the highly important task, a task of which I fully realize the responsibility, of asking this House, on behalf of His Majesty's Government, to read a second time the Bill which has been printed and circulated. I desire to avoid going into details upon this necessarily complicated and technical measure. I have flooded the House, in response to requests, and in order to give information to it as far as I possibly could, with a series of elaborate documents, and these will obviate, because I will assume that the House has mastered these documents, a large amount of technical disquisition. But in view of certain criticisms I want once again to repeat the origin of this Bill. When I took office two years ago much work leading up to the preparation of a Bill of this kind had already been done. Dispatches containing schemes for reform had passed between the Government of India and my predecessor, and out of their proposals and his criticism of them had emerged this principle, that to my predecessor no reform of the Government of India would be acceptable which did not involve the transfer of responsibility from these Houses to the people of India. I took up the work where the Chancellor of the Exchequer left it, and the pronouncement of the 20th August followed, a part of which was that my acceptance of the Viceroy's invitation to proceed to India had been authorized by His Majesty's Government. No sooner was that pronouncement made than I appointed a very important India Office Committee, presided over by Sir William Duke, an ex-Lieut.-Governor of Bengal, a member of my Council and an Indian

Civil Servant—I repeat all his qualifications because it is suggested in some quarters that this Bill arose spontaneously in the minds of the Viceroy and myself without previous inquiry or consideration, under the influence of Mr. Lionel Curtis. I have never yet been able to understand that you approach the merits of any discussion by vain efforts to approximate to its authorship. I do not even now understand that India or the empire owes anything more or anything less than a great debt of gratitude to the patriotic and devoted services Mr. Curtis has given to the consideration of this problem. But this Committee, presided over by Sir William Duke, sat at the India Office from the 20th August until I left for India, accompanied by Sir William Duke, Lord Donoughmore, and Mr. Charles Roberts, on the 20th of October. We held repeated conferences in the enforced leisure of a long sea voyage, and discussed the problem almost daily on board ship up to the time when we reached India, where we were joined by Mr. Bhupendra Nath Basu and Sir William Vincent, a member of the Viceroy's Executive Council. Spontaneously, as a necessary consequence of all these deliberations, as a necessary consequence of the terms of the pronouncement of the 20th August, and as a necessary and inevitable consequence of an unprejudiced study of the question we reached the conclusion upon which this Bill is based, a conclusion reached after listening to innumerable deputations, after six months of conference with non-officials and officials, after continuous discussion with the Government in the provinces and at Delhi with the heads of all the local governments. From the time I returned to

London, a new India Office Committee, presided over by Mr. Charles Roberts, and containing a large number of those Civil Servants who have taken part in this discussion, and whose services I have had the privilege to command, have sat upon and discussed all the criticisms that have reached us on the Bill. Sir William Duke, Sir James Brunyate, and Sir Thomas Holderness were members. Sir James Meston, the present Finance Member of the Government of India, was home last year and helped in the deliberations of this Committee. In recent months it has been assisted by Sir Frank Sly, Mr. Feetham, Mr. Stephenson, and Mr. Muddiman.

This Committee has been concerned in drafting the Bill, and in considering all dispatches and telegrams and criticisms upon the scheme originally proposed. After this prolonged discussion and deliberation of almost exactly two years in extent, I now ask with some confidence for the Second Reading of the Bill, which I do not hesitate to say has been as carefully prepared and considered in all its aspects as it is possible to consider a measure of this kind.

I ask for the Second Reading of the Bill to-day for two reasons. First of all, there is so much general agreement on all sides in India and here as to its provisions, so much general agreement and such important points of difference on methods side by side, that I do not believe there is any way of getting on until we examine the details of the measure in a Committee representing Parliament. Second Reading points, as I think I shall show, are points on which there is general agreement, both in India and here. There are very important differences—differences which I do not wish to minimize—as to methods, and you will never get to a discussion of those methods infinitely technical, until you have a small body constituted which will take evidence and consider the alternative merits or demerits of the different plans. It is our intention, if the House gives a Second Reading to this measure to-day, to ask that it should be referred to a Joint Committee of both Houses, and that that Joint Committee should consider all the questions that are involved. I cannot emphasize too strongly that it is the Government's wish that that Committee should discuss the matter not only from the point of view of detailed examination, but from the point of view of the examination of alternative methods. Let it have free scope. Let the House appoint a Committee to go into the whole question, and, as I have said before, so recently as a fortnight ago, although I believe from the bottom of my heart that you dare not and ought not to do less than we propose in this Bill, I shall be glad, and the Government will be glad, to take the advice of the Committee on any alternative method which really and actually promises at least as much.

I would only add one thing. We have so many responsibilities in this House, so many important questions needing consideration, that perhaps India looms quite small to many Members ; but this problem to 315,000,000 of people eagerly awaiting, so far as they are politically educated, the decision of this House—to India this subject is all-important. Let no man join in this Debate, let no man accept the incalculably responsible task of helping—and we want help, it is a difficult enough problem to require help—of helping on the Committee unless he is prepared to go there constructively, and not destructively, to help on as perfect a plan as can be devised, and not with the intention to delay or thwart legislation, which in my mind, and in the minds of the House I hope, it is absolutely essential to carry out.

The second reason why I would urge the assistance of the House in the passage of the Second Reading to-day is the impatience—I think the legitimate impatience—with which India is waiting a start upon the policy enunciated now two years ago. That policy was announced, and this Bill was drawn up with a view to meeting existing conditions in India. Believe me, my experience of India, my experience of the Government of India now extending over something like six years of office, make me confident that there is no more fallacious platitude, no more obvious fallacy than that which is on the lips of so many critics of Indian affairs—that it is a country which never changes, a country which undergoes none of the emotions which other countries experience. One old Indian friend of mine, who has been engaged upon public affairs in this country, who has been absent from his own fourteen months only, and who returned to it the other day, told me when last I saw him that he thought politically it was a different place to fourteen months ago. The War, the causes of the War, the objects of the War, the speeches of those who conducted the political aspects of the War have had their effect from one end of India to the other, and have even reached, as the documents which I published themselves show, the Government of Madras.

The pronouncement of the 20th August promised that substantial steps in the direction of responsible government should be taken as soon as possible. There is no use for pronouncements that are not fulfilled; there is no use for pronouncements which take geological epochs to fulfil. Doubts are already beginning to appear. It is suggested already—unworthily suggested, wickedly suggested, but still suggested—that we made the announcement and declared the intention of His Majesty's Government in order to secure loyalty from the Indian peoples during the War, and that now we have achieved victory we are not going on with our purpose. I only mention that to show that, in my opinion, as in the opinion of the Governor of Bombay, delay, inexcusable delay, unnecessary delay, would be fatal to our purpose. For that reason, after two years' consideration of this problem, I venture to suggest to the House that I have shown no undue haste in bringing this Bill before the House of Commons. First it used to be said, ' Oh, you must not introduce the Bill until the opinions of the local governments have been published and we have had an opportunity of reading them.' I promised the opinions of the local governments, and the opinions of the local governments have been published in accordance with that promise. To a very large extent they are irrelevant, because, despite the letters which have been published and the arguments they have used in them, they have produced, at a subsequent date, an alternative plan, about which I shall have something to say later on. But they are published. Now, when they are published, comes the new argument, ' You are hurrying on the Second

Reading of the Bill, when we have not had time to read the papers.' So, first you say, ' Do not take the Bill, because we want the papers.' Then, when the papers do appear, you say, ' Give us time to read the papers.' In other words, for the man who does not want to do something, the day on which you ask him to do something is always the wrong day.·

I have published also, in order to avoid discussion to-day, two White Papers. One White Paper explains, as clearly and as concisely as I could do it, the actual effect of the Clauses of the Bill. The other White Paper shows what the existing Government of India Act, passed in 1915, will look like if these Amendments are made in it, for this Bill has been drafted with a view to automatic consolidation and the Government of India Act, 1915, embraces a very large number of Statutes. It is suggested that when this Bill has been passed by the Houses of Parliament it shall be automatically included in the existing Act, and will itself disappear as a separate Act. In order to see the effect of that process—the best form of legislation, I venture to think, when you have a previous Statute—I have published and circulated a copy. That, I hope, will avoid the necessity at this stage of going into details. A few more words I must say as to the form of the Bill. In the first place, it may be said—it has been said—that we propose to rely so much on rules and regulations under the Bill that the Bill itself is only a skeleton. I need not remind the House that there are many precedents for that procedure, in fact, in almost every Statute referring to the Government of India I think that procedure has been adopted. But

I would also remind the House that deliberately, of intention, in accordance with the terms of the pronouncement of the 20th August, this Bill does not pretend to give to India a Constitution that will endure. It is transitional; it is a bridge between government by the agents of Parliament and government by the representatives of the peoples of India. It must be in such a form that it shall not be static, but fluid—that alterations can be made in it from time to time, and that you should not form a rigid Constitution by Statute which could not be altered except by trespassing at intervals upon the over-burdened and over-mortgaged time of this House. Therefore we have resorted to the plan of precedent, of asking that details shall be accomplished by rules. Let me hasten to add that this is one of the points upon which I approach this problem with an open mind. If there is anything which it is suggested should be done by rule which the House would prefer to be done by Statute, let us by all means, in the Committee stage, incorporate it in the Statute, although let us try at the same time to avoid rigidity, which, I believe, would be fatal to our purpose. I would add also that it is not our intention to prevent the control by Parliament of these rules and regulations. The Bill provides that they shall be submitted to both Houses. The principle which it is intended to embody in these rules it is intended should be submitted to the Joint Committee which it is proposed to set up; and the policy of the rules, if not the actual wording of the rules, will therefore be carefully considered at the same time as the Bill itself. I regard that as essential. It has always been said that the

Morley-Minto reforms were largely spoiled by the rules made under it. I am not at the moment prepared to argue whether or not that is so, but I want on this occasion to avoid any possibility of that charge being levelled. Therefore I hope that Parliament will not lose control of the Bill until the policy which is to be embodied in the rules has also been laid down by Parliament.

I come now to the Bill itself. What I would like to do, if I may, is to start afresh and try to take the House with me, if I can and if it is not too ambitious a project, in realizing that if you start from the place where the authors of this Bill started, the form of the Bill and the recommendations of the Bill are inevitable. Where did we start ? We started with the pronouncement of the 20th August 1917. I propose to ask : Is there anybody who questions to-day the policy of that pronouncement ? It is no use accepting it unless you mean it ; it is no use meaning it unless you act upon it ; and it is no use acting upon it unless your actions are in conformity with it. Therefore I take it that Parliament, or at any rate this House, will agree that the policy of the pronouncement of the 20th August must be the basis of our discussion —the progressive realization of responsible government, progressive realization, realization by degrees, by stages, by steps—and those steps must at the outset be substantial. That pronouncement was made in order to achieve what I believe is the only logical, the only possible, the only acceptable meaning of Empire and Democracy, namely, an opportunity to all nations flying the imperial flag to control their own destinies. [An HON. MEMBER : 'Nations ! '] I will come to nations in a moment.

I will beg no question. The hon. member raises the question of nations. Whether it be a nation or not, we have promised to India the progressive realization of responsible government. We have promised to India and given to India a representation like that of the Dominions on our Imperial Conference. India is to be an original member of the League of Nations. Therefore I say, whatever difficulties there may be in your path, your imperial task is to overcome those difficulties and to help India on the path of nationality, however much you may recognize—and I propose to ask the House to consider them—the difficulties which lie in the path.

Supposing for a moment there are those who consider that empire has justified itself when you give to a country satisfactory law and order, adequate peace, decent institutions, and a certain measure of prosperity under the defence that you have provided ; supposing, in other words, there are people who believe that you have fulfilled your mission when you have run the country as an estate, and not as a country at all ; even then, approaching it from the other point, there are large proposals in this Bill which command assent from them. There are the proposals for devolution, the proposals for decentralization. I have heard no critic in these two years who has not told me that it is absolutely essential to get greater freedom for the Government of India from the India Office. I have hardly met a critic who has not told me that it is absolutely essential for the local governments to get more freedom from the Government of India. I think that is agreed. I do not think that anybody questions that, from the point of view of administrative convenience, if on no higher grounds, government by dispatch, with all its cumbrous machinery, all its necessarily delaying methods, all the difficulties attending upon considering and reconsidering plans and projects over thousands of miles of land and thousands of miles of sea, all that ought to be got rid of. I ask Parliament to assent to this proposition, that you cannot get rid of it unless you substitute something else for it. Now and to-day you cannot have a Government more bureaucratic and less dependent upon Parliament, without being dependent upon anything else, than you have at present. The only possible substitute for government by dispatch is government by vote. The only possible way of really achieving devolution and making the unit, when you have chosen the unit, responsible for the management of its own affairs, is to make the Government of that unit responsible to the representatives of the people. If you simply say, 'Let us have an irresponsible Government in a province, and let the Government of India not interfere, and the Secretary of State not interfere, and Parliament not interfere,' you have a policy which is merely the enthronement of bureaucracy and the very negation of the progressive realization of responsible government.

Therefore I go a step farther. In order to realize responsible government, and in order to get devolution, upon which there is general agreement, you must gradually get rid of government by the agents of Parliament and replace it by government by the agents of the representatives of the peoples of India. In other words, you have to choose your unit of government, and you have got in that

unit to create an electorate which will control the
Government. What is the unit that you are choosing
to be ? Some people would say, Let us be content
with the unit of the local government area—the
parish council (I am not using terms of art, but
terms which have significance for this country)
the county council, the rural district council, the
municipalities—in other words, that you should
give responsible self-government in the area
of local government. That is already being
done under the terms of the Joint Report, but
that is not enough, for two reasons. The first
is this : The policy of complete local self-government was adopted by Lord Ripon in 1883, and we
are now proceeding to carry it out, after a delay of
something like thirty-five years. It is not enough
to answer the new conditions arising out of the
world war by fulfilling a promise made thirty-five
years ago, and therefore that is one reason why
you must give something more than local self-
government. But there is another reason. You
are not writing on a clear, clean slate. You are
writing, and rightly, in continuation of chapters
which have been written before. You are building
on foundations that already exist. It is in the
province that you must look for your unit, because
it is in the provinces that the great educational
results of Lord Morley's Reform Bill have been
achieved. He made the Legislative Councils representative to some extent of the people, with a very
small electorate and practically no powers beyond
powers of criticism. But it is the existence of
those councils which has awakened the appetite
for self-government, and have added to the
appreciation of self-government in India, and it is

therefore, to my mind, absolutely inevitable that we should proceed to devote ourselves to taking the Morley-Minto councils a stage farther in their development. Therefore it is to the provinces that we go, and the provinces are beginning to be the units of local patriotism in India. I do not say that as time goes on you will not substantially modify the size and boundaries of your provinces. Some of them are very artificial. But when you do, it should be in conformity with the wishes of the inhabitants of the provinces, and not by executive action.

If I have carried the House with me in the suggestion that the province is the unit in which we shall start a progressive realization of responsible government, what are the difficulties that we have to face ? They were suggested in the Joint Report. I will emphasize them again. It does India no good purpose to attempt to avoid them, but they are not arguments against our purpose. They are arguments which we must overcome. The difficulties are these. Under the system of education which has been given to India by British rulers, education has not been spread wide. You have a very small fraction of the population highly educated and a very large proportion of the population not educated at all. You have, secondly, great differences of race and religion and great difficulties arising out of the harsh customs and precepts of caste. I cannot help believing that there is no better way of getting over these difficulties than by representative institutions. There is no greater stimulus to education, there is no better way of promoting community of action or of overcoming the acerbities of caste than by setting to the population a common task to do together, to work out the prosperity of their country. Many of those who write on India assure us of the insuperable obstacles presented by caste. It can only be a gradual process to get rid of these harshnesses and acerbities to which I refer. But every step you take in this direction brings you nearer to the day when the population will not suffer as a consequence of differences of caste. It has begun. It is idle to say there is no difference of recent years in the conditions. When you realize the fact that men of all castes find themselves in the same third-class railway carriage, the way in which soldiers write to me that men of all castes mess together, the work which is being done by the members of the higher caste in helping the conditions and devoting themselves to the social problems afforded by the lower castes, you will realize that those problems are on the way to being solved. The other day I came across a case of a co-operative society run by a committee consisting of Brahmins, non-Brahmins, caste Hindus, and Panchamas. They met to discuss this movement of co-operation, which has grown enormously in India, under a tree of three levels—the Brahmins on one terrace, the non-Brahmins a little lower down, and the Panchamas a little lower still. They discussed the business of the co-operative society in that way. Do you imagine that that is going to endure? Some one will have a difference with some one else in discussing the management of affairs and will talk to him. There is no better way of promoting democratic customs than by working them through democratic institutions.

Despite all these difficulties, I therefore say the

essence of the problem is to train the electors. I desire to express, on behalf of the Government of India and the India Office, and, I hope, of this House, our appreciation of the excellent work done by Lord Southborough's Committee. An electorate has been formed ; that is to say, proposals have been made to put 5,000,000 voters on the register. But you do not form an electorate by that mere process. You have to get them to vote and you have to get them to understand what a vote means. You have to get them to appreciate the results of a vote. There is only one way of doing that, and that is to make the vote of some value. If a man is asked to vote, and then nothing happens as the result of it, nothing that he can see, nothing that he can appreciate, nothing that he can either reward or punish by the transference or maintenance of his vote, you will never train an electorate. Therefore it is a necessary step for the training of an electorate that you must give it power through its representative. If the result of a vote is that a certain person is elected, if he can not only criticize but get things done, if he can do things, if he can be held responsible for the things he does, then the man who wants to turn him out will soon undertake the task of training the electorate to a realization of the importance of a vote. And therefore in order to train your electorate, which is the only way in which you can transfer the power from this House and its agents to the people of India, you have to give the electorate which you create men responsible to it to carry out its demands.

If I have carried the House thus far, the next step must be that you have to choose a part of the

provincial functions which at the outset you will
entrust to the representatives of the people.
Any one who has followed me in what I have said
about education, about caste, and about religious
differences, will realize that it is not right to entrust
them with everything at the same moment. There
are some things, such as the maintenance of peace
and order—I will take the definition which Lord
Chelmsford and I suggested in the Report—things
in which mistakes are irretrievable, things in
which the electorate at the outset should not be
able to enforce its demands, things like Land
Revenue, which you should keep from the control
of the representatives of the people. Immediately
you say that, if there is any one in the House who
has gone so far with me, I do not know whether
they realize it, but they have swallowed the awful,
terrible, much criticized principle of dyarchy.

An Hon .Member : Say ' duality.'

Mr. Montagu : Duality. I have endeavoured
to lead them, as I was led myself, to realize that
the only way to achieve our purpose was to
reserve for the present and for the present only,
certain functions of government under the control
of the agents of this House, and to transfer other
functions to the representatives of the people.
That is what Mr. Feetham's Committee proposes
to do. That is what the India Office Committee,
and that is what the Government of India and
ourselves in discussion in India came to the conclusion was inevitable—to separate the functions
of government, to transfer some, to reserve others,
and to proceed by gradually taking the functions
that are at present reserved and transferring them.
Having decided that certain functions are to be

transferred and that other functions are to be reserved, the question next to be decided is, What is the form of ministry that you will set up to conduct them ?   Is it to be one or is it to be two ? I submit with great confidence to the House that immediately you try and preserve one ministry, always acting together and sharing responsibility for all acts, you obscure the lesson of responsibility. Let us take a particular reserved function—say police—and a particular transferred function—say education.   You say, ' It is our intention that the people shall have their way at once in education. It is our intention that, as far as police is concerned, for the moment those who administer it shall carry out the wishes of the Houses of Parliament as the trustees of the Indian people.'   If the man in charge of education and the man in charge of police are both equally members of the same Government, each sharing responsibility for the acts of the other, both equally responsible for police and education, the one or the other may at any moment have to carry out a policy of which he does not approve.   The man responsible for this House may have to carry out an educational policy of which he does not approve.   The man responsible to the Indian electorate may have to carry out a police policy of which he does not approve.   If you separate the two functions, if you separate the Government into two parts, when a man who is responsible for education goes to his constituency, he says, ' It is quite true that I have carried out a certain education policy.   That is quite right, I am answerable for that, and I am prepared to defend it.   With regard to police policy I am not responsible.   I am there only in a consultative capacity, with no direct responsibility at all. Your only way of modifying the police policy is so to show the House of Commons the excellence of the way in which you have used your educational policy, so that in ten years' time they will transfer to you the police policy too, but at present my responsibility ceases with the transferred subject.' By this means, it seems to me, you can make clear, both to the electorate and to the individual who exercises power on behalf of the electorate, the extent of his responsibility, and in no other way. The logical sequence to that form of argument would be that you would have two Governments completely separate in the same area, with separate funds, separate finances, separate legislatures, separate executive staffs. I would suggest most respectfully to the House that that is impossible, and for this reason. I cannot reiterate too often that the basis of this whole policy is its transitional nature. You want to lead on to something else at the earliest possible moment. If you have two Houses, with two staffs, two purses, the net result would be that the people concerning themselves with transferred subjects would never have anything to say on reserved subjects. But if reserved subjects are to become transferred subjects one day, it is absolutely essential that, during the transitional period, although there is no direct responsibility for them, there should be opportunities of influence and consultation. Therefore, although it seems necessary to separate the responsibility, there ought to be every room that you can possibly have for consultation and joint deliberation on the same policy, and for acting together for the purposes of consultation and deliberation, as the Bill provides, in one Government.

Colonel WEDGWOOD : And criticism ?

Mr. MONTAGU : And criticism. This procedure would be absolutely indefensible if it were not for the fact that it was transitional, and if it were not for the fact that at stated periods it is proposed to hold a Parliamentary inquiry into its working, with a view to further stages. By that means there is a certain method of progress. By that means everything that happens will come under review, and the attitude adopted by each part of the Government to the affairs of the other part will be one of the prime factors in the decision of the Commission that reviews.

I have dealt now with the local governments, and the way in which the scheme is evolved. I know it is a very hard thing, I know that it is more than difficult to explain so complicated a procedure, particularly for one who has been saturated for two years past with this sort of argument and discussion. But I have endeavoured as shortly as I possibly could to portray the arguments once again. They are portrayed in the memorandum which I have issued, and the Government of India's dispatch, which have led up to this Bill. I do not think the time has yet come for a similar movement in the Government of India. I think that there we must take the step of one stage only, namely, to make the Legislative Assembly more representative, to give it greater power of influencing and criticizing, but not, at this moment, of responsibility ; and we must make the Government of India itself more elastic in its composition, less stereotyped, by altering certain

I

of the statutory provisions which govern its executive formation. We must also add to its power of dealing with its own work, because we relieve it of the necessity of controlling a large number of provincial functions. In so far as the provincial Government has got to defer to its legislature by statute, that is to say in transferred subjects, you have a government which is responsible to the electorate. Therefore there is no necessity to control it by the Government of India and you get the devolution which the men who want to perfect administration desire. Therefore the Government of India will not be concerned, generally speaking, with transferred subjects, and the Secretary of State will not be concerned with transferred subjects. Therefore, this House will not be concerned with transferred subjects. Therefore, so far as transferred subjects are concerned, we shall have parted with our trusteeship and surrendered it to the representatives of the people of India. There is much more to be done with the Government of India. We have to release it from unnecessary administrative control by the India Office, and for that purpose, incidentally to this Bill, I am awaiting the details of Lord Crewe's Committee's Report, but so far as that is concerned, most of its recommendations, except as regards the composition of the Council, will be administrative and not statutory. At the same time, as was mentioned in the Joint Report, there is very much reason to believe that the secretariat system wants reconsideration and overhauling. I think it is understaffed, and I do not think it is modelled for the transaction of the complicated business which falls to the office at the present moment. The House will be glad to learn that Sir Herbert Llewellyn Smith, one of the most experienced British Civil Servants, has been good enough to accept my invitation, given to him on behalf of the Government of India, to visit India, to consider the secretariat arrangements in the Government of India, and Sir George Lloyd has also invited him to consider those of Bombay.

Colonel WEDGWOOD : Does that include the staffs of ministers who deal with transferred subjects, or will they arrange their own staffs ?

Mr. MONTAGU : Ultimately, of course, the ministers will arrange their own staffs, but I want them at the moment to take over their departments as going concerns. This question of the secretariat, however, is for the Government of India primarily, and nothing else.

Before I sit down, there are some very important matters with which I must deal. The first is that of the alternative schemes which have been presented and which have been rejected in this Bill. There is the Congress and Moslem-League scheme. I will not detain the House with the details of that. It was prepared before the pronouncement of the 20th August 1917. It does not attempt to realize responsible government, but it leaves an irremovable executive at the mercy of a legislature which can paralyse it but not direct it. I do not believe that this House will ever agree to set up a constitution in India which will leave an executive, that is not removable, at the mercy of a legislature which cannot control it. Much more formidable is another alternative proposal, which comes from the heads of the majority of the local governments. Although I cordially agree with the Government of India in rejecting this proposal, I hope the House will believe that I do not underestimate its importance. It is the work of no arm-chair critics. It is the work of the most experienced administrators in India. It is the work of men who are entitled above all others to have their opinions carefully weighed, and, although I believe them to be wrong and desire to show why I believe them to be wrong, and that we shall have to argue this in Committee, yet it is with no sense of disrespect to them that I challenge their conclusions. It is a powerful array. The Government of Madras had no part or share in the elaboration of this alternative proposal, nor had the Government of Bombay, but the heads of five local governments approved the alternative proposal. Yet the Governor of Bengal, Lord Ronaldshay, and the Lieutenant-Governor of Bihar and Orissa, Sir Edward Gait, preferred the scheme of the Bill and the Joint Report. That is the position. But although I do not want to discredit them, I want to suggest that really their views are accidental in this sense, that it must not be assumed that whatever the composition of those governments, and whoever had been their heads, the same results would have ensued. For instance, the Chief Commissioner for Assam prefers the scheme of the majority of local governments. But the late Chief Commissioner of Assam, who left only a few months previously—he came home about a year ago—would have preferred, I know, the scheme of the Joint Report and this Bill. The present Lieutenant-Governor of the United Provinces prefers the alternative scheme of the local governments, but his predecessor would have preferred the scheme of the Joint Report. A great deal depends upon personality.

But although these gentlemen are entitled to give a very weighty opinion, they are not unprejudiced. Where men have grown up under a system, they do not like to see it altered. Their proposal is the existing system with another man added to the Executive Council. Nothing much worse than the Morley-Minto scheme— an alleged unity of government, but no real unity of government, because one-half of the Government is in their own words ' necessarily influenced by the opinions of the Legislative Council ', and the other half not. And there is no certainty of control by the legislature because on all subjects, if the Governor certifies it is in the interests of his Province, he can override it. It is the same system with just another Indian member added to the Executive Council. Let me put it to this House. After all, the Civil Servant in India is not very different from the Civil Servant in this country. Whoever heard of a political reform in any office in this country coming out of the Civil Service. This House is the place for political reform. You will never get it carried out by the Civil Service. As time goes on, that service must carry out the wishes of those who dictate the policy. It must be first in this House, and ultimately in India, that that policy which the Civil Service is to carry out must be dictated to it.

Colonel YATE : Why did you send Sir Llewellyn Smith to make reforms in India ? Is he not a Civil Servant ?

Mr. MONTAGU : I am very much obliged to my hon. and gallant friend. His intervention in debate is always valuable. He has given me the opportunity of pointing my argument. I am using a Civil Servant to advise me on administrative changes as to how the secretariat can carry out most efficiently the orders and wishes of its political superiors. That is exactly the function of a Civil Servant. And this is what ultimately, when India is a self-governing country, I hope to see the position of the Civil Service. It is quite true that in what I have said about the local governments' alternative plan I have included Lord Willingdon, because, although he is not a Civil Servant, and although he has a plan of his own, he would, I am certain, have preferred the plan of the majority of local governments to the plan of the Bill. But then Lord Willingdon prefers to rely upon those qualities which he possesses, which made him an astonishing success in the Government of Bombay. He brings all the qualities that ensure for him great popularity and all the qualities which made him in this House a successful Whip. He says, in effect, under a Governor such as Lord Willingdon a more elastic arrangement would be far preferable to the arrangement of dyarchy of the Bill.

Under the scheme as we propose it to this House, if in any province a governor can so influence his advisers—and there are governors and governors, and lieutenant-governors and lieutenant-governors—if the circumstances of a particular province make it possible, there is nothing in the Bill which would prevent a governor trying to discharge all the reserved functions as if they were transferred. He can call his government together and say, ' I do not believe much in this dual form of government. Let us see if we cannot get on together. Unless I am driven to it I will use none of the powers given to me under this Bill. We will always consult together. I will do my best to work the scheme in deference to the wishes of the legislature on all subjects, and I will only use my exceptional powers on reserved subjects if I am compelled to.' Perhaps if he is lucky he will go through his term of office without being called upon to use them. Therefore, under my scheme, Lord Willingdon would get all he proposes in his letter. But suppose there is another governor, who says, ' I am not going to consult you. I like the good old way. I believe that good government, or what I think is good government, is far better than self-government, than the scheme under the Bill. I know what is good for you better than you know yourselves.' Under the scheme of the Bill, whatever the personality of the Governor, the transferred subjects are guaranteed to be representatives of the people. Under the alternative scheme, under the wide use of certification and of the local government majority, nothing is guaranteed to them at all. The time, I submit, is not one in which you can be content that certain members of your alleged united government should be ' necessarily influenced by the opinions of the Legislative Council '. What you want, if you are to launch India upon this road, is that the Government on certain subjects must respond to the wishes of the people. In other words, unless you have that, and more than the local governments suggest, then there is no progressive realization of responsible government.

Lastly, I come to the scheme of the Indo-British Association. This is a body which gets very angry

when I suggest that it does not intend to carry out
the pronouncement of the 20th August in any
adequate way, and it has done great harm in
India by leading people to suppose that it has more
influence on the decisions of Parliament than
I hope it is ever likely to have. What are its
proposals ? ' Financial delegation as between the
Secretary of State and the Government of India.'
As a matter of administration, they are in agreement with the Bill and with the Joint Report.
But that does not lead to any ·progressive realization of responsible government. ' The reorganization of the India Office intended not only to
remedy obsolete procedure, but to obtain more
recent knowledge of India.' They are in agreement
with the Joint Report on a matter of administration. They are suggesting the work on which
Lord Crewe's Committee is now engaged. But
that does not lead to the progressive realization
of responsible government. ' Decentralization in
India as between the Government of India and the
Provinces in domestic matters and the trans-
formation into a federal system.' Once again
they are in agreement with the Bill and with the
Joint Report. But that in itself does not lead them
any nearer to the progressive realization of responsible government. Then there are two points
about municipal and local government and elementary education. These are not constitutional
points at all. And then there comes their one
controversial and constructive programme. ' In
every Province place one or two districts in charge
of a wholly Indian official staff and extend that, if
it proves satisfactory, into a Division and finally
into a whole Province.' That scheme is a scheme

of bureaucrats for the consumption of bureaucrats, intended for the enthronement of bureaucracy. ' Let me, if I am in charge of a Province, be not controlled in any sense by my legislative councils.' I have got somewhere—I will refer to it if I am challenged—their qualifying statement ' that the powers of the provincial government are to remain unimpaired '. They are not to be interfered with by the Legislative Council or by the Government of India or by the India Office. In other words, the Lord Sydenhams of the future can remain upon their throne, untrammelled by control from above and undismayed by criticism from below. How is that to lead to the progressive realization of responsible government ?

Brigadier-General CROFT : Was he a successful Governor ?

Mr. MONTAGU : I do not want to express an opinion on that. His record is available. I am not concerned with the authorship. It does not matter who is the author. I am only concerned to test the programme and see whether it fulfils the policy of the progressive realization of responsible government. And when I find that the association puts forward a policy which pretends to carry out the pronouncement but which more or less involves bureaucracy, I am entitled to criticize with all the strength in my power. What is the use of ousting a British Civil Servant and replacing him by an Indian Civil Servant ? The district officer is the very backbone of the administrative machine. I venture to predict that the Indians themselves would be last to wish to see the complete disappearance of the district officer, but we do no good by establishing an Indian bureaucracy instead of an English bureaucrat. Of the two bureaucrats, having regard to his training, I infinitely prefer at the present moment the English bureaucrat. If that is the best alternative scheme addressed to this House, and if we really desire to carry out the pledges made to India, then it is far better to carry the Bill as it stands than to pay any attention to this scheme. We shall never get on with all the work that we have got to do in India unless we have settled, as this Bill will settle, the constitutional question and its interminable discussion. I say it 'will settle'. What I mean is that I hope we shall receive from the Joint Committee an agreed Bill, that all these alternative schemes will be considered in far more detail than is possible this afternoon, and that somehow or other a Statute will pass, as a consequence of the Second Reading this afternoon, which will launch India on the road to complete self-government. There is so much other work to do in India that if we can once get a growing constitution for it to win for itself that goal which we have pronounced, we can turn our attention to the spread of education—to the perfection or at least to the improvement of education—we can turn our attention to the development of her great resources and her great industries, we can consider the reorganization of her defences. But before we can do anything and in order to make these things possible it seems to me to be essential to start her on this road of self-government.

I implore this House to show to India to-day that Parliament is receptive of the case for self-government and only seeks an opportunity of completing it by the demonstrable realization of the success of its stages. There is too much race prejudice in India at the present time. It is beyond this House to correct it. It does not exist only in India ; it exists in South Africa too. But Parliament can help to correct it in the Constitution. If we hold on to power in India and stand fast to the policy of subordination, race friction will continue and ought to continue. If we surrender our trusteeship to the great provinces of India as speedily as they are ready to take it over, then Indians will have something better and more worth doing than fiercely and impotently to criticize those who are at present the agents of Parliament.

Perorations on Indian affairs have a tendency to great similarity ; at least the perorations of my speeches on Indian affairs always seem so. I cannot, however—and I say it once again—believe that Parliament is going to afford any obstacle to the partnership of India in the British Empire. We have recently been so sympathetic to the national aspirations of Arabs, of Czecho-Slovaks, of Serbs, of Croats, and of Slovenes. Here is a country desirous of achieving nationality once again, I repeat, an original member of the League of Nations, developed under our protecting care, imbued to a greater and greater degree with our political thought. Let us pass this Bill and start it, under the aegis of the British flag, on the road which we ourselves have travelled, despite all the acknowledged difficulties of area, of caste, of religion, of race and of education. If you do that, if you pass this Bill and modify it until it becomes a great Statute, I can say—we can say—as I should like to say with the authority of the House to the peoples of India, ' The future and the date upon which you realize the future goal of self-government are with you. You are being given great responsibility to-day, and the opportunities of consultation and influence on other matters in which for thé present we keep responsibility. You will find in Parliament every desire to help and to complete the task which this Bill attempts, if you devote yourselves to use with wisdom, with self-restraint, with respect for minorities, the great opportunities with which Parliament is entrusting you.' That is the message which it seems to me— I say it with all deference—this House should send to the Indian peoples to-day, when you are start-ing to fulfil the pronouncement of the 20th of August. That message cannot be sent unless the House is determined to pass without delay, and with every desire that it should be improved before it is passed, a Statute which means the beginning of self-government, responsible government, in the Indian Empire.

10. Report of the Joint Select Committee on the Government of India Bill, 17 November, 1919

5. HAVING weighed the evidence and informa-tion before them, the Committee have made a number of changes in the Bill. Those of a more detailed or miscellaneous character are briefly discussed below under the clauses to which they relate. Those which are directed to the avoidance of the difficulties and dangers which have been pointed out, proceed on a simple and, in the Com-mittee's opinion, an indefeasible theory. That theory the Committee think it desirable to state at once. Ministers who enjoy the confidence of a

majority in their Legislative Council will be given the fullest opportunity of managing that field of government which is entrusted to their care.   In their work they will be assisted and guided by the Governor, who will accept their advice and promote their policy whenever possible.   If he finds himself compelled to act against their advice, it will only be in circumstances roughly analogous to those in which he has to override his Executive Council —circumstances which will be indicated in the Instrument of Instructions furnished to him on his appointment by His Majesty.   On the other hand, in and for that field of government in which Parliament continues to hold him responsible, the Provincial Governor in Council will remain equipped with the sure and certain power of fulfilling that responsibility.   The Committee will indicate in the course of this Report how they visualize the relations between the two parts of the provincial government, but they wish to place in the forefront of the Report their opinion that they see no reason why the relations should not be harmonious and mutually advantageous.   They regard it as of the highest importance that the Governor should foster the habit of free consultation between both halves of his Government, and indeed that he should insist upon it in all important matters of common interest.   He will thus ensure that ministers will contribute their knowledge of the people's wishes and susceptibilities, and the members of his Executive Council their administrative experience, to the joint wisdom of the Government.   But while the Committee anticipate much advantage from amicable and, as far as possible, spontaneous association for purposes of deliberation, they would not allow it to confuse the duties or obscure the separate responsibility which will rest on the two parts of the administration. Each side of the government will advise and assist the other; neither will control or impede the other. The responsibility for administrative and legislative action in their own field will be fixed beyond possibility of doubt on ministers and on the majorities of the provincial legislatures which support them; and they will be given adequate power to fulfil their charge. Similarly within that field for which he remains accountable to Parliament, the responsibility for action must be fixed on the Governor in Council, and he must possess unfailing means for the discharge of his duties. Finally, behind the provincial authorities stands the Government of India.

6. The change which this Bill will make in the political structure and life of India is very important. It marks a great step in the path of self-government, and it is a proof of the confidence reposed by His Majesty's Government in the loyalty, wisdom, and capacity of our Indian fellow subjects. At the same time it points to the desirability of keeping Parliament in closer touch with Indian affairs than has recently been possible. The Committee accordingly propose that a Standing Joint Committee should be appointed by both Houses of Parliament for that purpose. It should have no statutory functions, but a purely advisory and consultative status; and among its tasks is one of high importance, the consideration of amendments to rules made under this Bill. For the plan on which the Bill has been drafted, and in the opinion of the Committee rightly drafted,

will necessitate the completion of some of its main
provisions by a large number of rules and other
documents which will have to be framed before the
machinery established by the Bill can come into
working order. Many of these rules and documents will be drafted in India for the approval
of the Secretary of State. When they come to
England it may be found convenient that the
present Committee be reappointed to advise
Parliament in regard to them.

7. The Committee will now proceed to indicate
the nature of the changes they have made in the
Bill, and also their suggestions for action to be
taken under it, either in the framing of rules or by
executive process hereafter.

PREAMBLE

... The Committee have enlarged the preamble so
as to include all parts of the announcement of the
20th August 1917. Their reason for doing so is
that an attempt has been made to distinguish
between the parts of this announcement, and to
attach a different value to each part according to
opinion. It has been said, for instance, that whereas
the first part is a binding pledge, the later part
is a mere expression of opinion of no importance.
But the Committee think that it is of the utmost
importance, from the very inauguration of these
constitutional changes, that Parliament should
make it quite plain that the responsibility for the
successive stages of the development of self-government in India rests on itself and on itself alone,
and that it cannot share this responsibility with,
much less delegate it to, the newly elected legislatures of India.

They also desire to emphasize the wisdom and justice of an increasing association of Indians with every branch of the administration, but they wish to make it perfectly clear that His Majesty's Government must remain free to appoint Europeans to those posts for which they are specially required and qualified.

PART I

Clause 1.—The Committee wish to take this opportunity of acknowledging the debt they owe to the work of the two Committees on Franchise and Functions presided over by Lord Southborough. If they are not able to accept all the conclusions of these Committees, and if they recommend some additional provisions to those included in those reports, it does not mean that they are not very sensible of the value of the work done, without which, indeed, this constitutional change could not have been effected.

The lists of central, provincial, and transferred subjects included in the Functions Committee's Report have been somewhat altered after consultation with the India Office (*see* Appendix F *to the Minutes of Evidence*); and as so amended they are accepted by this Committee, subject to certain general observations at the end of this Report. It must not, however, be concluded that these partitions of the functions of government are absolutely clear-cut and mutually exclusive. They must in all cases be read with the reservations in the text of the Functions Committee's Report, and with due regard to the necessity for special procedure in cases where their orbits overlap.

The Committee have given much attention to

the difficult question of the principle on which the provincial revenues and balances should be distributed between the two sides of the provincial governments. They are confident that the problem can readily be solved by the simple process of common sense and reasonable give-and-take, but they are aware that this question might, in certain circumstances, become the cause of much friction in the provincial government, and they are of opinion that the rules governing the allocation of these revenues and balances should be framed so as to make the existence of such friction impossible. They advise that if the Governor, in the course of preparing either his first or any subsequent budget, finds that there is likely to be a serious or protracted difference of opinion between the Executive Council and his ministers on this subject, he should be empowered at once to make an allocation of revenue and balances between the reserved and transferred subjects, which should continue for at least the whole life of the existing Legislative Council. The Committee do not endorse the suggestion that certain sources of revenue should be allocated to reserved, and certain sources to transferred subjects, but they recommend that the Governor should allocate a definite proportion of the revenue, say, by way of illustration, two-thirds to reserved and one-third to transferred subjects, and similarly a proportion, though not necessarily the same fraction, of the balances. If the Governor desires assistance in making the allocation, he should be allowed at his discretion to refer the question to be decided to such authority as the Governor-General shall appoint. Further, the Committee are of opinion that it should be laid down from the first that, until an agreement which both sides of the Government will equally support has been reached, or until an allocation has been made by the Governor, the total provisions of the different expenditure heads in the budget of the Province for the preceding financial year shall hold good.

The Committee desire that the relation of the two sides of the Government in this matter, as in all others, should be of such mutual sympathy that each will be able to assist and influence for the common good the work of the other, but not to exercise control over it. The budget should not be capable of being used as a means for enabling ministers or a majority of the Legislative Council to direct the policy of reserved subjects ; but on the other hand the Executive Council should be helpful to ministers in their desire to develop the departments entrusted to their care. On the Governor personally will devolve the task of holding the balance between the legitimate needs of both sets of his advisers.

Clause 2.—This clause has been inserted to regularize the raising of loans by local governments on the special security of their own provincial revenues.

Clause 3.—The question has been raised as to the communications between the Governors of Provinces and the Secretary of State.[1] The question as to whether such communications shall in future take place, and as to the procedure to be adopted in them, may well be left to the Secretary of State. In the opinion of the Committee there is no cause at present for disturbing the existing

---

[1] See Parl. Papers Cmd. 123, p. 12 ; Cmd. 207, p. 45.

position, except to the extent to which the Secretary of State relaxes his powers of direction and control over local governments. To that extent the Government of India will also withdraw from intervention ; but India is not yet ripe for a true federal system, and the central government cannot be relegated to functions of mere inspection and advice. The Committee trust that there will be an extensive delegation, statutory and otherwise, to provincial governments of some powers and duties now in the hands of the Government of India ; and they trust also that the control of that Government over provincial matters will be exercised with a view to preparing the provinces for the gradual transfer of power to the provincial government and legislature.

Clause 4.—The Committee are of opinion that the ministers selected by the Governor to advise him on the transferred subjects should be elected members of the Legislative Council, enjoying its confidence and capable of leading it. A minister will have the option of resigning if his advice is not accepted by the Governor ; and the Governor will have the ordinary constitutional right of dismissing a minister whose policy he believes to be either seriously at fault or out of accord with the views of the Legislative Council. In the last resort the Governor can always dissolve his Legislative Council and choose new ministers after a fresh election ; but if this course is adopted the Committee hope that the Governor will find himself able to accept such views as his new ministers may press upon him regarding the issue which forced the dissolution. The Committee are of opinion that in no province will there be need for less than two ministers, while in some provinces more will be required. In these circumstances they think that it should be recognized from the commencement that ministers may be expected to act in concert together. They probably would do so ; and in the opinion of the Committee it is better that they should, and therefore that the fact should be recognized on the face of the Bill. They advise that the status of ministers should be similar to that of the members of the Executive Council, but that their salaries should be fixed by the Legislative Council. Later on in this Report it will be suggested that Indian members of the Council of India in London should be paid a higher scale of remuneration than those members of the Council domiciled in the United Kingdom. The same principle might suggest to the Legislative Council that it was reasonable for the ministers of the provincial government domiciled in India to be paid on a lower scale of remuneration than the European members.

Provision has been made in this clause for the appointment, at the Governor's discretion, of non-official members of the Legislative Council to fill a rôle somewhat similar to that of the Parliamentary Under-Secretary in this country.

Clause 5.—The Committee are of opinion that the normal strength of an Executive Council, especially in the smaller provinces, need not exceed two members. They have not, however, reduced the existing statutory maximum of four ; but if in any case the Council includes two members with service qualifications, neither of whom is by birth an Indian, they think that it should also include two unofficial Indian members.

Clause 6.—The Committee desire at this point to give a picture of the manner in which they think that, under this Bill, the government of a Province should be worked. There will be many matters of administrative business, as in all countries, which can be disposed of departmentally ; but there will remain a large category of business, of the character which would naturally be the subject of Cabinet consultation. In regard to this category the Committee conceive that the habit should be carefully fostered of joint deliberation between the members of the Executive Council and the ministers, sitting under the chairmanship of the Governor. There cannot be too much mutual advice and consultation on such subjects, but the Committee attach the highest importance to the principle that, when once opinions have been freely exchanged and the last word has been said, there ought then to be no doubt whatever as to where the responsibility for the decision lies. Therefore, in the opinion of the Committee, after such consultation, and when it is clear that the decision lies within the jurisdiction of one or other half of the Government, that decision in respect of a reserved subject should be recorded separately by the Executive Council, and in respect of a transferred subject by the ministers, and all acts and proceedings of the Government should state in definite terms on whom the responsibility for the decision rests. It will not always, however, be clear, otherwise than in a purely departmental and technical fashion, with whom the jurisdiction lies in the case of questions of common interest. In such cases it will be inevitable for the Governor to occupy the position of informal arbitrator between the two parts of his administration ; and it will equally be his duty to see that a decision arrived at on one side of his government is followed by such consequential action on the other side as may be necessary to make the policy effective and homogeneous.

The position of the Governor will thus be one of great responsibility and difficulty, and also of great opportunity and honour. He may have to hold the balance between divergent policies and different ideals, and to prevent discord and friction. It will also be for him to help with sympathy and courage the popular side of his government in their new responsibilities. He should never hesitate to point out to ministers what he thinks is the right course or to warn them if he thinks they are taking the wrong course. But if, after hearing all the arguments, ministers should decide not to adopt his advice, then, in the opinion of the Committee, the Governor should ordinarily allow ministers to have their way, fixing the responsibility upon them, even if it may subsequently be necessary for him to veto any particular piece of legislation. It is not possible but that in India, as in all other countries, mistakes will be made by ministers, acting with the approval of a majority of the Legislative Council, but there is no way of learning except through experience and by the realization of responsibility.

In the debates of the Legislative Council members of the Executive Council should act together and ministers should act together, but members of the Executive Council and ministers should not oppose each other by speech or vote ; members of the Executive Council should not be required to support

either by speech or vote proposals of ministers of
which they do not approve, nor should ministers
be required to support by speech or vote proposals
of the Executive Council of which they do not
approve ; they should be free to speak and vote
for each other's proposals when they are in agreement with them. All other official members of the
Legislative Council should be free to speak and vote
as they choose.

Clause 7.—The Committee have altered the
first schedule to the Bill, so as to show only the
total strength of the Legislative Council in each
Province. They have retained the provision, now
in sub-clause (2), that at least 70 per cent. of the
members shall be elected, and not more than 20
per cent. shall be officials. This general stipulation
will govern the distribution of the seats in each
Province ; but in certain respects the detailed
arrangements will require further consideration,
and proposals should be called for from the
Government of India in regard to them. . . .

Clause 9.—The Committee have considered
carefully the question who is to preside over the
Legislative Councils in the provinces. They are
of opinion that the Governor should not preside,
and they advise that, for a period of four years,
the President should be appointed by the Governor.
Wherever possible it would be a great advantage
if some one could be found for this purpose who
had had parliamentary experience. The Legislative
Council should itself elect a Vice-President, and at
the end of four years the nominated President
would disappear, and the President and Vice-
President would be elected by the councils. The
Committee attribute the greatest importance to

this question of the Presidency of the Legislative Council. It will, in their opinion, conduce very greatly to the successful working of the new councils if they are imbued from the commencement with the spirit and conventions of parliamentary procedure as developed in the Imperial Parliament. The Committee will recur to this subject in dealing with the question of the President of the Legislative Assembly of India.

Clause 11.—The Committee think that the provincial budget should be submitted to the vote of the Legislative Council, subject to the exemption from this process of certain charges of a special or recurring character which have been set out in the Bill. In cases where the Council alter the provision for a transferred subject, the Committee consider that the Governor would be justified, if so advised by his ministers, in resubmitting the provision to the Council for a review of their former decision ; but they do not apprehend that any statutory prescription to that effect is required. Where the Council have reduced a provision for a reserved subject which the Governor considers essential to the proper administration of the subject concerned, he will have a power of restoration. The Committee wish it to be perfectly clear that this power is real and that its exercise should not be regarded as unusual or arbitrary ; unless the Governor has the right to secure supply for those services for which he remains responsible to Parliament, that responsibility cannot justly be fastened upon him.

Whenever the necessity for new taxation arises, as arise it must, the questions involved should be threshed out by both parts of the Government in consultation together, and it is especially important that in this matter both parts of the Government should, if possible, be in agreement when the proposals of the Government are laid before the legislature.

Clause 13.—The Committee have rejected the plan of Grand Committees as drafted originally in the Bill. They have done so because in their opinion the Grand Committee did not give the Governor the power of securing legislation in a crisis in respect of those matters for which he is held responsible, and because in respect of ordinary legislation about reserved subjects it perpetuated the system of securing legislation by what is known as the 'official bloc', which has been the cause of great friction and heartburning. The responsibility for legislation on reserved subjects is with the Governor in Council, and, when the 'official bloc' has been put into operation, it has been put into operation by him, and is merely an indirect way of asserting his responsibility. The Committee think it much better that there should be no attempt to conceal the fact that the responsibility is with the Governor in Council, and they recommend a process by which the Governor should be empowered to pass an Act in respect of any reserved subject, if he considers that the Act is necessary for the proper fulfilment of his responsibility to Parliament. He should not do so until he has given every opportunity for the matter to be thoroughly discussed in the Legislative Council, and as a sensible man he should, of course, endeavour to carry the Legislative Council with him in the matter by the strength of his case. But if he finds that cannot be so, then he should have the power to proceed on his own responsibility. Acts passed on his sole responsibility should be reserved by the Governor-General for His Majesty's pleasure, and be laid before Parliament. His Majesty will necessarily be advised by the Secretary of State for India, and the responsibility for the advice to be given to His Majesty can only rest with the Secretary of State. But the Committee suggest that the Standing Committee of Parliament, whose appointment they have advised, should be specially consulted about Acts of this character. Provision, however, is made in the Bill for the avoidance of delay in case of a grave emergency by giving the Governor-General power to assent to the Act without reserving it, though this, of course, would not prevent subsequent disallowance by His Majesty in Council.

Clause 15.—The Committee have two observations to make on the working of this Clause. On the one hand, they do not think that any change in the boundaries of a Province should be made without due consideration of the views of the Legislative Council of the Province. On the other hand, they are of opinion that any clear request made by a majority of the members of a Legislative Council representing a distinctive racial or linguistic territorial unit for its constitution under this Clause, as a sub-province or a separate province, should be taken as a prima facie case on the strength of which a commission of inquiry might be appointed by the Secretary of State, and that it should not be a bar to the appointment of such a commission of inquiry that the majority of the Legislative Council of theProvince in question is opposed to the request of the minority representing such a distinctive territorial unit.

PART II

Clause 18.—As will be explained below, the Committee do not accept the device, in the Bill as drafted, of carrying government measures through the Council of State without reference to the Legislative Assembly, in cases where the latter body cannot be got to assent to a law which the Governor-General considers essential. Under the scheme which the Committee propose to substitute for this procedure, there is no necessity to retain the Council of State as an organ for government legislation. It should therefore be reconstituted from the commencement as a true Second Chamber. They recommend that it should consist of sixty members, of whom not more than twenty should be official members. The Franchise Committee advise that the non-official members should be elected by the same group of persons as elect the members of the Legislative Assembly and in the same constituencies. This is a plan which the Committee could, in no circumstances, accept. They hope and believe that a different system of election for the Council of State can be devised by the time the constitution embodied in this Bill comes into operation, and they recommend that the Government of India be enjoined forthwith to make suggestions accordingly, to which effect can be given without delaying the inauguration of the new constitution. If the advice of the Committee that it be reappointed for the purpose of considering the rules to be framed under this Bill be approved, it should have an opportunity of considering the proposals made for the election of the Council of State.

Clause 19.—For the Legislative Assembly the Committee are equally unwilling to accept, as a permanent arrangement, the method of indirect election proposed in the report of the Franchise Committee. If by no other course it were possible to avoid delay in bringing the constitution enacted by the Bill into operation, the Committee would acquiesce in that method for a preliminary period of three years. But they are not convinced that delay would be involved in preparing a better scheme of election, and they endorse the views expressed by the Government of India in paragraph 39 of its dispatch dealing with the subject. They accordingly advise that the Government of India be instructed at once to make recommendations to this effect at the earliest possible moment. These recommendations as embodied in draft rules would also be subject to examination by this Committee if reappointed.

Clause 20.—The Committee think that the President of the Legislative Assembly should for four years be a person appointed by the Governor-General. He should be qualified by experience in the House of Commons and a knowledge of parliamentary procedure, precedents, and conventions. He should be the guide and adviser of the Presidents of the Provincial Councils, and he should be chosen with a view to the influence which it is hoped he would have on the whole history of parliamentary procedure in India. He should be paid an adequate salary.

Clause 25.—This is a new provision for the submission of the Indian Budget to the vote of the Legislative Assembly, on the understanding that this body is constituted as a chamber reasonably representative in character and elected directly by suitable constituencies. The Committee consider it necessary (as suggested to them by the consolidated fund charges in the Imperial Parliament) to exempt certain charges of a special or recurring nature, which have been set out in the Bill, e.g. the cost of defence, the debt charges, and certain fixed salaries, from the process of being voted. But otherwise they would leave the Assembly free to criticize and vote the estimates of expenditure of the Government of India.[1] It is not, however, within the scheme of the Bill to introduce at the present stage any measure of responsible government into the central administration, and a power must be reserved to the Governor-General in Council of treating as sanctioned any expenditure which the Assembly may have refused to vote if he considers the expenditure to be necessary for the fulfilment of his responsibilities for the good government of the country. It should be understood from the beginning that this power of the Governor-General in Council is real, and that it is meant to be used if and when necessary.

Clause 26.—For reasons which prompted their rejection of the process of certification by a Governor to a grand committee in a Province, the Committee are opposed to the proposals in the Bill which would have enabled the Governor-General to refer to the Council of State, and to obtain by virtue of his official majority in that body any legislation which the lower chamber refuse to accept, but which he regards as essential to the discharge of his duties. The Committee have no hesitation in accepting the view that the

[1] Cf. Cmd. 207, pp. 41-3.

Governor-General in Council should in all circumstances be fully empowered to secure legislation
which is required for the discharge of his responsibilities ; but they think it is unworthy that such
responsibility should be concealed through the
action of a Council of State specially devised in
its composition to secure the necessary powers.
They believe that in such á case it would add
strength to the Government of India to act before
the world on its own responsibility.   In order,
however, that Parliament may be fully apprised
of the position and of the considerations which
led to this exceptional procedure, they advise that
all Acts passed in this manner should be laid
before Parliament, who would naturally consider
the opinion of the Standing Committee already
referred to.

Clause 28.—The recommendation of the Committee is that the present limitation on the
number of the members of the Governor-General's
Executive Council should be removed, that three
members of that Council should continue to be
public servants or ex-public servants who have
had not less than ten years' experience in the
service of the Crown in India ; that one member of
the Council should have definite legal qualifications,
but that those qualifications may be gained in
India as well as in the United Kingdom ; and that
not less than three members of the Council should
be Indians.   In this connexion it must be borne in
mind that the members of the Council drawn
from the ranks of the public servants will, as time
goes on, be more and more likely to be of Indian
rather than of European extraction.

Clause 29.—The Committee have inserted this

provision to allow of the selection of members of the legislature who will be able to undertake duties similar to those of the Parliamentary Under Secretaries in this country. It should be entirely at the discretion of the Governor-General to say to which departments these officers should be attached, and to define the scope of their duties.

PART III

Clause 30.—The Committee think that all charges of the India Office, not being ' agency ' charges, should be paid out of moneys to be provided by Parliament.

Clause 31.—The Committee are not in favour of the abolition of the Council of India.[1] They think that, at any rate for some time to come, it will be absolutely necessary that the Secretary of State should be advised by persons of Indian experience, and they are convinced that, if no such Council existed, the Secretary of State would have to form an informal one if not a formal one. Therefore they think it much better to continue a body which has all the advantages behind it of tradition and authority, although they would not debar the readjustment of its work so as to make it possible to introduce what is known as the portfolio system. They think, also, that its constitution may advantageously be modified by the introduction of more Indians into it and by shortening of the period of the service upon it, in order to ensure

---

[1] This was recommended by Lord Crewe's Committee on the Home Administration of Indian Affairs, Majority Report (Cmd. 207, pp. 9–11), which recommended an Advisory Committee instead; objections were raised by members of that Committee, see pp. 32, 33, 48–52.

a continuous flow of fresh experience from India and to relieve Indian members from the necessity of spending so long a period as seven years in England.

Clause 33.—The Committee have given most careful consideration to the relations of the Secretary of State with the Government of India, and through it with the provincial governments. In the relations of the Secretary of State with the Governor-General in Council the Committee are not of opinion that any statutory change can be made, so long as the Governor-General remains responsible to Parliament; but in practice the conventions which now govern these relations may wisely be modified to meet fresh circumstances caused by the creation of a Legislative Assembly with a large elected majority. In the exercise of his responsibility to Parliament, which he cannot delegate to any one else, the Secretary of State may reasonably consider that only in exceptional circumstances should he be called upon to intervene in matters of purely Indian interest where the Government and the Legislature of India are in agreement.

This examination of the general proposition leads inevitably to the consideration of one special case of non-intervention. Nothing is more likely to endanger the good relations between India and Great Britain than a belief that India's fiscal policy is dictated from Whitehall in the interests of the trade of Great Britain. That such a belief exists at the moment there can be no doubt. That there ought to be no room for it in the future is equally clear. India's position in the Imperial Conference opened the door to negotiation between India and the rest of the Empire, but negotiation without power to legislate is likely to remain ineffective. A satisfactory solution of the question can only be guaranteed by the grant of liberty to the Government of India to devise those tariff arrangements which seem best fitted to India's needs as an integral portion of the British Empire. It cannot be guaranteed by statute without limiting the ultimate power of Parliament to control the administration of India, and without limiting the power of veto which rests in the Crown ; and neither of these limitations finds a place in any of the Statutes in the British Empire. It can only therefore be assured by an acknowledgement of a convention. Whatever be the right fiscal policy for India, for the needs of her consumers as well as for her manufacturers, it is quite clear that she should have the same liberty to consider her interests as Great Britain, Australia, New Zealand, Canada, and South Africa. In the opinion of the Committee, therefore, the Secretary of State should as far as possible avoid interference on this subject when the Government of India and its Legislature are in agreement, and they think that his intervention, when it does take place, should be limited to safeguarding the international obligations of the Empire or any fiscal arrangements within the Empire to which His Majesty's Government is a party.[1]

The relations of the Secretary of State and of the Government of India with provincial governments should, in the Committee's judgement, be regulated by similar principles, so far as the reserved subjects are concerned. It follows, therefore, that in purely provincial matters, which are

---

[1] Cf. Cmd. 207, pp. 41, 42.

K

reserved, where the provincial government and legislature are in agreement, their view should ordinarily be allowed to prevail, though it is necessary to bear in mind the fact that some reserved subjects do cover matters in which the central government is closely concerned. Over transferred subjects, on the other hand, the control of the Governor-General in Council, and thus of the Secretary of State, should be restricted in future within the narrowest possible limits, which will be defined by rules under sub-clause 3 of Clause 1 of the Bill.

Rules under this clause will be subsidiary legislation of sufficient moment to justify their being brought especially to the notice of Parliament. The Secretary of State might conveniently discuss them with the Standing Committee whose creation has been recommended in this Report ; and Parliament would no doubt consider the opinion of this body when the rules come, as it is proposed that they should do, for acceptance by positive resolution in both Houses. The same procedure is recommended by the Committee for adoption in the case of rules of special or novel importance under other clauses of the Bill. It must be for the Secretary of State to decide which of the many rules that will fall to be drafted by the Government of India can be sufficiently dealt with by the ordinary process of lying on the table of Parliament for a certain number of days. In deciding this point, however, he may naturally have recourse to the advice of the Standing Committee, should it happen to be in session, and obtain their assistance in determining which rules deserve to be made the subject of the more formal procedure by positive resolution.

Clause 35.—This clause carries out the recommendation of Lord Crewe's Committee to appoint a High Commissioner for India, to be paid out of Indian revenues, who will perform for India functions of agency, as distinguished from political functions, analogous to those now performed in the offices of the High Commissioners of the Dominions.

PART IV

Clause 36.—The Committee do not conceal from themselves that the position of the public services in working the new constitutions in the provinces will, in certain circumstances, be difficult. They are of opinion that these services have deserved the admiration and gratitude of the whole Empire. They know that some members of the services regard the wisdom of the proposed changes with grave misgiving, and that some fear that those changes will not tend to the welfare of the Indian masses. They are convinced, however, that the services will accept the changing conditions and the inevitable alteration in their own position, and devote themselves in all loyalty to making a success, so far as in them lies, of the new constitution.

In the provinces, officers serving in a reserved department will be controlled by the Governor in Council, and in a transferred department by the Governor acting with ministers, but in both cases alike the personal concurrence of the Governor should be regarded as essential in the case of all orders of any importance prejudicially affecting the position or prospects of officers appointed by the Secretary of State.

The Committee think that every precaution should be taken to secure to the public servants the career in life to which they looked forward when they were recruited, and they have introduced fresh provisions into this clause to that end. If friction occurs, a re-adjustment of persons and places may often get over the difficulty, and the Governor must always regard it as one of his most important duties to establish a complete understanding between his ministers and the officers through whom they will have to work. But if there are members of the service whose doubts as to the changes to be made are so deeply-rooted that they feel they cannot usefully endeavour to take part in them, then the Committee think it would only be fair to those officers that they should be offered an equivalent career elsewhere, if it is in the power of His Majesty's Government to do so, or, in the last resort, that they should be allowed to retire on such pension as the Secretary of State in Council may consider suitable to their period of service.

PART V

Clause 41.—The Committee are of opinion that the Statutory Commission should not be appointed until the expiration of ten years, and that no changes of substance in the constitution, whether in the franchise or in the lists of reserved and transferred subjects or otherwise, should be made in the interval. The Commission will be fully empowered to examine the workings of the constitutions in all their details in the provinces, and to advise whether the time has come for full responsible government in each province, or in the alternative whether and to what extent the powers of self-government already granted should be extended, or modified, or restricted. It should be clearly understood, also, that the Commission should be empowered to examine into the working of the Government of India and to advise in respect of the Government of India no less than in respect of the provincial governments. . . .

11. The Committee are impressed by the objections raised by many witnesses to the manner in which certain classes of taxation can be laid upon the people of India by executive action without, in some cases, any statutory limitation of the rates and, in other cases, any adequate prescription by statute of the methods of assessment. They consider that the imposition of new burdens should be gradually brought more within the purview of the Legislature. And in particular, without expressing any judgement on the question whether the land revenue is a rent or tax, they advise that the process of revising the land revenue assessments ought to be brought under closer regulation by statute as soon as possible. At present the statutory basis for charging revenue on the land varies in different provinces ; but in some at least the pitch of assessment is entirely at the discretion of the executive government. No branch of the administration is regulated with greater elaboration or care ; but the people who are most affected have no voice in the shaping of the system, and the rules are often obscure and imperfectly understood by those who pay the revenue. The Committee are of opinion that the time has come to embody in the law the main principles by which the land revenue is determined,

the methods of valuation, the pitch of assessment, the periods of revision, the graduation of enhancements, and the other chief processes which touch the well-being of the revenue-payers. The subject is one which probably would not be transferred to ministers until the electorate included a satisfactory representation of rural interests, those of the tenantry as well as of the landlords ; and the system should be established on a clear statutory basis before this change takes place.

12. The Committee have not hitherto touched on the subject of education in India, and it is far too large for them to make any attempt to deal with it adequately: They have accepted the recommendation of the Functions Committee that, subject to certain reservations about the Universities, the responsibility for the whole field of education in each province should be transferred to ministers. They attach much importance, however, to the educational advancement of the depressed and backward classes, and they trust that the subject will receive special attention from ministers. They are also impressed by the advantage of Boards such as Sir Michael Sadler has advised in Bengal, for the assistance of ministers in controlling the different grades of education, and they trust that ministers will see their way from the outset to constitute such Boards in every province. The Committee would similarly commend to ministers the advisability of creating local government departments in the provinces.

13. The Committee attach the greatest importance to the formation in each provincial government of a strong department of Finance which will serve both sides of the Government alike.

11. *William Adamson, House of Commons, 5 December, 1919*

THE political consciousness of India has been awakening within recent years, and her people have been pressing for reforms. All the evidence goes to confirm the idea that that pressure will continue until her people are able to obtain complete self-government. That is a very legitimate aspiration on the part of the Indian people, and it embodies one of the principles which have been brought into great prominence in the course of the world conflict from which we are just emerging. The aim of the best type of British statesmen who have interested themselves in the government of our great Indian Dependency has been to lead her people up by gradual stages to a position in which they would be able to exercise the full rights and responsibilities of citizenship within the Empire, a position in which they would be able to exercise all the duties and responsibilities of self-government. How this can best be accomplished is the problem which faces the House and the people of this country to-day, and I hope we are going to discharge that great responsibility in such a way as will assist the people of India to build up a strong united nation, well able to exercise all the duties of self-government. In August, 1917, the present Government, in declaring its policy regarding the future government of India, indicated that they were in complete sympathy with the progressive realization of this aim, and this Bill has been brought forward with that object in view. The Labour party are prepared

to admit that the Bill is a definite move in the
right direction, our principal criticism being that
it does not go far enough, and that we are failing
to take the fullest advantage of the help of the
people of India themselves to assist us in the
successful accomplishment of the great task we
have in hand. The Bill gives to the people of India
a measure of control in the various Provinces, but
no real control in the Central Government. This is
a mistake and will rob us of the sympathetic co-
operation of some of the best elements of the population of India.

We also regret the very limited franchise which
this Bill provides. There may be practical
difficulties in the way of the full enfranchisement
of the people of India at this juncture, but on the
face of it it is absurd that only 5,000,000 out of
a total population of 250,000,000 have been
enfranchised by this Bill. Especially do we
regret that the industrial workers are entirely
excluded. There might have been something to
have been said for the exceptional treatment of
the industrial workers of India if there had been no
industrial problems facing her people and demand-
ing solutions at their hands, but the industrial
development of our great Indian Dependency has
provided a considerable crop of industrial problems.
While we are glad to note that the industrial
workers of India are beginning to build up a trade-
union movement, whereby they will be able to protect their conditions of employment in the coming
days, we are disappointed that in this Bill we have
failed to provide the Indian working class movement with that political safety valve which has
been provided in our own and other industrial
countries. We are fully aware of the great value

that political freedom has been to our own nation. It has given the working classes an alternative to direct action, and an opportunity of working out their own destinies along constitutional lines, along the lines of evolution and against revolution, and the working classes of this country have taken full advantage of that opportunity. They have used that alternative to the greatest possible degree. To such an extent is that the case that there is a strong probability that Labour will assume the responsibilities of government in this country in the not distant future. That is an opportunity which you are denying to the industrial worker of India, and you force him back upon the alternative to that, namely, direct action. In our opinion that is a profound mistake, which may prove very costly to the Empire and to the people of India themselves. We regret also the exclusion of the women of India from the opportunity of standing on a political equality with the men. Our experience in this country, especially within the last five years, has taught us the great value of men and women facing the problems of national life together. Notwithstanding the defects, from our point of view, of this Bill, however, as a party we welcome the measure as a step in the right direction. We hope it will prove a success, and so justify a further instalment of political power at no distant date. I hope the people of India themselves will accept the measure in the right spirit as a step towards the realization of their ideals of self-government, and will do their best to make it a success, and so inspire the people of this country with the necessary confidence to trust them with a much larger measure of self-government in the very near future.

12. *Lord Carmichael, House of Lords, 12 December, 1919*

MY LORDS, I moved the adjournment of the Debate last night on behalf of Lord Harris, who, however, is not able to be present, so I will now make the few remarks that I desire to offer. I think I am entitled to say something, as it is not very long since I was a Governor of a Presidency in India. Some of your Lordships who know about recent affairs in India probably look upon me as holding views on the subject of this Bill which may be considered rather advanced—probably more advanced than those of most members of your Lordships' House ; and I admit that this certainly is the case, although I trust that your Lordships will believe me when I say that the views I do hold are views of the correctness of which I am perfectly convinced.

I dare say if I had not gone to India at the time when I did, or if I had gone to another part of India, I should not hold these views. I am not surprised that most members of this House do not look at these things quite as I do, because, if I had never been in India, or if I had gone to India before the passing of the Morley-Minto reforms—and I think even if I had not gone to India before the visit of the King-Emperor—I should not have thought as I do now. I am inclined to believe that if I had stayed on in Madras, where I first went as Governor, and ·had not gone to Bengal, I might have looked at things rather differently, and I probably should not have taken the view that, even if this Bill had gone a good deal farther than

LORD CARMICHAEL, 1919267

it does go, it should not be opposed, on general principles at any rate. That is the point of view from which I look at the Bill, and I congratulate my noble friend the Under-Secretary of State for India (Lord Sinha) on the present form in which the Bill is ; and, were he here I should congratulate my noble friend the Earl of Selborne and his colleagues on the form which has been adopted as the result of their labours on the Joint Committee.

I do not pretend that I look upon the Bill as a perfect Bill—I certainly do not. If it were any use I should make criticisms on some matters on which probably most members of this House would agree with me. I do not love the idea of the dyarchy any more, I think probably, than most members of this House, or most of those who have any knowledge of Indian administration. But I realize that no other alternative has been offered. Looking at it simply from the point of view of my own experience as a Governor in India, I believe there are just as many good arguments to be used against a scheme put forward by certain Lieutenant-Governors as there are to be used against the idea of the dyarchy. In any case, whatever is done will be somewhat in the nature of an experiment ; in any case there will be difficulty, and I recognize that there will be danger ; and I think in any case the point of view of a past Governor like myself would be that we have to make the best of whatever is brought forward.

Personally I do not much mind what the form of the Bill is as long as something is done, and as long as there is sufficient elasticity to make whatever is done into something which will lead to a better state of affairs in India. I recognize as fully as anybody in this House that there is danger. I, perhaps, see some of the dangers which most members of this House do not see—or perhaps I see them a little more clearly. I recognize, and I think the Under-Secretary recognizes, that a very large number of the people of India cannot be said by their best friends, if they speak honestly at this moment, to be very suitable for self-government. But I believe that a great many of them are suitable for it, and I think that we ought not to wait until everyone is suitable. I know that many of those who are politically-minded—which I think is the expression used nowadays about those in India who take an interest in politics (they are a small proportion of the people of India) —have not been hitherto, and are not at this moment, very much enamoured of the present state of affairs. I would go farther and say that many of them do not like government by us. Personally I do not see why they should; and I will say at this moment that if I were an Indian I should hold very advanced views—views which many of your Lordships would look upon as extreme —and I should think that I was fully justified in holding them. But where I differ from many of my friends, especially from those who know India, is that I do not believe they will continue to be hostile to us. By ' us ' I mean those people of Great Britain who govern India from the executive point of view at present.

No one regrets more than I do the way in which Indians who are most fully informed on political matters dislike and distrust—I think honestly distrust—us. When I first went to Madras, and had not the experience I afterwards got, nothing gave me greater anxiety than the feeling that Indians who knew and cared most about politics thoroughly distrusted me. I say ' me ' definitely, because many of them told me that they distrusted me ; they did not distrust me in any personal sense, but they did not see how I could be in a position really to deal honestly with them. That caused me a great deal of anxiety, especially as I know it was honest distrust on their part, which they were not ashamed to avow to me, though they were not anxious to avow it to me ; in fact, they would not do it for a long time until they began to trust me to a certain extent. I do not believe that this distrust need go on. I know that there are some men—with longer knowledge of India than I have ; knowledge acquired at an earlier stage than I acquired mine—who believe (you have only to look at the newspapers from time to time to learn it) that the politically-minded Indians will not give up that distrust. But that is not my experience.

Oddly enough, I got my Indian mail this morning and I have in my pocket letters from two Bengalis. These are both young men who at one time certainly held views which were not friendly to us, views which would have been looked upon by myself as dangerous, but they were honestly held —it was some time, I confess, before they would confide in me sufficiently to tell me their real ideas —but they are men with whom I had a good deal of conversation and with whom I have had a good deal of correspondence. I am delighted to say that both their letters are about this Bill. They are not exactly the letters with which I dare say many of your Lordships would sympathize fully, but they say, and I am sure they honestly mean it, that in this Bill they see a prospect of hope which leads them to think that, after all, they have, perhaps, been wrong in the attitude which they held, believing hónestly that it was impossible that British government of India could ever be such as they would gladly support. I am not going to deal with that very much. I have mentioned it merely because I know that some of your Lordships are aware that I am in sympathy—more, perhaps, than most who have been in India—with views which are looked upon as somewhat extreme. I am going farther to admit that possibly in the definition of what views were extreme and what were moderate I would go farther in the direction of extremism than a great many of my friends would in saying that certain views were moderate.

We have all been younger than we now are. Some of us have modified our views—I know I have—on many points ; and as we grow older I think we learn a certain amount of sense. One thing which, perhaps, people in this country forget is that in India those who take an interest in politics are on the whole younger than the men who take an interest in politics here. It is rather difficult for us in this country to realize—it was very difficult for me to realize it when I first went to India—how much the very young count in matters of that sort. It is only when people begin to be educated—you may call it half-educated or three-quarter educated if you like—in Western ideas, that as a rule men of the upper classes (so to speak), or of the upper middle classes, in India take an interest in politics. Every year the number of men who are so educated becomes larger and larger. That, I think, is to our credit. I think any of your Lordships who have ever electioneered—as some of you have done and as I myself have done—will remember that the younger men did not count so much from the voting point of view as those who were rather older ; but in India the more numerous body taking an interest in politics is always the youngest men, and, therefore, the men who have least experience. Though it is not necessarily so, at any rate you would still think they had all the enthusiasm and all the certainty of youth. It is in favour of British government that these men as they grow older and learn more will think more correctly ; and I am conceited enough to think that if Indians think more correctly they will think more as their governors do.

I have said enough upon that. I do not want to take up the time of the House, but there is one small matter at which I want to ask Lord Sinha to look. Perhaps in this I may be looked upon— I know that I am so looked upon by some of my friends—as somewhat reactionary. It is not often that I am looked upon as a reactionary. I do not quite know what 'reactionary' means, but generally it seems to me to mean, in the opinion of anybody who uses the term, that he thinks rather differently from you. I have no doubt many of your Lordships read *The Times* newspaper, and perhaps that is the quickest way of getting at the point. If so, although I know some of your Lordships to whom I have spoken missed it, others may have seen the letter from Professor Berriedale Keith, of Edinburgh University. He is a friend of mine, but he has not written to me about this matter, and I am speaking my own opinion. On December 1 he wrote to *The Times* drawing attention to a point which may be thought a small point, but which he says is of the highest constitutional importance. I confess that I regard it as of very high importance, and it may have escaped consideration. Mr. Keith draws attention to the Amendment in Part II of the Schedule—I am not going to deal with it, because I am sure that Lord Sinha will know what I mean—by which an addition is made to a clause in the Government of India Act, 1915, saying that the Ministers appointed under this Act, as is the case with Governors, Lieutenant-Governors, the Chief Commissioner, and members of the Executive Council of the Governor-General or Lieutenant-Governor, are not to be subject to the original jurisdiction.

∮ There was a reply in *The Times* on Wednesday, December 3, from Sir Edward Chamier, which gave an explanation. No doubt it is the explanation which those who speak for the Government thought was good enough to put forward. It may be the only explanation. A further letter from Professor Keith appeared on Monday, December 8, in which he returned to the point. I am not a lawyer and do not pretend to be one. I have been a Governor in Australia, and a Governor in India, and I am an ordinary, commonplace man here. However, I do not think that this is a very important point. I quite see that it may be said that the new Ministers should be put on the same footing as the Executive Council or as the Governors. Possibly they should be. I am not certain myself that Governors ought to be in that

position. However, this is a question with which
constitutional lawyers can deal. Looking to the
future—perhaps looking rather far ahead—I think
that point ought to be fully considered. Perhaps
it has been already, but the public ought to know
that it has been more fully considered than the
public at present think it has been. I do not
believe that very much attention would be drawn
to it in India, but my knowledge of India leads me
to suppose that it is the sort of point which might
come up some years hence. The only people in
India who consider that sort of point wish India
to be on a level with those other States which make
up the British Empire, and I do not believe that
they want their Ministers to be in a different
position. No doubt these points will be looked
into when we get into Committee, where there
will be members of your Lordships' House who are
learned in the law and in a far better position than
I am to judge. I hope the Government will
consider it and be able to satisfy us on the matter,
because if they do not satisfy us they are raising
up difficulty in India in the future.

I said I would not say very much about my ideas
as to where this Bill is defective, because there
will be criticism from other members of this House,
with much of which I shall agree. Where I differ
from some members is that I feel more strongly
than perhaps they do, that the greatest danger is
to do nothing, and that the next greatest danger
is to do something which seems in any way
to detract from the authority of the Viceroy and
from what I would almost call the veneration in
which he is held in India. That is why I wish to
see something done. This Bill has been put forward

and nothing else, at any rate, has been more definitely proposed. What certainly weighs with me is that it is put forward on the strength of recommendations made by the Viceroy and by the Secretary of State, from which I might differ and do differ, in some respects, but I think it would be most unfortunate for India if we go very far from what they have recommended. That is the reason, more than any other, which weighs with me in being perfectly willing to sink my dislike of some of the provisions of the Bill, about which I know some of your Lordships hold very strong views.

I am not going to press my own view that I think the Bill might have gone farther than it does in certain directions, because I can hardly expect your Lordships to agree with me. As I said a little while ago, if I had gone to India at an earlier date than I did, or if I had gone to a different part of India than that to which I did go, I believe I should not have held the views I do hold. I believe however that those views will be generally held before very long in this country, though it takes a little time for them to spread. Only the younger men among officials think as I do, and I do not wonder at it ; but I am not going to dwell on that. I am not sorry, because I know this is merely a step in the right direction. At least, I regard it as a step in the right direction, and I think all your Lordships admit that it is. There are very few members of your Lordships' House interested in India who do not agree that a good deal has to be done.

I think we ought to be very thankful to the noble Earl, Lord Selborne, and the other members of the Select Committee for the Report they have made. It is a most important document, and I do not think that the Under-Secretary of State overstated the case yesterday when he dwelt upon its importance. For my own part I feel extremely thankful—and I think all friends of India ought to feel thankful—also to my noble friend Lord Sydenham. He and I do not agree on a good many points, but there are others on which we agree very closely. Lord Sydenham has pointed out dangers which he feels, and some of them I feel too, but we have drawn different conclusions, probably because he was not in Bengal in the years when I was there. However, we need not go into that. He is not going to change his mind, and I am afraid I am too stupid or too obstinate to change mine. On one or two other points probably Lord Sydenham will agree with me. This Bill when it becomes an Act will undoubtedly give us a great deal of cause for thought. I assume we are going to pass it, and in that case we are taking a step which would have astonished us if we had known ten years ago that we should take it. We are taking a step which, I think, will surprise people in European countries. At present they are thinking, as we are, of the War, but those interested in politics will be surprised to find that Great Britain is taking this step.

The eyes of the whole world, indeed, will be on India to see what is the result. It lies, and must lie, with the people of India themselves, more than with anyone else, to make this Bill a success. Lord Sinha dealt with this point yesterday, and it is one which he was right to emphasize. Perhaps I can speak on this point more effectively than most people, as owing to circumstances there are

Indians who fancy that I more than many other Englishmen sympathize with their advanced views. Those who are politically-minded in India, to whatever party and to whatever class they belong, are not, as a rule, very satisfied with their present position. I know that there are differences of opinion; that there are extremists and moderates, and that hitherto, perhaps naturally, the extremists have counted for more as a force than the moderates.

There was nothing I regretted more while I was in India than the position in which some of the moderate Indian reformers found themselves. I knew many of them. I have talked with them in Bengal, and I knew some of them in Madras. I did my best to try to know what they were really thinking, and I know that many moderate reformers, those whom the Government looked upon as moderate men, felt very bitterly their position. They were never sure when, to use a common expression, they might be 'put in the cart'. They were never sure when the Government would back them up, and I confess that, after all, one had as a Governor to think more of the views put forward by the extremists than by the moderates.

But neither the extremists nor the moderates had very much power of getting anything done. They could criticize, and of course it was the criticism of the extremists that was most listened to. The moderates made suggestions to me and to my officers. They were not often very practical. How could they be? These people have no experience in administration. When I stood for a constituency in this country I had to listen to people putting forward views which were not exactly practical; and is it any wonder that

impracticable views should be held by men who
never had, and thought they would never have,
the chance of having any real responsibility ?
I do not blame the officials of the Government
in India. They are all over-worked. The worst
thing in India is the fact that every official from
top to bottom is over-worked. Not one, from the
Viceroy down to the most newly-joined officer, but
is expected to do far more than any man ought to
be expected to do. They try to do the work, but
are very much over-worked, and when people are
in that state they cannot have the patience, or
show the patience, which is expected from them
by men who were in the position of Lord Sinha
when I first went to Bengal—intelligent men who
thought on political questions, who had ideas
well worth considering, and who wished to put
them before those who alone could give effect to
them. The officials had not the time to give to the
consideration of these matters, and therefore
brushed them aside, civilly I hope, though perhaps
not always civilly. I know this from my own
experience. You have to brush the proposal aside
because you have not the time to deal with it and
explain to the man the real position. I do not
wonder that the moderate man has often felt that
he might just as well be an extremist.

One of the best results of this Bill when it
becomes an Act will be that it will give some sense
of confidence to the moderate politically-minded
Indians. From my knowledge of the Bengalis
I do not think that the politically-minded Bengali
is as bold as he might be. The politically-minded
Madrasi is a much bolder man. That is my
experience. I was only a short time in Madras,

but the number of Madrasis who told me I was wrong and gave me good reasons why they thought I was wrong—sometimes they were right—was much larger than the number of Bengalis who expressed their opinion. This is probably due to the fact that in Madras they have for a long time had a series of Governors, whereas I was the first Governor in Bengal. I know many of your Lordships will think, as I think, that a Lieutenant-Governor is much more likely to have real knowledge about Indian affairs than a Governor has. I see just on my right one or two of your Lordships whose knowledge of Indians matters is far greater than mine can be. As to any details I bow to them, certainly, but I do not believe that the ordinary Indian would be as willing to be convinced by them as he would be by me, simply because he knows that they have been brought up in the Indian Civil Service, and he believes that they have got into traditions which, unfortunately but undoubtedly, have aroused a certain amount of distrust among Indians.

I think there is an advantage in having a Governor rather than a Lieutenant-Governor, and a Governor who comes from this country—or I don't care where—but who has not been a Civil Servant in India. I said I do not care where he comes from. I think—it is a fad of my own—that a Governor might sometimes come from another part than the British Isles. However, there is a great advantage in there being in the province one man who is ignorant—I do not care how ignorant—who even may be a fool, but who can ask questions, and whose questions must be answered—who has the right to ask questions and who, when something happens which he thinks is wrong, has a right to inquire into it. I have asked many questions. I used to ask questions in Madras, and also in Bengal, and I do not mind saying this—that when I went to Bengal, I think that sometimes some of my officers did not quite like my asking the questions which I did ask. They had an idea—a very natural idea—that I, as the first Governor after a change which they did not like quite as much as they might, should have sympathized with them, and that I was wasting their time, and that sort of thing ; still they had to answer those questions, and I do not think it was at all a bad thing that they had to do so, because I hope that, when I was in Bengal, amongst Indians the idea grew up that there was one man who was always to be blamed for anything that happened in Bengal, and that man was the Governor.

I have said again and again to them ' Well, if it is wrong I am to blame for it. Either I ought to have done it otherwise, or I ought to have seen that the person dealing with it was capable of dealing with it.' That is not a position in which any Lieutenant-Governor who has been a member of the Civil Service ever can be or can be expected to be in. I say that the Indians must themselves make this Bill a success. If the moderate men prevail, as I hope they will, then this step will lead to success and will lead to further success, but I think it will lie with us—with the Government— to help the moderate men. It will lie with the members of the Civil Service to a great extent to help them, and I believe they will do so. I know myself that members of the Civil Service are not enamoured of this Bill. Many of them are against it, and I do not wonder at it. Their idea is, and it is a quite correct idea, that they have so far ' run the show', to use a common expression, very well. I think they have. And they do not quite see why we should alter the system. But I feel sure of this, that if we alter the system they will do their very best to make it a success.

I know there are some of them who think that they will not have the power, so to speak ,that they have hitherto had. My own view is that with the Ministers the Civil Service will have a very great deal of influence—more influence than they have with any member of an Executive ·Council. I believe that the Indian gentlemen who become Ministers will certainly want to make a success of their own work. They will be men of intelligence, and they will know that they themselves have no administrative or executive experience, and their first idea will be to rely on the officers who have. I am talking from some experience of Indian Executive Councillors, and my idea is that the Indian Executive Councillors listen to their secretaries and persons who advise them in a way which a secretary cannot complain of. I have discussed matters with my own executive councillors and I always found that my Indian executive councillors when they differed from me, as they sometimes did, quoted to me the views of their secretary, or some other member of the Indian Civil Service, far more than my English executive councillors did. I have not myself the slightest doubt that, at any rate at first, the danger will rather be that the Indian ministers will rely a little bit too much on individual members of the Indian Civil Service, and on English members of the Indian Civil Service.

I shall say no more on that. I just want to say a word or two on two other points. Another person who will be in a great difficulty is undoubtedly the Governor. I am speaking feelingly in this. I think the Governor under the new system will be in a very difficult position. That has been recognized in Lord Selborne's report, and we will have to take care that good men go out as Governors. I know that it will be said it is difficult to find Governors, and still more to find good ones, but I think the future of this Bill will lie with them to a very great extent. One other thing, I am very glad to see that the Joint Committee have recommended that the matter of Europeans in Bengal should, at any rate, be considered. I have always found as a Governor that a great deal of help could be given by non-official Europeans. They do not take much interest in politics. Many of them are Scotsmen, and I am a Scotsman, and I quite sympathize with them. They were attending to their own business, but I often felt that if only they would help me to attend to mine a little more than they did it would help matters on. I hope when it comes to dealing with the rules that they will be considered very fully.

13. *Government of India Act, 1919 (9 & 10 Geo. 5, c. 101)*

WHEREAS it is the declared policy of Parliament to provide for the increasing association of Indians in every branch of Indian administration, and for the gradual development of self-governing institutions, with a view to the progressive realization of responsible government in British India as an integral part of the empire :

And whereas progress in giving effect to this policy can only be achieved by successive stages, and it is expedient that substantial steps in this direction should now be taken :

And whereas the time and manner of each advance can be determined only by Parliament, upon whom responsibility lies for the welfare and advancement of the Indian peoples :

And whereas the action of Parliament in such matters must be guided by the co-operation received from those on whom new opportunities of service will be conferred, and by the extent to which it is found that confidence can be reposed in their sense of responsibility :

And whereas concurrently with the gradual development of self-governing institutions in the Provinces of India it is expedient to give to those Provinces in provincial matters the largest measure of independence of the Government of India, which is compatible with the due discharge by the latter of its own responsibilities :

Be it therefore enacted by the King's most Excellent Majesty, by and with the advice and consent of the Lords Spiritual and Temporal, and Commons, in this present Parliament assembled, and by the authority of the same, as follows :

PART I

LOCAL GOVERNMENTS

Classification of central and provincial subjects

1.—(1) Provision may be made by rules under the Government of India Act, 1915,[1] as amended by the Government of India (Amendment) Act,

[1] 5 & 6 Geo. 5, c. 61.

1916 [1] (which Act, as so amended, is in this Act
referred to as ' the principal Act ') :
- (a) for the classification of subjects, in relation
  to the functions of government, as central
  and provincial subjects, for the purpose
  of distinguishing the functions of local
  governments and local legislatures from
  the functions of the Governor-General in
  Council and the Indian legislature ;
- (b) for the devolution of authority in respect of
  provincial subjects to local governments,
  and for the allocation of revenues or other
  moneys to those governments ;
- (c) for the use under the authority of the Governor-General in Council of the agency of
  local governments in relation to central
  subjects, in so far as such agency may be
  found convenient, and for determining the
  financial conditions of such agency ; and
- (d) for the transfer from among the provincial
  subjects of subjects (in this Act referred
  to as ' transferred subjects ') to the administration of the governor acting with
  ministers appointed under this Act, and
  for the allocation of revenues or moneys
  for the purpose of such administration.

(2) Without prejudice to the generality of the
foregoing powers, rules made for the above-men-
tioned purposes may—
- (i) regulate the extent and conditions of such
  devolution, allocation, and transfer ;
- (ii) provide for fixing the contributions payable
  by local governments to the Governor-
  General in Council, and making such con-

[1] 6 & 7 Geo. 5, c. 37

tributions a first charge on allocated revenues or moneys ;

(iii) provide for constituting a finance department in any province, and regulating the functions of that department ;

(iv) provide for regulating the exercise of the authority vested in the local government of a province over members of the public services therein ;

(v) provide for the settlement of doubts arising as to whether any matter does or does not relate to a provincial subject or a transferred subject, and for the treatment of matters which affect both a transferred subject and a subject which is not transferred ; and

(vi) make such consequential and supplemental provisions as appear necessary or expedient ;

Provided that, without prejudice to any general power of revoking or altering rules under the principal Act, the rules shall not authorize the revocation or suspension of the transfer of any subject except with the sanction of the Secretary of State in Council.

(3) The powers of superintendence, direction, and control over local governments vested in the Governor-General in Council under the principal Act shall, in relation to transferred subjects, be exercised only for such purposes as may be specified in rules made under that Act, but the Governor-General in Council shall be the sole judge as to whether the purpose of the exercise of such powers in any particular case comes within the purposes so specified.

(4) The expressions ' central subjects ' and ' provincial subjects ' as used in this Act mean subjects so classified under the rules.

Provincial subjects, other than transferred subjects, are in this Act referred to as ' reserved subjects '.

Borrowing powers of local governments

2.—(1) The provision in subsection (1) of section thirty of the principal Act, which gives power to local governments to raise money on real or personal estate within the limits of their respective governments by way of mortgage or otherwise, shall have effect as though that provision conferred a power on local governments to raise money on the security of their allocated revenues, and to make proper assurances for that purpose.

(2) Provision may be made by rules under the principal Act as to the conditions under which the power to raise loans on the security of allocated revenues shall be exercised.

(3) The provision in subsection (1) of section thirty of the principal Act, which enables the Secretary of State in Council with the concurrence of a majority of votes at a meeting of the Council of India to prescribe provisions or conditions limiting the power to raise money, shall cease to have effect as regards the power to raise money on the security of allocated revenues.

Revised system of local government in certain provinces

3.—(1) The presidencies of Fort William in Bengal, Fort St. George, and Bombay, and the provinces known as the United Provinces, the

Punjab, Bihar and Orissa, the Central Provinces, and Assam, shall each be governed, in relation to reserved subjects, by a governor in council, and in relation to transferred subjects (save as otherwise provided by this Act) by the governor acting with ministers appointed under this Act.

The said presidencies and provinces are in this Act referred to as ' governor's provinces ' and the two first-named presidencies are in this Act referred to as the presidencies of Bengal and Madras.

(2) The provisions of section forty-six to fifty-one of the principal Act, as amended by this Act, shall apply to the United Provinces, the Punjab, Bihar and Orissa, the Central Provinces, and Assam, as they apply to the presidencies of Bengal, Madras, and Bombay : Provided that the governors of the said provinces shall be appointed after consultation with the Governor-General.

Appointment of ministers and council secretaries

4.—(1) The governor of a governor's province may, by notification, appoint ministers, not being members of his executive council or other officials, to administer transferred subjects, and any ministers so appointed shall hold office during his pleasure.

There may be paid to any minister so appointed in any province the same salary as is payable to a member of the executive council in that province, unless a smaller salary is provided by vote of the legislative council of the province.

(2) No minister shall hold office for a longer period than six months, unless he is or becomes an elected member of the local legislature.

(3) In relation to transferred subjects, the gover-

nor shall be guided by the advice of his ministers, unless he sees sufficient cause to dissent from their opinion, in which case he may require action to be taken otherwise than in accordance with that advice : Provided that rules may be made under the principal Act for the temporary administration of a transferred subject where, in cases of emergency, owing to a vacancy, there is no minister in charge of the subject, by such authority and in such manner as may be prescribed by the rules.

(4) The governor of a governor's province may at his discretion appoint from among the non-official members of the local legislature council secretaries, who shall hold office during his pleasure, and discharge such duties in assisting members of the executive council and ministers, as he may assign to them.

There shall be paid to council secretaries so appointed such salary as mäy be provided by vote of the legislative council.

A council secretary shall cease to hold office if he ceases for more than six months to be a member of the legislative council.

Qualification of members of local Executive Councils

5.—(1) The provision in section forty-seven of the principal Act, that two of the members of the executive council of the governor of a province must have been for at least twelve years in the service of the Crown in India, shall have effect as though ' one ' were substituted for ' two ', and the provision in that section that the Commander-in-Chief of His Majesty's Forces in India, if resident at Calcutta, Madras, or Bombay, shall, during his continuance there, be a member of the governor's council, shall cease to have effect.

(2) Provision may be made by rules under the principal Act as to the qualifications to be required in respect of members of the executive council of the governor of a province in any case where such provision is not made by section forty-seven of the principal Act as amended by this section.

Business of governor in council and governor with ministers

6.—(1) All orders and other proceedings of the government of a governor's province shall be expressed to be made by the government of the province, and shall be authenticated as the governor may by rule direct, so, however, that provision shall be made by rule for distinguishing orders and other proceedings relating to transferred subjects from other orders and proceedings.

Orders and proceedings authenticated as aforesaid shall not be called into question in any legal proceeding on the ground that they were not duly made by the government of the province.

(2) The governor may make rules and orders for the more convenient transaction of business in his executive council and with his ministers, and every order made or act done in accordance with those rules and orders shall be treated as being the order or the act of the government of the province.

The governor may also make rules and orders for regulating the relations between his executive council and his ministers for the purpose of the transaction of the business of the local government:

Provided that any rules or orders made for the

purposes specified in this section which are repugnant to the provisions of any rules made under the principal Act as amended by this Act shall, to the extent of that repugnancy, but not otherwise, be void.

Composition of governors' legislative councils

7.—(1) There shall be a legislative council in every governor's province, which shall consist of the members of the executive council and of members nominated or elected as provided by this Act.

The governor shall not be a member of the legislative council, but shall have the right of addressing the council, and may for that purpose require the attendance of its members.

(2) The number of members of the governors' legislative councils shall be in accordance with the table set out in the First Schedule to this Act ; and of the members of each council not more than twenty per cent. shall be official members, and at least seventy per cent. shall be elected members :
Provided that—

(a) subject to the maintenance of the above proportions, rules under the principal Act may provide for increasing the number of members of any council, as specified in that schedule ; and

(b) the governor may, for the purposes of any Bill introduced or proposed to be introduced in his legislative council, nominate, in the case of Assam one person, and in the case of other provinces not more than two persons, having special knowledge or experience of the subject-matter of the

Bill, and those persons shall, in relation to the Bill, have for the period for which they are nominated all the rights of members of the council, and shall be in addition to the numbers above referred to ; and

(c) members nominated to the legislative council of the Central Provinces by the governor as the result of elections held in the Assigned Districts of Berar shall be deemed to be elected members of the legislative council of the Central Provinces.

(3) The powers of a governor's legislative council may be exercised notwithstanding any vacancy in the council.

(4) Subject as aforesaid, provision may be made by rules under the principal Act as to—

(a) the term of office of nominated members of governors' legislative councils, and the manner of filling casual vacancies occurring by reason of absence of members from India, inability to attend to duty, death, acceptance of office, resignation duly accepted, or otherwise ; and

(b) the conditions under which and manner in which persons may be nominated as members of governors' legislative councils ; and

(c) the qualification of electors, the constitution of constituencies, and the method of election for governors' legislative councils, including the number of members to be elected by communal and other electorates, and any matters incidental or ancillary thereto ; and (*d*) the qualifications for being and for being nominated or elected a member of any such council ; and

(*e*) the final decision of doubts or disputes as to the validity of any election ; and

(*f*) the manner in which the rules are to be carried into effect :

Provided that rules as to any such matters as aforesaid may provide for delegating to the local government such power as may be specified in the rules of making subsidiary regulations affecting the same matters.

(5) Subject to any such rules, any person who is a ruler or subject of any State in India may be nominated as a member of a governor's legislative council.

Sessions and duration of governors' legislative councils

8.—(1) Every governor's legislative council shall continue for three years from its first meeting :

Provided that—

(*a*) the council may be sooner dissolved by the governor ; and

(*b*) the said period may be extended by the governor for a period not exceeding one year, by notification in the official gazette of the province, if in special circumstances (to be specified in the notification) he so think fit ; and

(*c*) after the dissolution of the council the governor shall appoint a date not more than six months or, with the sanction of the Secretary of State, not more than nine months from the date of dissolution for the next session of the council.

(2) A governor may appoint such times and places for holding the sessions of his legislative council as he thinks fit, and may also, by notification or otherwise, prorogue the council.

(3) Any meeting of a governor's legislative council may be adjourned by the person presiding.

(4) All questions in a governor's legislative council shall be determined by a majority of votes of the members present other than the person presiding, who shall, however, have and exercise a casting vote in the case of an equality of votes.

Presidents of governors' legislative councils

9.—(1) There shall be a president of a governor's legislative council, who shall, until the expiration of a period of four years from the first meeting of the council as constituted under this Act, be a person appointed by the governor, and shall thereafter be a member of the council elected by the council and approved by the governor :

Provided that, if at the expiration of such period of four years the council is in session, the president then in office shall continue in office until the end of the current session, and the first election of a president shall take place at the commencement of the next ensuing session.

(2) There shall be a deputy-president of a governor's legislative council who shall preside at meetings of the council in the absence of the president, and who shall be a member of the council elected by the council and approved by the governor.

(3) The appointed president of a council shall hold office until the date of the first election of a president by the council under this section, but

he may resign office by writing under his hand addressed to the governor, or may be removed from office by order of the governor, and any vacancy occurring before the expiration of the term of office of an appointed president shall be filled by a similar appointment for the remainder of such term.

(4) An elected president and a deputy-president shall cease to hold office on ceasing to be members of the council. They may resign office by writing under their hands addressed to the governor, and may be removed from office by a vote of the council. with the concurrence of the governor.

(5) The president and the deputy-president shall receive such salaries as may be determined, in the case of an appointed president, by the governor, and in the case of an elected president or deputy-president, by Act of the local legislature.

Powers of local legislatures

10.—(1) The local legislature of any province has power, subject to the provisions of this Act, to make laws for the peace and good government of the territories for the time being constituting that province.

(2) The local legislature of any province may, subject to the provisions of the subsection next following, repeal or alter as to that province any law made either before or after the commencement of this Act by any authority in British India other than that local legislature.

(3) The local legislature of any province may not, without the previous sanction of the Governor-General, make or take into consideration any law—

(a) imposing or authorizing the imposition of

any new tax unless the tax is a tax scheduled as exempted from this provision by rules made under the principal Act ; or

(b) affecting the public debt of India, or the customs duties, or any other tax or duty for the time being in force and imposed by the authority of the Governor-General in Council for the general purposes of the government of India, provided that the imposition or alteration of a tax scheduled as aforesaid shall not be deemed to affect any such tax or duty ; or

(c) affecting the discipline or maintenance of any part of His Majesty's naval, military, or air forces ; or

(d) affecting the relations of the government with foreign princes or states ; or

(e) regulating any central subject ; or

(f) regulating any provincial subject which has been declared by rules under the principal Act to be, either in whole or in part, subject to legislation by the Indian Legislature, in respect of any matter to which such declaration applies ; or

(g) affecting any power expressly reserved to the Governor-General in Council by any law for the time being in force ; or

(h) altering or repealing the provisions of any law which, having been made before the commencement of this Act by any authority in British India other than that local legislature, is declared by rules under the principal Act to be a law which cannot be repealed or altered by the local legislature without previous sanction ; or

(i) altering or repealing any provision of an Act of the Indian Legislature made after the commencement of this Act, which by the provisions of that Act may not be repealed or altered by the local legislature without previous sanction :

Provided that an Act or a provision of an Act made by a local legislature, and subsequently assented to by the Governor-General in pursuance of this Act, shall not be deemed invalid by reason only of its requiring the previous sanction of the Governor-General under this Act.

(4) The local legislature of any province has not power to make any law affecting any Act of Parliament.

Business and procedure in governors' legislative councils

11.—(1) Subsections (1) and (3) of section eighty of the principal Act (which relate to the classes of business which may be transacted at meetings of local legislative councils) shall cease to apply to a governor's legislative council, but the business and procedure in any such council shall be regulated in accordance with the provisions of this section.

(2) The estimated annual expenditure and revenue of the province shall be laid in the form of a statement before the council in each year, and the proposals of the local government for the appropriation of provincial revenues and other moneys in any year shall be submitted to the vote of the council in the form of demands for grants. The council may assent, or refuse its assent, to a demand, or may reduce the amount therein referred to either by a reduction of the whole

grant or by the omission or reduction of any of the items of expenditure of which the grant is. composed :

Provided that—

(a) the local government shall have power, in relation to any such demand, to act as if it had been assented to, notwithstanding the withholding of such assent or the reduction of the amount therein referred to, if the demand relates to a reserved subject, and the governor certifies that the expenditure provided for by the demand is essential to the discharge of his responsibility for the subject ; and

(b) the governor shall have power in cases of emergency to authorize such expenditure as may be in his opinion necessary for the safety or tranquillity of the province, or for the carrying on of any department ; and

(c) no proposal for the appropriation of any such revenues or other moneys for any purpose shall be made except on the recommendation of the governor, communicated to the council.

(3) Nothing in the foregoing subsection shall require proposals to be submitted to the council relating to the following heads of expenditure :

(i) contributions payable by the local government to the Governor-General in Council ; and

(ii) interest and sinking fund charges on loans ; and

(iii) expenditure of which the amount is prescribed by or under any law ; and

(iv) salaries and pensions of persons appointed by or with the approval of His Majesty or by the Secretary of State in Council; and

(v) salaries of judges of the high court of the province and of the advocate-general.

If any question arises whether any proposed appropriation of moneys does or does not relate to the above heads of expenditure, the decision of the governor shall be final.

(4) Where any Bill has been introduced or is proposed to be introduced, or any amendment to a Bill is moved or proposed to be moved, the governor may certify that the Bill or any clause of it or the amendment affects the safety or tranquillity of his province or any part of it or of another province, and may direct that no proceedings or no further proceedings shall be taken by the council in relation to the Bill, clause or amendment, and effect shall be given to any such direction.

(5) Provision may be made by rules under the principal Act for the purpose of carrying into effect the foregoing provisions of this section and for regulating the course of business in the council, and as to the persons to preside over meetings thereof in the absence of the president and deputy-president, and the preservation of order at meetings; and the rules may provide for the number of members required to constitute a quorum, and for prohibiting or regulating the asking of questions on, and the discussion of, any subject specified in the rules.

(6) Standing orders may be made providing for the conduct of business and the procedure to be

followed in the council, in so far as these matters are not provided for by rules made under the principal Act. The first standing orders shall be made by the governor in council, but may, subject to the assent of the governor, be altered by the local legislatures. Any standing order made as aforesaid which is repugnant to the provisions of any rules made under the principal Act, shall, to the extent of that repugnancy but not otherwise, be void.

(7) Subject to the rules and standing orders affecting the council, there shall be freedom of speech in the governors' legislative councils. No person shall be liable to any proceedings in any court by reason of his speech or vote in any such council, or by reason of anything contained in any official report of the proceedings of any such council.

Return and reservation of Bills

12.—(1) Where a Bill has been passed by a local legislative council, the governor, lieutenant-governor or chief commissioner may, instead of declaring that he assents to or withholds his assent from the Bill, return the Bill to the council for reconsideration, either in whole or in part, together with any amendments which he may recommend, or, in cases prescribed by rules under the principal Act may, and if the rules so require shall, reserve the Bill for the consideration of the Governor-General.

(2) Where a Bill is reserved for the consideration of the Governor-General, the following provisions shall apply :—

(a) The governor, lieutenant-governor or chief

commissioner may, at any time within six months from the date of the reservation of the Bill, with the consent of the Governor-General, return the Bill for further consideration by the council with a recommendation that the council shall consider amendments thereto :

(*b*) After any Bill so returned has been further considered by the council, together with any recommendations made by the governor, lieutenant-governor or chief commissioner relating thereto, the Bill, if re-affirmed with or without amendment, may be again presented to the governor, lieutenant-governor, or chief commissioner :

(*c*) Any Bill reserved for the consideration of the Governor-General shall, if assented to by the Governor-General within a period of six months from the date of such reservation, become law on due publication of such assent, in the same way as a Bill assented to by the governor, lieutenant-governor or chief commissioner, but, if not assented to by the Governor-General within such period of six months, shall lapse and be of no effect unless before the expiration of that period either—

(i) the Bill has been returned by the governor, lieutenant-governor or chief commissioner, for further consideration by the council ; or

(ii) In the case of the council not being in session, a notification has been published of an intention so to return the Bill at the commencement of the next session.

(3) The Governor-General may (except where the

Bill has been reserved for his consideration), instead of assenting to or withholding his assent from any Act passed by a local legislature, declare that he reserves the Act for the signification of His Majesty's pleasure thereon, and in such case the Act shall not have validity until His Majesty in Council has signified his assent and his assent has been notified by the Governor-General.

Provision for case of failure to pass legislation in governors' legislative councils

13.—(1) Where a governor's legislative council has refused leave to introduce, or has failed to pass in a form recommended by the governor, any Bill relating to a reserved subject, the governor may certify that the passage of the Bill is essential for the discharge of his responsibility for the subject, and thereupon the Bill shall, notwithstanding that the council have not consented thereto, be deemed to have passed, and shall, on signature by the governor, become an Act of the local legislature in the form of the Bill as originally introduced or proposed to be introduced in the council or (as the case may be) in the form recommended to the council by the governor.

(2) Every such Act shall be expressed to be made by the governor, and the governor shall forthwith send an authentic copy thereof to the Governor-General, who shall reserve the Act for the signification of His Majesty's pleasure, and upon the signification of such assent by His Majesty in Council, and the notification thereof by the Governor-General, the Act shall have the same force and effect as an Act passed by the local legislature and duly assented to :

Provided that, where in the opinion of the Governor-General a state of emergency exists which justifies such action, he may, instead of reserving such Act, signify his assent thereto, and thereupon the Act shall have such force and effect as aforesaid, subject however to disallowance by His Majesty in Council.

(3) An Act made under this section shall, as soon as practicable after being made, be laid before each House of Parliament, and an Act which is required to be presented for His Majesty's assent shall not be so presented until copies thereof have been laid before each House of Parliament for not less than eight days on which that House has sat.

Vacation of seats in local legislative councils

14.　An official shall not be qualified for election as a member of a local legislative council, and, if any non-official member of a local legislative council, whether elected or nominated, accepts any office in the service of the Crown in India, his seat on the council shall become vacant :

Provided that for the purposes of this provision a minister shall not be deemed to be an official and a person shall not be deemed to accept office on appointment as a minister.

Constitution of new provinces, &c., and provision as to backward tracts

15.—(1) The Governor-General in Council may, after obtaining an expression of opinion from the local government and the local legislature affected, by notification, with the sanction of His Majesty previously signified by the Secretary of State in Council, constitute a new governor's province, or place part of a governor's province under the administration of a deputy-governor to be appointed by the Governor-General, and may in any such case apply, with such modifications as appear necessary or desirable, all or any of the provisions of the principal Act or this Act relating to governors' provinces, or provinces under a lieutenant-governor or chief commissioner, to any such new province or part of a province.

(2) The Governor-General in Council may declare any territory in British India to be a ' backward tract ', and may, by notification, with such sanction as aforesaid, direct that the principal Act and this Act shall apply to that territory subject to such exceptions and modifications as may be prescribed in the notification. Where the Governor-General in Council has, by notification, directed as aforesaid, he may, by the same or subsequent notification, direct that any Act of the Indian Legislature shall not apply to the territory in question or any part thereof, or shall apply to the territory or any part thereof subject to such exceptions or modifications as the Governor-General thinks fit, or may authorize the governor in council to give similar directions as respects any Act of the local legislature.

Saving

16.—(1) The validity of any order made or action taken after the commencement of this Act by the Governor-General in Council or by a local government which would have been within the powers of the Governor-General in Council or of such local government if this Act had not been passed, shall not be open to question in any legal proceedings on the ground that by reason of any provision of this Act or of any rule made by virtue of any such provision such order or action has ceased to be within the powers of the Governor-General in Council or of the government concerned.

(2) Nothing in this Act, or in any rule made thereunder, shall be construed as diminishing in any respect the powers of the Indian legislature as laid down in section sixty-five of the principal Act, and the validity of any Act of the Indian legislature or any local legislature shall not be open to question in any legal proceedings on the ground that the Act affects a provincial subject or a central subject, as the case may be, and the validity of any Act made by the governor of a province shall not be so open to question on the ground that it does not relate to a reserved subject.

(3) The validity of any order made or action taken by a governor in council, or by a governor acting with his ministers, shall not be open to question in any legal proceedings on the ground that such order or action relates or does not relate to a transferred subject, or relates to a transferred subject of which the minister is not in charge.

PART II

GOVERNMENT OF INDIA

Indian legislature

17. Subject to the provisions of this Act, the Indian legislature shall consist of the Governor-General and two chambers, namely, the Council of State and the Legislative Assembly.

Except as otherwise provided by or under this

Act, a Bill shall not be deemed to have been passed by the Indian legislature unless it has been agreed to by both chambers, either without amendment or with such amendments only as may be agreed to by both chambers.

Council of State

18.—(1) The Council of State shall consist of not more than sixty members nominated or elected in accordance with rules made under the principal Act, of whom not more than twenty shall be official members.

(2) The Governor-General shall have power to appoint, from among the members of the Council of State, a president and other persons to preside in such circumstances as he may direct.

(3) The Governor-General shall have the right of addressing the Council of State, and may for that purpose require the attendance of its members.

Legislative Assembly

19.—(1) The Legislative Assembly shall consist of members nominated or elected in accordance with rules made under the principal Act.

(2) The total number of members of the Legislative Assembly shall be one hundred and forty. The number of non-elected members shall be forty, of whom twenty-six shall be official members. The number of elected members shall be one hundred :

Provided that rules made under the principal Act may provide for increasing the number of members of the Legislative Assembly as fixed by this section, and may vary the proportion which the classes of members bear one to another, so, however, that at least five-sevenths of the members of the Legislative Assembly shall be elected members, and at least one-third of the other members shall be non-official members.

(3) The Governor-General shall have the right of addressing the Legislative Assembly, and may for that purpose require the attendance of its members.

President of Legislative Assembly

20.—(1) There shall be a president of the Legislative Assembly, who shall, until the expiration of four years from the first meeting thereof, be a person appointed by the Governor-General, and shall thereafter be a member of the Assembly elected by the Assembly and approved by the Governor-General :   •

Provided that, if at the expiration of such period of four years the Assembly is in session, the president then in office shall continue in office until the end of the current session, and the first election of a president shall take place at the commencement of the ensuing session.

(2) There shall be a deputy-president of the Legislative Assembly, who shall preside at meetings of the Assembly in the absence of the president, and who shall be a member of the Assembly elected by the Assembly and approved by the Governor-General.

(3) The appointed president shall hold office until the date of the election of a president under this section, but he may resign his office by writing under his hand addressed to the Governor-General, or may be removed from office by order of the Governor-General, and any vacancy occurring before the expiration of his term of office shall be

filled by a similar appointment for the remainder of such term.

(4) An elected president and a deputy-president shall cease to hold office if they cease to be members of the Assembly. They may resign office by writing under their hands addressed to the Governor-General, and may be removed from office by a vote of the Assembly with the concurrence of the Governor-General.

(5) A president and deputy-president shall receive such salaries as may be determined, in the case of an appointed president by the Governor-General, and in the case of an elected president and a deputy-president by Act of the Indian legislature.

Duration and sessions of Legislative Assembly and Council of State

21.—(1) Every Council of State shall continue for five years, and every Legislative Assembly for three years, from its first meeting :

Provided that—

(a) either chamber of the legislature may be sooner dissolved by the Governor-General ; and

(b) any such period may be extended by the Governor-General if in special circumstances he so thinks fit ; and

(c) after the dissolution of either chamber the Governor-General shall appoint a date not more than six months, or, with the sanction of the Secretary of State, not more than nine months after the date of dissolution for the next session of that chamber.

(2) The Governor-General may appoint such times and places for holding the sessions of either chamber of the Indian legislature as he thinks fit, and may also from time to time, by notification or otherwise, prorogue such sessions.

(3) Any meeting of either chamber of the Indian legislature may be adjourned by the person presiding.

(4) All questions in either chamber shall be determined by a majority of votes of members present other than the presiding member, who shall, however, have and exercise a casting vote in the case of an equality of votes.

(5) The powers of either chamber of the Indian legislature may be exercised notwithstanding any vacancy in the chamber.

Membership of both chambers

22.—(1) An official shall not be qualified for election as a member of either chamber of the Indian legislature, and, if any non-official member of either chamber accepts office in the service of the Crown in India, his seat in that chamber shall become vacant.

(2) If an elected member of either chamber of the Indian legislature becomes a member of the other chamber, his seat in such first-mentioned chamber shall thereupon become vacant.

(3) If any person is elected a member of both chambers of the Indian legislature, he shall, before he takes his seat in either chamber, signify in writing the chamber of which he desires to be a member, and thereupon his seat in the other chamber shall become vacant.

(4) Every member of the Governor-General's

Executive Council shall be nominated as a member of one chamber of the Indian legislature, and shall have the right of attending in and addressing the other chamber, but shall not be a member of both chambers.

Supplementary provisions as to composition of Legislative Assembly and Council of State

23.—(1) Subject to the provisions of this Act, provision may be made by rules under the principal Act as to—

(a) the term of office of nominated members of the Council of State and the Legislative Assembly, and the manner of filling casual vacancies occurring by reason of absence of members from India, inability to attend to duty, death, acceptance of office, or resignation duly accepted, or otherwise ; and

(b) the conditions under which and the manner in which persons may be nominated as members of the Council of State or the Legislative Assembly ; and

(c) the qualification of electors, the constitution of constituencies, and the method of election for the Council of State and the Legislative Assembly (including the number of members to be elected by communal and other electorates) and any matters incidental or ancillary thereto ; and

(d) the qualifications for being or for being nominated or elected as members of the Council of State or the Legislative Assembly ; and

(e) the final decision of doubts or disputes as to the validity of an election ; and

(f) the manner in which the rules are to be carried into effect.

(2) Subject to any such rules, any person who is a ruler or subject of any state in India may be nominated as a member of the Council of State or the Legislative Assembly.

Business proceedings in Indian legislature

24.—(1) Subsections (1) and (3) of section sixty-seven of the principal Act (which relate to the classes of business which may be transacted by the Indian legislative council) shall cease to have effect.

(2) Provision may be made by rules under the principal Act for regulating the course of business and the preservation of order in the chambers of the Indian legislature, and as to the persons to preside at the meetings of the legislative assembly in the absence of the president and the deputy-president ; and the rules may provide for the number of members required to constitute a quorum, and for prohibiting or regulating the asking of questions on, and the discussion of, any subject specified in the rules.

(3) If any Bill which has been passed by one chamber is not, within six months after the passage of the Bill by that chamber, passed by the other chamber either without amendments or with such amendments as may be agreed to by the two chambers, the Governor-General may in his discretion refer the matter for decision to a joint sitting of both chambers : Provided that standing orders made under this section may provide for

meetings of members of both chambers appointed for the purpose, in order to discuss any difference of opinion which has arisen between the two chambers.

(4) Without prejudice to the powers of the Governor-General under section sixty-eight of the principal Act, the Governor-General may, where a Bill has been passed by both chambers of the Indian legislature, return the Bill for reconsideration by either chamber.

(5) Rules made for the purpose of this section may contain such general and supplemental provisions as appear necessary for the purpose of giving full effect to this section.

(6) Standing orders may be made providing for the conduct of business and the procedure to be followed in either chamber of the Indian legislature in so far as these matters are not provided for by rules made under the principal Act. The first standing orders shall be made by the Governor-General in Council, but may, with the consent of the Governor-General, be altered by the chamber to which they relate.

Any standing order made as aforesaid which is repugnant to the provisions of any rules made under the principal Act shall, to the extent of that repugnancy but not otherwise, be void.

(7) Subject to the rules and standing orders affecting the chamber, there shall be freedom of speech in both chambers of the Indian legislature. No person shall be liable to any proceedings in any court by reason of his speech or vote in either chamber, or by reason of anything contained in any official report of the proceedings of either chamber.

Indian budget

25.—(1) The estimated annual expenditure and revenue of the Governor-General in Council shall be laid in the form of a statement before both chambers of the Indian legislature in each year.

(2) No proposal for the appropriation of any revenue or moneys for any purpose shall be made except on the recommendation of the Governor-General.

(3) The proposals of the Governor-General in Council for the appropriation of revenue or moneys relating to the following heads of expenditure shall not be submitted to the vote of the legislative assembly, nor shall they be open to discussion by either chamber at the time when the annual statement is under consideration, unless the Governor-General otherwise directs—

> (i) interest and sinking fund charges on loans ; and
>
> (ii) expenditure of which the amount is prescribed by or under any law ; and
>
> (iii) salaries and pensions of persons appointed by or with the approval of His Majesty or by the Secretary of State in Council ; and
>
> (iv) salaries of chief commissioners and judicial commissioners ; and
>
> (v) expenditure classified by the order of the Governor-General in Council as—
>
>> (a) ecclesiastical ;
>>
>> (b) political ;
>>
>> (c) defence.

(4) If any question arises whether any proposed appropriation of revenue or moneys does or does not

relate to the above heads, the decision of the Governor-General on the question shall be final.

(5) The proposals of the Governor-General in Council for the appropriation of revenue or moneys relating to heads of expenditure not specified in the above heads shall be submitted to the vote of the legislative assembly in the form of demands for grants.

(6) The legislative assembly may assent or refuse its assent to any demand or may reduce the amount referred to in any demand by a reduction of the whole grant.

(7) The demands as voted by the legislative assembly shall be submitted to the Governor-General in Council, who shall, if he declares that he is satisfied that any demand which has been refused by the legislative assembly is essential to the discharge of his responsibilities, act as if it had been assented to, notwithstanding the withholding of such assent, or the reduction of the amount therein referred to, by the legislative assembly.

(8) Notwithstanding anything in this section, the Governor-General shall have power, in cases of emergency, to authorize such expenditure as may, in his opinion, be necessary for the safety or tranquillity of British India or any part thereof.

Provision for case of failure to pass legislation

26.—(1) Where either chamber of the Indian legislature refuses leave to introduce, or fails to pass in a form recommended by the Governor-General, any Bill, the Governor-General may certify that the passage of the Bill is essential for the safety, tranquillity or interests of British India or any part thereof, and thereupon—

(a) If the Bill has already been passed by the other chamber, the Bill shall, on signature by the Governor-General, notwithstanding that it has not been consented to by both chambers, forthwith become an Act of the Indian legislature in the form of the Bill as originally introduced or proposed to be introduced in the Indian legislature, or (as the case may be) in the form recommended by the Governor-General ; and

(b) If the Bill has not already been so passed, the Bill shall be laid before the other chamber, and, if consented to by that chamber in the form recommended by the Governor-General, shall become an Act as aforesaid on the signification of the Governor-General's assent, or, if not so consented to, shall, on signature by the Governor-General, become an Act as aforesaid.

(2) Every such Act shall be expressed to be made by the Governor-General, and shall, as soon as practicable after being made, be laid before both Houses of Parliament, and shall not have effect until it has received His Majesty's assent, and shall not be presented for His Majesty's assent until copies thereof have been laid before each House of Parliament for not less than eight days on which that House has sat ; and upon the signification of such assent by His Majesty in Council, and the notification thereof by the Governor-General, the Act shall have the same force and effect as an

Act passed by the Indian legislature and duly assented to :

Provided that, where in the opinion of the Governor-General a state of emergency exists which justifies such action, the Governor-General may direct that any such Act shall come into operation forthwith, and thereupon the Act shall have such force and effect as aforesaid, subject, however, to disallowance by His Majesty in Council.

Supplemental provisions as to powers of Indian legislature

27.—(1) In addition to the measures referred to in subsection (2) of section sixty-seven of the principal Act, as requiring the previous sanction of the Governor-General, it shall not be lawful without such previous sanction to introduce at any meeting of either chamber of the Indian legislature any measure—

(a) regulating any provincial subject, or any part of a provincial subject, which has not been declared by rules under the principal Act to be subject to legislation by the Indian legislature ; or

(b) repealing or amending any Act of a local legislature ; or

(c) repealing or amending any Act or ordinance made by the Governor-General.

(2) Where in either chamber of the Indian legislature any Bill has been introduced, or is proposed to be introduced, or any amendment to a Bill is moved, or proposed to be moved, the Governor-General may certify that the Bill, or any clause of it, or the amendment, affects the safety or tranquillity of British India, or any part thereof,

and may direct that no proceedings, or that no further proceedings, shall be taken by the chamber in relation to the Bill, clause, or amendment, and effect shall be given to such direction.

Composition of Governor-General's executive council

28.—(1) The provision in section thirty-six of the principal Act, imposing a limit on the number of members of the Governor-General's executive council, shall cease to have effect.

(2) The provision in section thirty-six of the principal Act as to the qualification of members of the council shall have effect as though the words ' at the time of their appointment ' were omitted, and as though after the word ' Scotland ' there were inserted the words ' or a pleader of the High Court ' and as though ' ten years ' were substituted for ' five years '.

(3) Provision may be made by rules under the principal Act as to the qualifications to be required in respect of members of the Governor-General's executive council, in any case where such provision is not made by section. thirty-six of the principal Act as amended by this section.

(4) Subsection (2) of section thirty-seven of the principal Act (which provides that when and so long as the Governor-General's executive council assembles in a province having a governor the governor shall be an extraordinary member of the council) shall cease to have effect.

Appointment of council secretaries

29.—(1) The Governor-General may at his discretion appoint, from among the members of the legislative assembly, council secretaries, who shall hold office during his pleasure and discharge such duties in assisting the members of his executive council as he may assign to them.

(2) There shall be paid to council secretaries so appointed such salary as may be provided by the Indian legislature.

(3) A council secretary shall cease to hold office if he ceases for more than six months to be a member of the legislative assembly.

PART III

SECRETARY OF STATE IN COUNCIL

Payment of salary of Secretary of State, &c., out of moneys provided by Parliament

30. The salary of the Secretary of State, the salaries of his under-secretaries, and any other expenses of his department may, notwithstanding anything in the principal Act, instead of being paid out of the revenues of India, be paid out of moneys provided by Parliament, and the salary of the Secretary of State shall be so paid.

Council of India

31. The following amendments shall be made in section three of the principal Act in relation to the composition of the Council of India, the qualification, term of office, and remuneration of its members :—

(1) The provisions of subsection (1) shall have effect as though ' eight ' and ' twelve ' were substituted for ' ten ' and ' fourteen ' respectively, as the minimum and maximum number of members, provided that the council, as constituted at the time of

the passing of this Act, shall not be affected by this provision, but no fresh appointment or re-appointment thereto shall be made in excess of the maximum prescribed by this provision.

(2) The provisions of subsection (3) shall have effect as if ' one-half ' were substituted for ' nine ' and ' India ' were substituted for ' British India '.

(3) In subsection (4) ' five years ' shall be substituted for ' seven years ' as the term of office of members of the council, provided that the tenure of office of any person who is a member of the council at the time of the passing of this Act shall not be affected by this provision.

(4) The provisions of subsection (8) shall cease to have effect and in lieu thereof the following provisions shall be inserted :

' There shall be paid to each member of the Council of India the annual salary of twelve hundred pounds ; provided that any member of the council who was at the time of his appointment domiciled in India shall receive, in addition to the salary hereby provided, an annual subsistence allowance of six hundred pounds.

' Such salaries and allowances may be paid out of the revenues of India or out of moneys provided by Parliament.'

(5) Notwithstanding anything in any Act or rules, where any person in the service of the Crown in India is appointed a member of the council before completion of the

period of such service required to entitle him to a pension or annuity, his service as such member shall, for the purpose of any pension or annuity which would be payable to him on completion of such period, be reckoned as service under the Crown in India whilst resident in India.

Further provisions as to Council of India

32.—(1) The provision in section six of the principal Act which prescribes the quorum for meetings of the Council of India shall cease to have effect, and the Secretary of State shall provide for a quorum by directions to be issued in this behalf.

(2) The provision in section eight of the principal Act relating to meetings of the Council of India shall have effect as though ' month ' were substituted for ' week '.

(3) Section ten of the principal Act shall have effect as though the words ' all business of the ' council or committees thereof is to be transacted ' were omitted, and the words ' the business of the ' Secretary of State in Council or the Council of ' India shall be transacted, and any order made or ' act done in accordance with such direction shall, ' subject to the provisions of this Act, be treated ' as being an order of the Secretary of State in ' Council ' were inserted in lieu thereof.

Relaxation of control of Secretary of State

33. The Secretary of State in Council may, notwithstanding anything in the principal Act, by rule regulate and restrict the exercise of the powers of superintendence, direction, and control,

vested in the Secretary of State and the Secretary
of State in Council, by the principal Act, or
otherwise, in such manner as may appear necessary
or expedient in order to give effect to the purposes
of this Act.

Before any rules are made under this section
relating to subjects other than transferred subjects,
the rules proposed to be made shall be laid in
draft before both Houses of Parliament, and such
rules shall not be made unless both Houses by
resolution approve the draft either without
modification or addition, or with modifications
or additions to which both Houses agree, but upon
such approval being given the Secretary of State
in Council may make such rules in the form in
which they have been approved, and such rules
on being so made shall be of full force and effect.

Any rules relating to transferred subjects made
under this section shall be laid before both Houses
of Parliament as soon as may be after they are
made, and, if an Address is presented to His
Majesty by either House of Parliament within the
next thirty days on which that House has sat after
the rules are laid before it praying that the rules
or any of them may be annulled, His Majesty in
Council may annul the rules or any of them, and
those rules shall thenceforth be void, but without
prejudice to the validity of anything previously
done thereunder.

Correspondence between Secretary of State and India

34. So much of section five of the principal
Act as relates to orders and communications
sent to India from the United Kingdom and to
orders made in the United Kingdom, and sections

eleven, twelve, thirteen, and fourteen of the principal Act, shall cease to have effect, and the procedure for the sending of orders and communications to India and in general for correspondence between the Secretary of State and the Governor-General in Council or any local government shall be such as may be prescribed by order of the Secretary of State in Council.

High Commissioner for India

35. His Majesty may by Order in Council make provision for the appointment of a High Commissioner for India in the United Kingdom, and for the pay, pension, powers, duties, and conditions of employment of the High Commissioner and of his assistants ; and the Order may further provide for delegating to the High Commissioner any of the powers previously exercised by the Secretary of State or the Secretary of State in Council, whether under the principal Act or otherwise, in relation to making contracts, and may prescribe the conditions under which he shall act on behalf of the Governor-General in Council or any local government.

PART IV

THE CIVIL SERVICES IN INDIA

The civil services in India

36.—(1) Subject to the provisions of the principal Act and of rules made thereunder, every person in the civil service of the Crown in India holds office during His Majesty's pleasure, and may be employed in any manner required by a proper authority within the scope of his duty, but no person in that service may be dismissed by any authority subordinate to that by which he was appointed, and the Secretary of State in Council may (except so far as he may provide by rules to the contrary) reinstate any person in that service who has been dismissed.

If any such person appointed by the Secretary of State in Council thinks himself wronged by an order of an official superior in a governor's province, and on due application made to that superior does not receive the redress to which he may consider himself entitled, he may, without prejudice to any other right of redress, complain to the governor of the province in order to obtain justice, and the governor is hereby directed to examine such complaint and require such action to be taken thereon as may appear to him to be just and equitable.

(2) The Secretary of State in Council may make rules for regulating the classification of the civil services in India, the methods of their recruitment, their conditions of service, pay and allowances, and discipline and conduct. Such rules may, to such extent and in respect of such matters as may be prescribed, delegate the power of making rules to the Governor-General in Council or to local governments, or authorize the Indian legislature or local legislatures to make laws regulating the public services :

` Provided that every person appointed before the commencement of this Act by the Secretary of State in Council to the civil service of the Crown in India shall retain all his existing or accruing rights, or shall receive such compensation for the loss of any of them as the Secretary of State in Council may consider just and equitable.

(3) The right to pensions and the scale and condi-tions of pensions of all persons in the civil service of the Crown in India appointed by the Secretary of State in Council shall be regulated in accordance with the rules in force at the time of the passing of this Act. Any such rules may be varied or added to by the Secretary of State in Council and shall have effect as so varied or added to, but any such variation or addition shall not adversely affect the pension of any member of the service appointed before the date thereof.

Nothing in this section or in any rule thereunder shall prejudice the rights to which any person may, or may have, become entitled under the provisions in relation to pensions contained in the East India Annuity Funds Act, 1874.[1]

(4) For the removal of doubts, it is hereby declared that all rules or other provisions in operation at the time of the passing of this Act, whether made by the Secretary of State in Council or by any other authority, relating to the civil service of the Crown in India, were duly made in accordance with the powers in that behalf, and are confirmed, but any such rules or provisions may be revoked, varied, or added to by rules or laws made under this section.

Appointments to the Indian Civil Service

37.—(1) Notwithstanding anything in section ninety-seven of the principal Act, the Secretary of State may make appointments to the Indian Civil Service of persons domiciled in India, in accordance with such rules as may be prescribed by the Secretary of State in Council with the

---

[1] 37 & 38 Vict. c. 12.

concurrence of the majority of votes at a meeting of the Council of India.

Any rules made under this section shall not have force until they have been laid for thirty days before both Houses of Parliament.

(2) The Indian Civil Service (Temporary Provisions) Act, 1915 [1] (which confers power during the war and for a period of two years thereafter to make appointments to the Indian Civil Service without examination), shall have effect as though 'three years' were substituted for 'two years'.

Public service commission

38.—(1) There shall be established in India a public service commission, consisting of not more than five members, of whom one shall be chairman, appointed by the Secretary of State in Council. Each member shall hold office for five years, and may be re-appointed. No member shall be removed before the expiry of his term of office, except by order of the Secretary of State in Council. The qualifications for appointment, and the pay and pension (if any) attaching to the office of chairman and member, shall be prescribed by rules made by the Secretary of State in Council.

(2) The public service commission shall discharge, in regard to recruitment and control of the public services in India, such functions as may be assigned thereto by rules made by the Secretary of State in Council.

Financial control

39.—(1) An auditor-general in India shall be appointed by the Secretary of State in Council,

[1] 5 & 6 Geo. 5, c. 87.

and shall hold office during His Majesty's pleasure. The Secretary of State in Council shall, by rules, make provision for his pay, powers, duties, and conditions of employment, or for the discharge of his duties in the case of a temporary vacancy or absence from duty.

(2) Subject to any rules made by the Secretary of State in Council, no office may be added to or withdrawn from the public service, and the emoluments of no post may be varied, except after consultation with such finance authority as may be designated in the rules, being an authority of the province or of the Government of India, according as the post is or is not under the control of a local government.

Rules under Part IV

40. Rules made under this Part of this Act shall not be made except with the concurrence of the majority of votes at a meeting of the Council of India.

PART V

STATUTORY COMMISSION

41.—(1) At the expiration of ten years after the passing of this Act the Secretary of State, with the concurrence of both Houses of Parliament, shall submit for the approval of His Majesty the names of persons to act as a commission for the purposes of this section.

(2) The persons whose names are so submitted, if approved by His Majesty, shall be a commission for the purpose of inquiring into the working of the system of government, the growth of education,

and the development of representative institutions in British India, and matters connected therewith, and the commission shall report as to whether and to what extent it is desirable to establish the principle of responsible government, or to extend, modify, or restrict the degree of responsible government then existing therein, including the question whether the establishment of second chambers of the local legislatures is or is not desirable.

(3) The commission shall also inquire into and report on any other matter affecting British India and the provinces, which may be referred to the commission by His Majesty.

PART VI

GENERAL

Modification of s. 124 of principal Act

42. Notwithstanding anything in section one hundred and twenty-four of the principal Act, if any member of the Governor-General's Executive Council or any member of any local government was at the time of his appointment concerned or engaged in any trade or business, he may, during the term of his office, with the sanction in writing of the Governor-General, or, in the case of ministers, of the governor of the province, and in any case subject to such general conditions and restrictions as the Governor-General in Council may prescribe, retain his concern or interest in that trade or business, but shall not, during that term, take part in the direction or management of that trade or business.

Signification of Royal Assent

43. Any assent or disallowance by His Majesty, which under the principal Act is required to be signified through the Secretary of State in Council, shall, as from the passing of this Act, be signified by His Majesty in Council.

Power to make rules

44.—(1) Where any matter is required to be prescribed or regulated by rules under the principal Act and no special provision is made as to the authority by whom the rules are to be made, the rules shall be made by the Governor-General in Council, with the sanction of the Secretary of State in Council, and shall not be subject to repeal or alteration by the Indian legislature or by any local legislature.

(2) Any rules made under this Act or under the principal Act may be so framed as to make different provision for different provinces.

(3) Any rules to which subsection (1) of this section applies shall be laid before both Houses of Parliament as soon as may be after they are made, and, if an Address is presented to His Majesty by either House of Parliament within the next thirty days on which that House has sat after the rules are laid before it praying that the rules or any of them may be annulled, His Majesty in Council may annul the rules or any of them, and those rules shall thenceforth be void, but without prejudice to the validity of anything previously done thereunder :

Provided that the Secretary of State may direct that any rules to which this section applies shall be laid in draft before both Houses of Parliament, and in such case the rules shall not be made unless both Houses by resolution approve the draft either without modification or addition, or with modifications or additions to which both Houses agree, but, upon such approval being given, the rules may be made in the form in which they have been approved, and such rules on being so made shall be of full force and effect, and shall not require to be further laid before Parliament.

14. *Proclamation by the King-Emperor, 23 December, 1919*

GEORGE THE FIFTH, by the Grace of God of the
  United Kingdom of Great Britain and Ireland,
  and of the British Dominions beyond the Seas,
  King, Defender of the Faith, Emperor of India.
To My Viceroy and Governor-General, to the
  Princes of the Indian States, and to all My
  subjects in India, of whatsoever race or creed,
  Greeting.
1. Another epoch has been reached to-day in the annals of India. I have given My Royal Assent to an Act which will take its place among the great historic measures passed by the Parliament of this Realm for the better government of India and the greater contentment of her people. The Acts of 1773 and 1784 were designed to establish a regular system of administration and justice under the Honourable East India Company. The Act of 1833 opened the door for Indians to public office and employment. The Act of 1858 transferred the administration from the Company to the Crown, and laid the foundations of the public life

which exists in India to-day. The Act of 1861 sowed the seed of representative institutions, and the seed was quickened into life by the Act of 1909. The Act which has now become law entrusts elected representatives of the people with a definite share in the government and points the way to full responsible government hereafter. If, as I confidently hope, the policy which this Act inaugurates should achieve its purpose, the results will be momentous in the story of human progress ; and it is timely and fitting that I should invite you to-day to consider the past and to join me in My hopes of the future.

2. Ever since the welfare of India was confided to Us, it has been held as a sacred trust by Our Royal House and Line. In 1858 Queen Victoria, of revered memory, solemnly declared Herself bound to Her Indian subjects by the same obligations of duty as to all Her other subjects ; and She assured to them religious freedom, and the equal and impartial protection of the Law. In His message to the Indian people in 1903, My dear Father, King Edward VII, announced His determination to maintain unimpaired the same principles of humane and equitable administration. Again, in His Proclamation of 1908, he renewed the assurances which had been given fifty years before, and surveyed the progress which they had inspired. On My Accession to the Throne in 1910, I sent a message to the Princes and peoples of India, acknowledging their loyalty and their homage, and promising that the prosperity and happiness of India should always be to me of the highest interest and concern. In the following year I visited India with the Queen-Empress and

testified my sympathy for her people and My desire for their wellbeing.

3. While these are the sentiments of affection and devotion by which I and My predecessors have been animated, the Parliament and the people of this Realm and My officers in India have been equally zealous for the moral advancement of India. We have endeavoured to give to her people the many blessings which Providence has bestowed upon ourselves. But there is one gift which yet remains, and without which the progress of a country cannot be consummated—the right of her people to direct her affairs and safeguard her interests. The defence of India against foreign aggression is a duty of common imperial interest and pride. The control of her domestic concerns is a burden which India may legitimately aspire to take upon her own shoulders. The burden is too heavy to be borne in full until time and experience have brought the necessary strength ; but opportunity will now be given for experience to grow and for responsibility to increase with the capacity for its fulfilment.

4. I have watched with understanding and sympathy the growing desire of My Indian people for representative institutions. Starting from small beginnings, this ambition has steadily strengthened its hold upon the intelligence of the country. It has pursued its course along constitutional channels with sincerity and courage. It has survived the discredit which at times and in places lawless men sought to cast upon it by acts of violence committed under the guise of patriotism. It has been stirred to more vigorous life by the ideals for which the British Commonwealth fought in

the Great War, and it claims support in the part
which India has taken in our common struggles,
anxieties and victories.

In truth, the desire after political responsibility
has its source at the root of the British connexion
with India. It has sprung inevitably from the
deeper and wider studies of human thought and
history which that connexion has opened to the
Indian people. Without it the work of the British
in India would have been incomplete. It was
therefore with a wise judgement that the beginnings of representative institutions were laid many
years ago. Their scope has been extended stage
by stage until there now lies before us a definite
step on the road to responsible government.

5. With the same sympathy and with redoubled
interest I shall watch the progress along this road.
The path will not be easy, and in the march
towards the goal there will be need of perse-
verance and of mutual forbearance between all
sections and races of My people in India. I am
confident that those high qualities will be forthcoming. I rely on the new popular assemblies to
interpret wisely the wishes of those whom they
represent, and not to forget the interests of the
masses who cannot yet be admitted to the franchise. I rely on the leaders of the people, the
Ministers of the future, to face responsibility and
endure misrepresentation; to sacrifice much for the
common interest of the State, remembering that
true patriotism transcends party and communal
boundaries; and while retaining the confidence
of the legislatures to co-operate with My officers
for the common good in sinking unessential
differences and in maintaining the essential

standards of a just and generous government. Equally do I rely upon My officers to respect their new colleagues and to work with them in harmony and kindliness ; to assist the people and their representatives in an orderly advance towards free institutions ; and to find in these new tasks a fresh opportunity to fulfil, as in the past, their highest purpose of faithful service to My people.

6. It is My earnest desire at this time that, so far as possible, any trace of bitterness between My people and those who are responsible for My government should be obliterated. Let those who, in their eagerness for political progress, have broken the law in the past respect it in the future. Let it become possible for those who are charged with the maintenance of peaceful and orderly government to forget the extravagances which they have had to curb. A new era is opening. Let it begin with a common determination among My people and My officers to work together for a common purpose. I therefore direct My Viceroy to exercise, in My name and on My behalf, My Royal clemency to political offenders, in the fullest measure which in his judgement is compatible with the public safety. I desire him to extend it, on this condition, to persons who, for offences against the State or under any special or emergency legislation, are suffering imprisonment or restrictions upon their liberty. I trust that this leniency will be justified by the future conduct of those whom it benefits, and that all My subjects will so demean themselves as to render it unnecessary to enforce the laws for such offences hereafter.

7. Simultaneously with the new constitution in British India, I have gladly assented to the

establishment of a Chamber of Princes. I trust that its counsels may be fruitful of lasting good to the Princes and States themselves, may advance the interests which are common to their territories and to British India, and may be to the advantage of the Empire as a whole. I take the occasion again to assure the Princes of India of My determination ever to maintain unimpaired their privileges, rights and dignities.

8. It is My intention to send My dear son, the Prince of Wales, to India next winter to inaugurate on My behalf the new Chamber of Princes and the new constitution in British India. May he find mutual goodwill and confidence prevailing among those on whom will rest the future service of the country, so that success may crown their labours and progressive enlightenment attend their administration. And with all My people I pray to Almighty God that by His wisdom and under His guidance India may be led to greater prosperity and contentment, and may grow to the fullness of political freedom.   ·   GEORGE, R. I.

15. *The King-Emperor's Message to the Rulers of the Indian States on the Inauguration of the Chamber of Princes, February 1921*

GEORGE THE FIFTH, by the Grace of God of the United Kingdom of Great Britain and Ireland, and of the British Dominions beyond the Seas, King, Defender of the Faith, Emperor of India.

To My Viceroy and Governor-General, and to the Princes and Rulers of the Indian States: Greeting.

1. In My Royal Proclamation of December, 1919, I gave earnest of My affectionate care and regard for the Ruling Princes and Chiefs of the Indian States by signifying My assent to the establishment of a Chamber of Princes. During the year that has since passed My Viceroy and many of the Princes themselves have been engaged in framing for My approval a constitution for the Chamber and the rules and regulations necessary to ensure the smooth and efficient performance of its important functions.

This work is now complete, and it remains for Me to take the final steps to bring the Chamber into being, in the confident hope that the united counsels of the Princes and Rulers, assembled in formal conclave, will be fruitful of lasting good both to themselves and their subjects, and by advancing the interests that are common to their territories and to British India, will benefit My Empire as a whole. It is in this hope that I have charged My revered and beloved Uncle, His Royal Highness the Duke of Connaught and Strathearn, to perform on My behalf the ceremony of the inauguration of the Chamber of Princes.

2. It is My firm belief that a future full of great and beneficent activities lies before the Chamber thus established. To the Princes, long versed in the arts of government and statesmanship, it will open still wider fields of Imperial Service. It will afford them opportunities, of which, I am convinced, they will be prompt to avail themselves, of comparing experience, interchanging ideas, and framing mature and balanced conclusions on matters of common interest. Nor will less advantage accrue to My Viceroy and the officers serving under him,

to whom the prudent counsels and considered advice of the Chamber cannot fail to be of the greatest assistance. The problems of the future must be faced in a spirit of co-operation and mutual trust.

It is in this spirit that I summon the Princes of India to a larger share in My Councils. I do so in full reliance upon their devotion to My Throne and Person, proved as it has been both in long years of peace and in the terrible ordeal of the Great War, and in the confident anticipation that by this means the bonds of mutual understanding will be strengthened and the growing identity of interest between the Indian States and the rest of My Empire will be fostered and developed.

3. In My former Proclamation I repeated the assurance, given on many occasions by My Royal predecessors and Myself, of My determination ever to maintain unimpaired the privileges, rights, and dignities of the Princes of India. The Princes may rest assured that this pledge remains inviolate and inviolable. I now authorize My Viceroy to publish the terms of the Constitution of the new Chamber.

My Viceroy will take its counsel freely in matters relating to the territories of the Indian States generally, and in matters that affect those territories jointly with British India, or with the rest of My Empire. It will have no concern with the internal affairs of individual States or their Rulers or with the relations of Individual States to My Government, while the existing rights of the States and their freedom of action will be in no way prejudiced or impaired. It is My earnest hope that the Princes of India will take regular part in

the deliberations of the Chamber; but attendance
will be a matter of choice, not of constraint.
There will be no obligation upon any member to
record his opinion, by vote or otherwise, upon any
question that may come under discussion; and
it is further My desire that, at the discretion of
My Viceroy, an opportunity shall be given to any
Prince who has not taken a part in the deliberations
of the Chamber to record his views on any question
that the Chamber has had under its consideration.

4. I pray that the blessing of Divine Providence
may rest upon the labours of the Chamber; that
its deliberations may be inspired by true wisdom
and moderation; and that it may seek and find
its best reward in promoting the general weal and
in increasing the strength and unity of the mighty
Empire over which I have been called upon to rule.

16. *H.R.H. the Duke of Connaught's Address
to the Indian Assembly on its Inauguration, 9 February 1921*

Your Excellency and Gentlemen of the Indian
  Legislature,
I am the bearer of a message from His Majesty the
  King-Emperor. It is this :
As you know, it had been the intention of His
Majesty to send the Prince of Wales, the heir to the
throne, with His greetings and His authority to
open the chambers of the new Indian Legislature.
Events did not permit of his coming, and I received
His Majesty's commands to perform these functions
on His behalf. In me the King selected the eldest
member of the Royal house, and the only surviving
son of Queen Victoria, whose love and care for

India will ever live in its people's memory. I have myself a deep affection for India, having served it for years and made many friends among its Princes and leaders. It is thus with no common pleasure that I am here, to receive you on this memorable occasion.

Throughout the centuries Delhi has witnessed the pomp and ceremony of many historic assemblages. Two at least of these are remembered by most of you. Twenty years ago I took part in that brilliant concourse which celebrated the accession of my late brother, King Edward the Seventh. Nine years later, amid circumstances of unforgettable splendour, King George the Fifth and his Queen received in person the homage of the Princes and people of India. Our ceremony to-day may lack the colour and romance of the gatherings I have mentioned though it does not yield to them in the sincerity of its loyalty. But it strikes a new and a different note ; it marks the awakening of a great nation to the power of its nationhood.

In the annals of the world there is not, so far as I know, an exact parallel for the constitutional change which this function initiates ; there is certainly no parallel for the method of that change. Political freedom has often been won by revolution, by tumult, by civil war, as the price of peace and public safety. How rarely has it been the free gift of one people to another, in response to a growing wish for greater liberty, and to growing evidence of fitness for its enjoyment. Such, however, is the position of India to-day ; and I congratulate most warmly those of you, old in the service of your motherland, who have striven, through good report and ill, for the first instal-

ment of that gift, and to prove India worthy of it.
I trust that you, and those who take up your
mantles after you will move faithfully and steadfastly along the road which is opened to-day.

When India became a Dependency of the British
Crown she passed under British guardianship,
which has laboured with glorious results to protect
India from the consequences of her own history
at home, and from the complications of international pressure abroad. Autocratic, however,
as was the Government then inaugurated, it was
based on principles laid down by Her late Majesty
Queen Victoria in that proclamation of 1858, of
which the keynote is contained in the following
passage : ' In their prosperity will be our strength ;
in their contentment our security, and in their
gratitude our best reward.' And, though there
have been occasions on which the tranquillity of
this great country has been endangered by dis-
turbances and disorders, which have necessitated
the use of military force, speaking on behalf of
His Majesty and with the assent of His Government,
I repudiate in the most emphatic manner the idea
that the administration of India has been, or ever
can be, based on principles of force or terrorism.

All governments are liable to be confronted with
situations which can be dealt with only by measures
outside the ordinary law ; but the employment of
such measures is subject to clear and definite limitations ; and His Majesty's Government have always
insisted, and will always insist, on the observance
of these limitations as jealously in the case of
India as in that of England herself.

As His Excellency the Viceroy has observed, the
principle of autocracy has been abandoned. Its

.retention would have been incompatible with that contentment which had been declared by Her late Majesty Queen Victoria to be the aim of British rule, and would have been inconsistent with the legitimate demands and aspirations of the Indian people, and the stage of political development which they have attained. Henceforward, in an ever-increasing degree, India will have to bear her own burdens. They are not light. The times which have seen the conception and birth of the new constitution are full of trouble. The war which ended two years ago has done more than alter the boundaries of nations. The confusion which it brought in its train will abate in time ; but the world has not passed unchanged through the fire. New aspirations have awakened, new problems been created, and old ones invested with a stinging urgency.

India has escaped the worst ravages of the war and its sequels, and is thus in some respects better fitted than many other countries to confront the future. Her material resources are unimpaired, her financial system is sound, and her industries are ready for rapid expansion. But she cannot hope to escape altogether the consequences of the world-wide struggle. The countries of the earth are linked together as never before. A contagious ferment of scepticism and unrest is seething everywhere in the minds of men, and its workings are plainly visible in India. She has other problems peculiarly her own. Inexperience in political methods will be irksome at times. The electorates will have to be taught their powers and responsibilities. And difficulties which are negligible in smaller and homogeneous countries will arise in handling questions of religion and race and custom.

Gentlemen of the Indian Legislature, such are the labours which await you. They will have to be carried on under the eyes of a watching world, interested but not uncritical, of the sister nations who welcome you into their partnership in the British Empire, of that wider Council of Nations which look to India as the future guide of the unknown forces of Asia. Your individual responsibility is great. You may perhaps be apprehensive that the arena for practical issues of immediate moment will be rather the provincial councils than the central legislature. You may feel that the ministers in the provinces will be in closer touch with popular causes and have larger opportunities of public service. But this is true only in a very limited sense.

It is the clear intention of the Act of 1919 that the policy and decisions of the Government of India should be influenced to an extent incomparably greater than they have been in the past by the views of the Indian Legislature ; and the Government will give the fullest possible effect, consistent with their own responsibilities to Parliament, to this principle of the new constitution. From now onwards your influence will extend to every sphere of the central government. It will be felt in every part of its administration. You are concerned, not with one province but with all British India, and statesmanship could not ask for a nobler field of exercise. Upon the manner in which your influence is exerted, upon the wisdom and foresight displayed in your deliberations, upon the spirit in which you approach your great task,

will depend the progress of India towards the
goal of complete self-government.

To ensure, so far as political machinery can
ensure, that the legislature is fitly equipped for
those lofty duties, two chambers have been constituted. In the Council of State it has been the
intention of Parliament to create a true Senate, a
body of 'elder statesmen' endowed with mature
knowledge, experience of the world, and the con-
sequent sobriety of judgement. Its functions will
be to exercise a revising but not an overriding
influence for caution and moderation, and to
review and adjust the acts of the larger chamber.
To the Assembly it will fall to voice more directly
the needs of the people. Soldier and trader,
owners of land and dwellers in cities, Hindu and
Mahomedan, Sikh, and Christian, all classes and
communities will have in it their share of representation. Each class and each community can
bring its own contribution, its own special knowledge, to the common deliberations.

And may I say in passing that help will be
expected from the representatives of the British
non-official community. They have done great
service to the trade and industry of India in the
past ; will they now, with their special experience
of representative institutions in their own land,
lend their powerful aid in building up India's
political life and practice ?

In a legislature thus composed it is both inevitable and right that strong differences of opinion
and aims should manifest themselves. Struggle is
a condition of progress in the political as in the
natural world. Politics is in fact the process of
the clash of wills, sympathies, and interests,

striving for adjustment in the sphere of legislation and government. But it is the great virtue of representative institutions that they tend to replace the blind encounter of conflicting interests by reasoned discussion, compromise, toleration, and the mutual respect of honourable opponents. The extent to which a body of law-makers shows itself capable of controlling passion and prejudice is the measure of its capacity for enduring success.

For these reflections I make no apology. They must already have been present to your minds ; but they constitute the strongest plea for what all friends of India most desire to see—a greater unity of purpose among her varying communities. In all your deliberations let there be a conscious striving for unity in essentials, that unity which has been lacking in India in the past, but may yet become, if steadfastly nurtured, her greatest strength.

Gentlemen of the Indian Legislature, hitherto I have spoken of your duties. Let me close with a word on your privileges. On you, who have been elected the first members of the two chambers, a signal honour has fallen. Your names will go down to history as those whom India chose to lead the van of her march towards constitutional liberty. I pray that success will attend you, and that the result of your labours will be worthy of the trust that India has reposed in you.

Your Excellency, you are approaching the end of your Viceroyalty. In almost every country of the world the years just passed have been critical and anxious, in India no less, and I know well the vast and well-nigh overwhelming anxieties which you have been called upon to face.

I know well the high sense of duty which has always prompted you, the single purpose which has possessed you, the never-failing courage which has sustained you.

From the first moment you held one special object in view. You determined, God willing, to lead India to a definite stage in her constitutional advancement. Through all distractions and difficulties you held to that determination, and to-day, when your thoughts are turning to the Homeland, and to the hour when your mantle will pass to other shoulders, when you think regretfully, as all men must in such an hour, of all the things you would have wished to do had fortune been more kind, still as you look round this assembly, your Excellency must surely feel ' for this I have striven and in this I have won '.

I wish to offer my warm congratulations to you on the translation to-day into life and reality of that far-seeing scheme of political progress of which you and the Secretary of State were the authors. It must be no small pride to a statesman who had been directing the destinies of India during these difficult years, that he sees, while still in office, the foundations securely laid of that edifice which he helped to plan with infinite care, in face of much misunderstanding, and yet with the full assurance of a nation's future gratitude. I trust that your Excellency's successor and the devoted public servants who will be his agents and advisers, will find in the new Indian Legislature an alleviation of labour, a faithful mirror of India's needs and wishes, and a trusty link between themselves and the vast millions under their care.

And now I declare duly open the Council of

State and the Legislative Assembly constituted under the Government of India Act, 1919.

Gentlemen, I have finished my part in to-day's official proceedings. May I claim your patience and forbearance while I say a few words of a personal nature? Since I landed, I have felt around me bitterness and estrangement between those who have been and should be friends. The shadow of Amritsar[1] has lengthened over the fair face of India. I know how deep is the concern felt by His Majesty the King-Emperor at the terrible chapter of events in the Punjab. No one can deplore those events more intensely than I do myself.

I have reached a time of life when I most desire to heal wounds, and to reunite those who have been disunited. In what must be, I fear, my last visit to the India I love so well, here in the new capital inaugurating a new Constitution, I am moved to make you a personal appeal, put in simple words that come from my heart, not to be coldly and critically interpreted.

My experience tells me that misunderstandings usually mean mistakes on either side. As an old friend of India, I appeal to you all, British and Indians, to bury along with the dead past the mistakes and misunderstandings of the past, to forgive where you have to forgive, and to join hands and to work together to realize the hopes that arise from to-day.

[1] See Cmd. 534, 681, 705, as to the grave outbreak of unrest in the Punjab and the deplorable massacre at the Jallianwala Bagh on April 13, 1919.

INDEX

232   N

A LIST OF THE
WORLD'S
CLASSICS

Oxford University Press

THE WORLD'S CLASSICS

A SERIES in constant progress, containing over
four hundred volumes, and offering in a size
adapted for the pocket, and at a low price, the most
famous works in the English language, with more
than a few translations. Many of the volumes contain introductions by the best modern writers.

POCKET SIZE, 6 × 3¾ inches (as this list). Large
type, on thin opaque paper, in superfine art cloth.

A NUMBER of the volumes are also obtainable in
Pebble grain Moroccoette and in Natural grain
Morocco. These are specially recommended for
presentation.

THE VOLUMES are obtainable through any book-
seller.

IN THE FOLLOWING LIST the books are classified as below:

Anthologies	*Letters*
Autobiography	*Literary Criticism*
Biography	*Philosophy and Science*
Classics–Greek and Roman	*Poetry*
Drama	*Politics, Political Theory,*
Essays and Belles Lettres	*and Political Economy*
Fiction (Short Stories are	*Religion*
grouped separately)	*Short Stories*
History	*Travel and Topography*

AN INDEX OF AUTHORS is given at the end of
the list.

THE
WORLD'S CLASSICS

PRINTED ON OXFORD INDIA PAPER

The following Works are obtainable in superfine
maroon cloth, gilt lettered on back,
gilt top, and marker.

TWO VOLUMES IN ONE

BORROW. Lavengro *and* Romany Rye.

MAUDE (AYLMER). Life of Tolstoy.

TOLSTOY. Anna Karenina. Translated by *Louise*
and *Aylmer Maude*.

TROLLOPE. Last Chronicle of Barset.
 „ Orley Farm.
 „ Phineas Finn.
 „ Phineas Redux.

THREE VOLUMES IN ONE

DANTE. The Divine Comedy. Italian text and
translation by *M. B. Anderson*.

ENGLISH SHORT STORIES (Nineteenth and Twentieth
Centuries).

RABELAIS (FRANÇOIS). Gargantua *and* Pantagruel.

TOLSTOY. War and Peace. Revised translation by
Louise and *Aylmer Maude*.

COMPLETE LIST OF THE SERIES

¶ *Anthologies*

A BOOK OF AMERICAN VERSE. Selected and edited by *A. C. Ward* (428).

A BOOK OF NARRATIVE VERSE. Compiled by *V. H. Collins*. Introduction by *Edmund Blunden* (350).

A BOOK OF SCOTTISH VERSE. Compiled by *R. L. Mackie* (417).

AMERICAN CRITICISM. Representative Literary Essays. Chosen by *Norman Foerster* (354).

ENGLISH ESSAYS, chosen and arranged by *W. Peacock* (32).

ENGLISH ESSAYS, 1600–1900, chosen by *S. V. Makower* and *B. H. Blackwell* (172).

ENGLISH ESSAYS, MODERN. Two Series. Selected by *H. S. Milford* (280, 406).

ENGLISH PROSE from MANDEVILLE to RUSKIN, chosen and arranged by *W. Peacock* (45).

ENGLISH PROSE, chosen and arranged by *W. Peacock* in 5 volumes: I, WYCLIFFE to CLARENDON; II, MILTON to GRAY; III, WALPOLE to LAMB; IV, LANDOR to HOLMES; V, MRS. GASKELL to HENRY JAMES (219–23).

ENGLISH PROSE, Narrative, Descriptive, Dramatic (MALORY to STEVENSON), compiled by *H. A. Treble* (204).

ENGLISH SONGS AND BALLADS, compiled by *T. W. H. Crosland*. New edition, with the text revised, and additional poems (13).

ENGLISH SHORT STORIES (Nineteenth and Twentieth Centuries), selected by *H. S. Milford*. Three Series (193, 228, 315).

ENGLISH VERSE. Edited by *W. Peacock*. I, Early Lyrics to SHAKESPEARE (308); II, CAMPION to the Ballads (309); III, DRYDEN to WORDSWORTH (310); IV, SCOTT to ELIZABETH BROWNING (311); V, LONGFELLOW to RUPERT BROOKE (312).

LETTERS WRITTEN IN WAR-TIME (Fifteenth to Nineteenth Centuries), selected and arranged by *H. Wragg* (202).

A MISCELLANY OF TRACTS AND PAMPHLETS. Sixteenth to Nineteenth Centuries. Edited by *A. C. Ward* (304).

PALGRAVE'S GOLDEN TREASURY, with 188 pages of additional poems from LANDOR to BLUNDEN (133).

READING AT RANDOM. A 'World's Classics' Anthology. Edited by *Ben Ray Redman* (410).

¶ *Autobiography*

AKSAKOFF (SERGHEI). Trans. by *J. D. Duff*. A Russian Gentleman (241). Years of Childhood (242). A Russian Schoolboy (261).

CELLINI (BENVENUTO) (300).

DE QUINCEY (THOMAS). Confessions of an Opium-Eater (23).

FRANKLIN (BENJAMIN). The Autobiography, edited from his original manuscript by *John Bigelow* (250).

GIBBON (EDWARD). Autobiography. Introduction by *J. B. Bury* (139).

HAYDON (BENJAMIN ROBERT). The Autobiography. Introduction and Epilogue by *Edmund Blunden* (314).
HUNT (LEIGH). Autobiography. Intro. *Edmund Blunden* (329).
MILL (JOHN STUART). Autobiography. Introduction by *Harold J. Laski* (262).
TOLSTOY. A Confession, and What I believe. Translated by *Aylmer Maude* (229).
TROLLOPE (ANTHONY). Autobiography. Introduction by *Michael Sadleir* (239).

¶ Biography

CARLYLE. The Life of John Sterling. Introduction by *W. Hale White* (' *Mark Rutherford* ') (144).
CRABBE, LIFE OF. By his Son. Introduction by *E. M. Forster* (404).
DOBSON (AUSTIN). Four Frenchwomen: Charlotte Corday, Madame Roland, Princess de Lamballe, Madame de Genlis (248).
EMERSON. Representative Men. (With *English Traits*) (30).
FRANCIS OF ASSISI (ST.). The Little Flowers; and The Life of Brother Giles. Translated into English verse by *James Rhoades* (265).
GASKELL (MRS.). The Life of Charlotte Brontë (214).
HOUGHTON (LORD). Life of Keats (364).
JOHNSON (SAMUEL). Lives of the Poets. 2 vols. (83, 84).
MAUDE (AYLMER). Life of Tolstoy. 2 vols. (383, 384).
SCOTT (SIR WALTER). Lives of the Novelists. Introduction by *Austin Dobson* (94).
TREVELYAN (SIR G. O.). Life of Macaulay. With a new Introduction by *G. M. Trevelyan*. 2 vols. (401, 402).
WALTON (IZAAK). Lives of Donne, Wotton, Hooker, Herbert, Sanderson. Introduction by *George Saintsbury* (303).

¶ The ' Classics ', Greek and Roman

AESCHYLUS. The Seven Plays. Translated into English Verse by *Lewis Campbell* (117).
ARISTOPHANES. The Acharnians, Knights, Birds, and Frogs. Translated by *J. Hookham Frere*. Intro. *W. W. Merry* (134).
HOMER. Translated by *Pope*. Iliad (18). Odyssey (36).
SOPHOCLES. The Seven Plays. Translated into English Verse by *Lewis Campbell* (116).
VIRGIL. The Aeneid, Georgics, and Eclogues. Translated by *John Dryden* (37).
—— The Aeneid, Georgics, and Eclogues. Translated by *James Rhoades* (227).

¶ Drama

BROWNING (ROBERT). Poems and Plays, 1833–42 (58).

CONGREVE (WILLIAM). Complete Works. 2 vols. Introduction by *Bonamy Dobrée.* I, The Comedies. II, The Mourning Bride, with Letters, Poems, and Miscellanies (276, 277).

EIGHTEENTH CENTURY COMEDY. FARQUHAR'S Beaux' Stratagem, STEELE'S Conscious Lovers, GAY'S Beggar's Opera, FIELDING'S Tom Thumb, GOLDSMITH'S She Stoops to Conquer (292).

EIGHTEENTH CENTURY, LESSER COMEDIES OF THE. Edited by *Allardyce Nicoll.* The five comedies are ARTHUR MURPHY'S The Way to keep him, GEORGE COLMAN'S The Jealous Wife, MRS. INCHBALD'S Everyone has his Fault, THOMAS MORTON'S Speed the Plough, and FREDERICK REYNOLDS'S The Dramatist (321).

FIVE ELIZABETHAN COMEDIES. Edited by *A. K. McIlwraith.* Contains GREENE'S Friar Bacon and Friar Bungay, PEELE'S The Old Wives' Tale, LYLY'S Campaspe, DEKKER'S Shoemaker's Holiday, and the anonymous Merry Devil of Edmonton (422).

FIVE PRE-SHAKESPEAREAN COMEDIES. Edited by *F. S. Boas.* Contains MEDWALL'S Fulgens and Lucrece, HEYWOOD'S The Four PP., UDALL'S Ralph Roister Doister, the anonymous Gammer Gurton's Needle, and GASCOIGNE'S Supposes (418).

GOETHE. Faust, Parts I and II. Translated by *Bayard Taylor.* Intro. by *Marshall Montgomery* and notes by *Douglas Yates* (380).

IBSEN, HENRIK. Peer Gynt. Trans. with an Introduction by *R. Ellis Roberts* (446).

MARLOWE'S Dr. Faustus (with GOETHE'S Faust, Part I, trans. *J. Anster*). Introduction by *Sir A. W. Ward* (135).

RESTORATION TRAGEDIES. DRYDEN'S All for Love, OTWAY'S Venice Preserved, SOUTHERNE'S Oronooko, ROWE'S Fair Penitent, and ADDISON'S Cato. Introduction by *Bonamy Dobrée* (313).

SHAKESPEARE. Plays and Poems. Preface by *A. C. Swinburne.* Introductions by *Edward Dowden.* 9 vols. Comedies. 3 vols. (100, 101, 102). Histories and Poems. 3 vols. (103, 104, 105). Tragedies. 3 vols. (106, 107, 108).

SHAKESPEARE, Six Plays by Contemporaries of. DEKKER, The Shoemaker's Holiday; WEBSTER, The White Devil; BEAUMONT and FLETCHER, The Knight of the Burning Pestle, and Philaster; WEBSTER, The Duchess of Malfi; MASSINGER, A New Way to pay Old Debts. Edited by *C. B. Wheeler* (199).

SHERIDAN. Plays. Introduction by *Joseph Knight* (79).

TOLSTOY. The Plays. Complete edition, including the posthumous plays. Translated by *Louise* and *Aylmer Maude* (243).

¶ Essays and Belles Lettres

BACON. The Essays, Civil and Moral (24).

CARLYLE. On Heroes and Hero-Worship (62). Past and Present. Introduction by *G. K. Chesterton* (153). Sartor Resartus (19).

TRACTS AND PAMPHLETS, from JOHN KNOX to H. G. WELLS (304).
WALTON and COTTON. The Compleat Angler. Introduction by
John Buchan (430).
WHITE (GILBERT). The Natural History of Selborne (22).
WHITMAN. Specimen Days in America (371).

¶ *Fiction* (For SHORT STORIES see separate heading)

AINSWORTH (W. HARRISON). The Tower of London (162).
AUSTEN (JANE). Emma (129). Pride and Prejudice (335). Mansfield Park (345). Northanger Abbey (355). Persuasion (356).
Sense and Sensibility (389).
BLACKMORE (R. D.). Lorna Doone. Introduction by *Sir Herbert Warren* (171).
BORROW (GEORGE). Lavengro (66). The Romany Rye (73).
BRONTË (ANNE). Agnes Grey (141). Tenant of Wildfell Hall (67).
BRONTË (CHARLOTTE). Jane Eyre (1). Shirley (14). Villette (47).
The Professor, and the Poems of the Brontës (78).
BRONTË (EMILY). Wuthering Heights (10).
BUNYAN. The Pilgrim's Progress (12). Mr. Badman (338).
BUTLER (SAMUEL). The Way of all Flesh. With an Essay by
Bernard Shaw (438).
CERVANTES. Don Quixote. 2 volumes (130, 131).
COBBOLD (REV. RICHARD). Margaret Catchpole (119).
COLLINS (WILKIE). The Moonstone. Introduction by *T. S. Eliot* (316). The Woman in White (226).
COOPER (J. FENIMORE). The Last of the Mohicans (163).
DEFOE. Captain Singleton (82). Robinson Crusoe. Part I (17).
DICKENS. Barnaby Rudge (286). Christmas Books (307). Edwin
Drood (263). Great Expectations (128). Hard Times (264).
Old Curiosity Shop (270). Oliver Twist (8). Pickwick Papers.
2 volumes (120, 121). Tale of Two Cities (38).
DISRAELI (BENJAMIN). Coningsby (381). Sybil (291).
ELIOT (GEORGE). Adam Bede (63). Felix Holt (179). The Mill
on the Floss (31). Romola (178). Scenes of Clerical Life (155).
Silas Marner, &c. (80).
FIELDING. Jonathan Wild (382). Joseph Andrews (334).
GALT (JOHN). The Entail. Introduction by *John Ayscough* (177).
GASKELL (MRS.). Cousin Phillis, and Other Tales, &c. (168).
Cranford, The Cage at Cranford, and The Moorland Cottage
(110). Lizzie Leigh, The Grey Woman, and Other Tales, &c.
(175). Mary Barton (86). North and South (154). Right at
Last, and Other Tales, &c. (203). Round the Sofa (190).
Ruth (88). Sylvia's Lovers (156). Wives and Daughters (157).
GOLDSMITH. The Vicar of Wakefield (4).
HARRIS (JOEL CHANDLER). Uncle Remus (361).
HAWTHORNE. House of the Seven Gables (273). The Scarlet
Letter (26). Tales (319).

FICTION

HOLME (CONSTANCE). Beautiful End (431). Crump Folk going Home (419). He-who-came? (440). The Lonely Plough (390). The Old Road from Spain (400). The Splendid Fairing (416). The Things which Belong—— (425). The Trumpet in the Dust (409).

KINGSLEY (HENRY). Geoffry Hamlyn (271). Ravenshoe (267). Austin Elliot (407).

LA MOTTE FOUQUÉ. Undine, Sintram, &c. (408).

LE FANU (J. S.). Uncle Silas. Intro. by *Montague R. James* (306).

LESAGE. Gil Blas. Edited *J. Fitzmaurice-Kelly*. 2 vols. (151, 152).

MARRYAT. Mr. Midshipman Easy (160). Jacob Faithful (439).

MELVILLE (HERMAN). Moby Dick (225). Typee (274). Omoo (275). White Jacket (253).

MORIER (J. J.). Hajji Baba (238). Hajji Baba in England (285).

PEACOCK (T. L.). Headlong Hall ; and Nightmare Abbey (339). Misfortunes of Elphin; and Crotchet Castle (244).

RABELAIS. Gargantua and Pantagruel. Translated by *Urquhart* and *Motteux*, with notes and map. 3 volumes (411–13).

SCOTT. Ivanhoe (29).

SMOLLETT. Roderick Random (353). Humphry Clinker (290).

STERNE. Sentimental Journey (333). Tristram Shandy (40).

STEVENSON (R. L.). Kidnapped; and Catriona (297). The Master of Ballantrae (441). Treasure Island (295).

STURGIS (HOWARD). Belchamber. Intro. by *Gerard Hopkins* (429).

SWIFT. Gulliver's Travels (20).

TAYLOR (MEADOWS). Confessions of a Thug (207).

THACKERAY. Henry Esmond (28).

TOLSTOY. Translated by *Louise* and *Aylmer Maude*. Anna Karenina. 2 volumes (210, 211). Childhood, Boyhood, and Youth (352). The Cossacks, &c. (208). Iván Ilých, and Hadji Murád (432). The Kreutzer Sonata, &c. (266). Resurrection, trans. by *L. Maude* (209). Twenty-three Tales (72). War and Peace. 3 volumes (233–5).

TROLLOPE. American Senator (391). Ayala's Angel (342). Barchester Towers (268). The Belton Estate (251). The Claverings (252). Cousin Henry (343). Doctor Thorne (298). Dr. Wortle's School (317). The Eustace Diamonds (357). Framley Parsonage (305). The Kellys and the O'Kellys (341). Lady Anna (443). Last Chronicle of Barset. 2 vols. (398, 399). Miss Mackenzie (278). Orley Farm. 2 vols. (423, 424). Phineas Finn. 2 vols. (447, 448). Phineas Redux. 2 vols. (450, 451). Rachel Ray (279). Sir Harry Hotspur (336). Tales of all Countries (397). The Three Clerks (140). The Warden (217). The Vicar of Bullhampton (272).

WATTS-DUNTON (THEODORE). Aylwin (52).

WHARTON (EDITH). The House of Mirth. With a new Introduction by the Author (437).

¶ History

BARROW (SIR JOHN). The Mutiny of the *Bounty* (195).
BUCKLE. The History of Civilization. 3 volumes (41, 48, 53).
CARLYLE. The French Revolution. Introduction by *C. R. L. Fletcher*. 2 volumes (125, 126).
FROUDE (J. A.). Short Studies on Great Subjects. Series I (269).
GIBBON. Decline and Fall of the Roman Empire. With Maps. 7 volumes (35, 44, 51, 55, 64, 69, 74).
IRVING (WASHINGTON). Conquest of Granada (150).
MACAULAY. History of England. 5 volumes (366–70).
MOTLEY. Rise of the Dutch Republic. 3 volumes (96, 97, 98).
PRESCOTT (W. H.). The Conquest of Mexico. 2 vols. (197, 198).

¶ Letters

BURKE. Letters. Selected, with Introduction, by *H. J. Laski* (237).
CHESTERFIELD. Letters. Selected, with an Introduction, by *Phyllis M. Jones* (347).
CONGREVE. Letters, in Volume II. See under *Drama* (277).
COWPER. Letters. Selected, with Intro., by *E. V. Lucas* (138).
DUFFERIN (LORD). Letters from High Latitudes. Illustrated (158).
GRAY (THOMAS). Letters. Selected by *John Beresford* (283).
JOHNSON (SAMUEL). Letters. Selected, with Introduction, by *R. W. Chapman* (282).
SOUTHEY. Selected Letters (169).
WHITE (GILBERT). The Natural History of Selborne (22).

¶ Literary Criticism

AMERICAN CRITICISM. Representative Literary Essays. Chosen by *Norman Foerster* (354).
COLERIDGE (S. T.) Lectures on Shakespeare (363).
ENGLISH CRITICAL ESSAYS. Selected and edited by *Edmund D. Jones*. 2 volumes: I, Sixteenth to Eighteenth Centuries (240); II, Nineteenth Century (206).
HAZLITT (WILLIAM). Characters of Shakespeare's Plays. Introduction by *Sir A. T. Quiller-Couch* (205). Lectures on the English Comic Writers. Introduction by *R. Brimley Johnson* (124). Lectures on the English Poets (255). The Spirit of the Age. (Essays on his contemporaries) (57).
HORNE (R. H.). A New Spirit of the Age (127).
JOHNSON (SAMUEL). Lives of the Poets. 2 volumes (83, 84).
MORE (PAUL ELMER). Selected Shelburne Essays (434).
SAINTE-BEUVE. Causeries du Lundi. (In English.) Two Series (372–3).
SHAKESPEARE CRITICISM. (HEMINGE and CONDELL to CARLYLE.) Selected and introduced by *D. Nichol Smith* (212).
SHAKESPEARE CRITICISM (1919–1935). Selected and introduced by *Anne Bradby* (436).

¶ Philosophy and Science

(For POLITICAL THEORY and RELIGION see separate headings)

AURELIUS (MARCUS). Thoughts. Translated by *John Jackson*(60).
BACON. The Advancement of Learning, and the New Atlantis. Introduction by *Professor Case* (93). Essays (24).
CARLYLE. Sartor Resartus (19).
DARWIN. The Origin of Species. With a new preface by *Major Leonard Darwin* (11).
REYNOLDS(SIR JOSHUA). Discourses, &c. Introduction by *A. Dobson* (149).
TOLSTOY. What then must we do? Trans. by *A. Maude* (281).
WHITE (GILBERT). The Natural History of Selborne (22).

¶ Poetry

ARNOLD (MATTHEW). Poems, 1849–67 (85).
BARHAM (RICHARD). The Ingoldsby Legends (9).
BLAKE (WILLIAM). Selected Poems (324).
BRONTË SISTERS, THE. The Professor, by CHARLOTTE BRONTË, and Poems by CHARLOTTE, EMILY, and ANNE BRONTË (78).
BROWNING (ELIZABETH BARRETT). Poems. A Selection (176).
BROWNING (ROBERT). Poems and Plays, 1833–42 (58). Poems, 1842–64 (137).
BURNS (ROBERT). Poems (34). Complete and in large type.
BYRON. Poems. A Selection (180).
CHAUCER, The Works of. 3 volumes: I (42); II (56); III, containing the whole of the Canterbury Tales (76).
COLERIDGE. Poems. Introduction by *Sir A. T. Quiller-Couch* (99).
CONGREVE (WILLIAM). Complete works in 2 volumes. Introductions by *Bonamy Dobrée*. I, The Comedies (276); II, The Mourning Bride, Poems, Miscellanies and Letters (277).
DANTE. Italian text and English verse-translation by *Melville B. Anderson*, on facing pages, with notes. 3 vols. (392–4). Translation only, with notes, in one volume (395).
DOBSON (AUSTIN). Selected Poems (249).
ENGLISH SONGS AND BALLADS. Compiled by *T. W. H. Crosland*. New edition, with revised text and additional poems, 1927 (13).
ENGLISH VERSE. Vols. I–V: Early Lyrics to SHAKESPEARE; CAMPION to the Ballads; DRYDEN to WORDSWORTH; SCOTT to E. B. BROWNING; LONGFELLOW to RUPERT BROOKE. Edited by *William Peacock* (308–312).
FRANCIS OF ASSISI (ST.). The Little Flowers of St. Francis. Translated into English Verse by *James Rhoades* (265).
GOETHE. Faust, Parts I and II. Translated by *Bayard Taylor*. Intro. by *Marshall Montgomery* and notes by *Douglas Yates* (380).
GOLDEN TREASURY, THE. With additional Poems (133).
GOLDSMITH. Poems. Introduction by *Austin Dobson* (123).
HERBERT (GEORGE). Poems. Introduction by *Arthur Waugh* (109).
HERRICK (ROBERT). Poems (16).

HOMER. Translated by *Pope*. Iliad (18). Odyssey (36).
HOOD. Poems. Introduction by *Walter Jerrold* (87).
IBSEN. Peer Gynt. Translated by *R. Ellis Roberts* (446).
KEATS. Poems (7).
KEBLE. The Christian Year (181).
LONGFELLOW. Hiawatha, Miles Standish, Tales of a Wayside Inn, &c. (174).
MACAULAY. Lays of Ancient Rome ; Ivry ; The Armada (27).
MARLOWE. Dr. Faustus (with GOETHE's Faust, Part I, trans. *J. Anster*). Introduction by *Sir A. W. Ward* (135).
MILTON. The English Poems (182).
MORRIS (WILLIAM). The Defence of Guenevere, Life and Death of Jason, and other Poems (183).
NARRATIVE VERSE, A BOOK OF. Compiled by *V. H. Collins*. With an Introduction by *Edmund Blunden* (350).
NEKRASSOV. Trans. by *Juliet Soskice*. Who can be happy and free in Russia ? A Poem (213). Poems (340).
PALGRAVE. The Golden Treasury. With additional Poems (133).
ROSSETTI (CHRISTINA). Goblin Market, &c. (184).
SCOTT (SIR WALTER). Selected Poems (186).
SCOTTISH VERSE, A BOOK OF. Compiled by *R. L. Mackie* (417).
SHAKESPEARE. Plays and Poems. Preface by *A. C. Swinburne.* Introductions by *Edward Dowden*. 9 volumes. Comedies. 3 volumes (100, 101, 102). Histories and Poems. 3 volumes (103, 104, 105). Tragedies. 3 volumes (106, 107, 108).
SHELLEY. Poems. A Selection (187).
TENNYSON. Selected Poems. Intro. by *Sir Herbert Warren* (3).
VIRGIL. The Aeneid, Georgics, and Eclogues. Translated by *Dryden* (37). Translated by *James Rhoades* (227).
WELLS (CHARLES). Joseph and his Brethren. A Dramatic Poem. Intro. by *A. C. Swinburne*, and Note by *T. Watts-Dunton* (143).
WHITMAN. A Selection. Introduction by *E. de Sélincourt* (218).
WHITTIER. Poems : A Selection (188).
WORDSWORTH. Poems : A Selection (189).

¶ Politics, Political Economy, Political Theory

BAGEHOT (WALTER). The English Constitution. With an Introduction by the *Earl of Balfour* (330).
BUCKLE. The History of Civilization. 3 volumes (41, 48, 53).
BURKE (EDMUND). Letters. Selected, with an Introduction, by *Harold J. Laski* (237). Works. 6 volumes. I: A Vindication of Natural Society; The Sublime and Beautiful, &c. (71). II: The Present Discontents; and Speeches and Letters on America (81). III: Speeches on India, &c. (111). IV: Writings on France, 1790–1 (112). V: Writings on Ireland, &c. (113). VI: A Letter to a Noble Lord; and Letters on a Regicide Peace (114).
ENGLISH SPEECHES, from BURKE to GLADSTONE. Selected and edited by *E. R. Jones* (191).
MACAULAY. Speeches. Selected, with Introduction and footnotes, by *G. M. Young* (433).

MACHIAVELLI. The Prince (43).
MAINE (SIR HENRY). Ancient Law (362).
MILL (JOHN STUART). On Liberty, Representative Government, and the Subjection of Women (170).
MILTON (JOHN). Selected Prose. Intro. *Malcolm W. Wallace* (293).
RUSKIN. 'A Joy for Ever', and The Two Paths. Illustrated (147). Time and Tide. and The Crown of Wild Olive (146). Unto this Last, and Munera Pulveris (148).
SMITH (ADAM). The Wealth of Nations. 2 volumes (54, 59).
SPEECHES AND DOCUMENTS ON BRITISH COLONIAL POLICY (1763–1917). Ed. *A. B. Keith.* 2 volumes (215, 216).
SPEECHES AND DOCUMENTS ON THE BRITISH DOMINIONS, 1918–31. Selected, with Introduction, by *A. B. Keith* (403).
SPEECHES AND DOCUMENTS ON INDIAN POLICY (1756–1921). Edited, with Introduction, by *A. B. Keith* (231, 232).
SPEECHES ON BRITISH FOREIGN POLICY (1738–1914). Edited by *Edgar R. Jones, M.P.* (201).
TOLSTOY. What then must we do ? Translated, with an Introduction, by *Avlmer Maude* (281).
TRACTS AND PAMPHLETS, A Miscellany of. Sixteenth to Nineteenth Centuries. Edited by *A. C. Ward* (304).

¶ Religion

THE OLD TESTAMENT. Revised Version. 4 vols. (385–8).
APOCRYPHA, THE, in the Revised Version (294).
THE FOUR GOSPELS, AND THE ACTS OF THE APOSTLES. Authorized Version (344).
THE NEW TESTAMENT. Revised Version (346).
À KEMPIS (THOMAS). Of the Imitation of Christ (49).
AURELIUS (MARCUS). Translated by *John Jackson* (60).
BUNYAN. The Pilgrim's Progress (12). Mr. Badman (338).
CONFUCIUS. The Analects. Trans. by *W. E. Soothill.* Introduction by *Lady Hosie* (442).
KORAN, THE. Translated by *E. H. Palmer.* Introduction by *Reynold A. Nicholson* (328).
TOLSTOY. Translated by *Aylmer Maude.* A Confession, and What I believe (229). On Life, and Essays on Religion (426). The Kingdom of God, and Peace Essays (445).

¶ Short Stories

AFRICA, STORIES OF. Chosen by *E. C. Parnwell* (359).
AUSTRIAN SHORT STORIES. Selected and translated by *Marie Busch* (337).
CRIME AND DETECTION. Two Series (301, 351). Stories by H. C. BAILEY, ERNEST BRAMAH, G. K. CHESTERTON. SIR A. CONAN DOYLE, R. AUSTIN FREEMAN, W. W. JACOBS, EDEN PHILPOTTS, 'SAPPER', DOROTHY SAYERS, and others.
CZECH TALES, SELECTED. Translated by *Marie Busch* and *Otto Pick* (288). Nine stories, including two by the BROTHERS CAPEK.

DICKENS. Christmas Books (307).
ENGLISH SHORT STORIES. Three Series. Selected by *H. S. Milford*. Introduction by *Prof. Hugh Walker* in Vol. I (193, 228, 315).
FRENCH SHORT STORIES. Eighteenth to Twentieth Centuries. Selected and translated by *K. Rebillon Lambley* (396).
GASKELL (MRS.). Introductions by *Clement Shorter*. Cousin Phillis, and Other Tales (168). Lizzie Leigh, The Grey Woman, and Other Tales, &c. (175). Right at Last, and Other Tales, &c. (203). Round the Sofa (190).
GERMAN SHORT STORIES. Translated by *E. N. Bennett*, with an Introduction by *E. K. Bennett* (415).
GHOSTS AND MARVELS and MORE GHOSTS AND MARVELS. Two Selections of Uncanny Tales made by *V. H. Collins*. Introduction by *Montague R. James* in Series I (284, 323).
HARTE (BRET). Short Stories (318).
HAWTHORNE (NATHANIEL). Tales (319).
IRVING (WASHINGTON). Tales (320).
PERSIAN (FROM THE). The Three Dervishes, and Other Stories. Translated from MSS. in the Bodleian by *Reuben Levy* (254).
POE (EDGAR ALLAN). Tales of Mystery and Imagination (21).
POLISH TALES BY MODERN AUTHORS. Translated by *Else C. M. Benecke* and *Marie Busch* (230).
RUSSIAN SHORT STORIES. Chosen and translated by *A. E. Chamot* (287).
SCOTT. Short Stories. With an Introduction by *Lord David Cecil* (414).
SHORT STORIES OF THE SOUTH SEAS. Selected by *E. C. Parnwell* (332).
SPANISH SHORT STORIES. Sixteenth Century. In contemporary translations, revised, with an Introduction, by *J. B. Trend* (326).
TOLSTOY. Nine Stories (1855-63) (420). Twenty-three Tales. Translated by *Louise* and *Aylmer Maude* (72).
TROLLOPE. Tales of all Countries (397).

¶ *Travel and Topography*

BORROW (GEORGE). The Bible in Spain (75). Wild Wales (224). Lavengro (66). Romany Rye (73).
DUFFERIN (LORD). Letters from High Latitudes (158).
MELVILLE (HERMAN). Typee (294). Omoo (275).
MORIER (J. J.). Hajji Baba of Ispahan. Introduction by *C. W. Stewart*, and a Map (238).
SMOLLETT (TOBIAS). Travels through France and Italy in 1765. Introduction (lxii pages) by *Thomas Seccombe* (90).
STERNE (LAURENCE). A Sentimental Journey. With Introduction by *Virginia Woolf* (333).

INDEX OF AUTHORS, ETC.

Further Volumes are in preparation.

December 1936